HOW TO STORE

JUST ABOUT ANYTHING

ALBERT JACKSON & DAVID DAY

HOW TO STORE

JUST ABOUT ANYTHING

ALBERT JACKSON & DAVID DAY

BCA

LONDON · NEW YORK · SYDNEY · TORONTO

**HOW TO STORE
JUST ABOUT ANYTHING**
was created exclusively for HarperCollins Publishers by

INKLINK
1-3 HIGHBRIDGE WHARF, GREENWICH, LONDON SE10 9PS

First published in 1992 by
HarperCollins Publishers
London

Copyright © 1992 HarperCollins Publishers

This edition published 1992 by BCA by
arrangement with HarperCollins Publishers

CN 9168

TEXT AND PROJECT DESIGN
**Albert Jackson
David Day**

EXECUTIVE ART DIRECTOR
Simon Jennings

DESIGN & ART DIRECTION
Alan Marshall

EDITOR
Peter Leek

ILLUSTRATIONS
**Robin Harris
David Day**

STUDIO PHOTOGRAPHY
**Neil Waving
Trevor Leak**

For HarperCollins:

EXECUTIVE EDITOR
Polly Powell

PUBLISHING DIRECTOR
Robin Wood

**The CIP catalogue record for this
book is available from the British Library**

TEXT SET IN
UNIVERS AND HELVETICA NARROW BY
Inklink, London

IMAGESETTING BY
Blackheath Publishing Services, London

COLOUR ORIGINATION
Colourscan, Singapore

PRINTED & BOUND BY
Graficromo, Spain

CONTENTS

Inklink are indebted to the following individuals, organizations and companies who generously supplied reference material, samples for photography and product photographs:

PRODUCTS/REFERENCE

C.F. Anderson & Son Ltd.,
Islington Green, London, N1

Atlanta Marketing Ltd.,
Combe Park, Bickerton, Newton Abbot,
Devon, TQ12

Desfab,
45 Croydon Road, Beckenham,
Kent, BR3

Disabled Living Foundation,
380/384 Harrow Road, London, W9

FIDOR,
1 Hanworth Road, Feltham,
Middlesex, TW13

Geliot Whitman Wheatsheaf,
Herschell Road, London, SE23

Häfele America Co.,
3091 Cheyenne Drive, Archdale,
NC 27263, USA

Susan Smith/Kevin Nolan,
Häfele UK Ltd.,
Swift Valley Industrial Estate,
Rugby, CV21

Interlübke Ltd
Unit 4, Greenwich High Road,
London, SE10

Magnet Ltd.,
Royd Ings Avenue, Keighley, West
Yorkshire, BD21

John Myland Ltd.,
80 Norwood High Street, London, SE27

Rustins Ltd.,
Waterloo Road, Cricklewood,
London, NW2

Shopkit Designs Ltd.,
100 Cecil Street, N. Watford,
Herts, WD2

Woodfit Ltd.,
Kem Mill, Whittle le Woods, Chorley,
Lancashire, PR6

PHOTOGRAPHS

Atlanta Marketing Ltd
Page 72

Jon Bouchier/Elizabeth Whiting Associates
Page 110

Camera Press
Pages 9, 38, 74, 84, 106

Bruce Greenlaw/Fine Homebuilding
Pages 26, 28, 31, 40, 118

Franke UK
Page 25

Häfele UK Ltd.
Pages 12, 22, 23, 44.

Interlübke Ltd
Pages 30, 42, 60, 92, 97

Ken Kirkwood
Pages 7, 10, 100, 121

Trevor Leak
Pages 16, 17, 138

Magnet Ltd
Page 34

Martin Moore & Co
Page 32

Neil Waving
Pages i, iii, 78, 99, 112, 122,
131-136, 140

Partridge Fine Arts PLC
Page 67

Pennard House Antiques
Page 54

Spike Powell/Elizabeth Whiting Associates
Page 48

Traditional Homes Magazine
Pages 18, 24, 50, 98

Shona Wood
Pages 15, 102

Chapter 1 DESIGNING AND PLANNING

Even for the professional designer, the truly innovative idea is the exception rather than the rule. Most of the time designers rework tried-and-tested concepts, attempting to balance the sometimes conflicting requirements imposed by economics, function and aesthetics. Indeed, when the roles of the designer and maker were not as strictly defined as they are today, craftsmen tended to copy what their fathers and grandfathers had made before them, any changes being the result of gradual assimilation. Familiarity with methods of construction, appreciating what materials will work best, and knowing what special fittings and fixings are available are essential ingredients for a successful design solution. The spark of originality is a bonus. This book sets out to provide a rich source of these ingredients, to be modified at your discretion and to be used as starting points from which to develop your own storage ideas.

BASIC PRINCIPLES

Despite their apparent complexity, practically all items of storage can be construed as boxes or shelves in various combinations. A chest of drawers, for example, is one large box standing on edge with a number of smaller boxes slotted into it. A traditional kitchen dresser is a similar assemblage of boxes in the form of cupboards and drawers with shelves stacked above them. Arranging such boxes and shelves so they are capable of carrying the loads for which they are intended is essentially what designing storage is about.

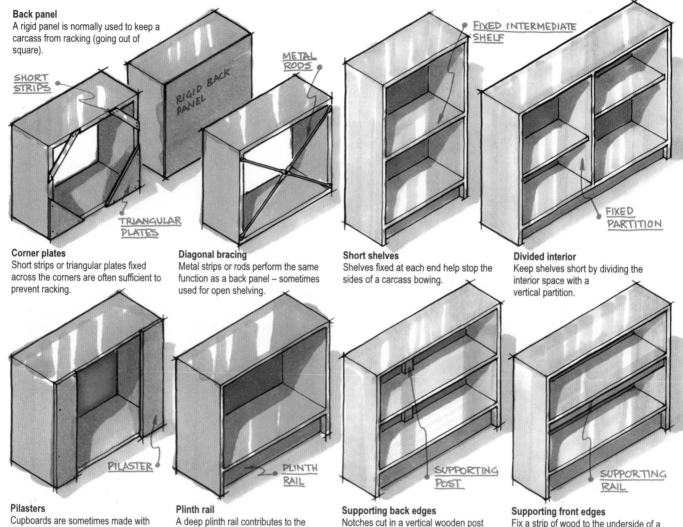

Back panel
A rigid panel is normally used to keep a carcass from racking (going out of square).

Corner plates
Short strips or triangular plates fixed across the corners are often sufficient to prevent racking.

Diagonal bracing
Metal strips or rods perform the same function as a back panel – sometimes used for open shelving.

Short shelves
Shelves fixed at each end help stop the sides of a carcass bowing.

Divided interior
Keep shelves short by dividing the interior space with a vertical partition.

Pilasters
Cupboards are sometimes made with vertical pilasters, plus a back panel.

Plinth rail
A deep plinth rail contributes to the rigidity of a carcass.

Supporting back edges
Notches cut in a vertical wooden post support the back edges of shelving.

Supporting front edges
Fix a strip of wood to the underside of a long shelf to stop it bending.

Constructing a rigid carcass
The top, bottom and side panels of a cupboard or bookcase are known collectively as the carcass. Strong corner joints would probably hold these four components together indefinitely so long as no additional load was applied to them. However, in normal use the joints would soon work loose and the carcass would collapse unless some measure was taken to tie the structure diagonally from corner to corner. The usual method is to attach a back panel, but there are also other methods which can be used singly or in combination.

Incorporating shelves
Once a box or carcass is rigid, shelves can be incorporated to make better use of the interior. Provided it is not too long, each end of a shelf can simply be attached to the sides of the carcass. If for some reason the carcass has to be wider than the optimum shelf length, either the interior space must be divided with a vertical partition to accommodate shorter shelves or longer ones must be supported in some way to prevent them bending under load. Shelves can be fixed or adjustable in height (see page 15).

These days most storage furniture is manufactured from man-made boards that remain dimensionally stable in all but the most extreme changes in humidity. However, if you opt for solid wood it is essential that you allow for the inevitable movement that occurs as wood shrinks and expands according to its moisture content. The greatest problems are associated with differential movement – wood shrinks and expands to a greater extent across the grain than along it. If cross-grain movement is restricted, stresses are eventually relieved by splits opening along the grain. Many of the common methods for dealing with differential movement are illustrated by traditional chest-of-drawer construction (see pages 62-3).

Fitting doors
Enclosing shelves with doors protects contents.

Incorporating drawers
Drawers are preferable for storing small items.

Developing the structure
Begin to develop storage by extending the sides and adding more shelving.

Developing storage

Having decided on the arrangement of shelves within the carcass, you might decide to enclose them with doors to protect the contents. You could also include drawers for storing smaller items.

Extending the sides of the carcass (or placing another box on top) affords the opportunity to incorporate still more shelving or another cupboard. By adapting the structure in similar ways it is possible to create all the more familiar forms of storage furniture. Details of their construction can be found throughout the book.

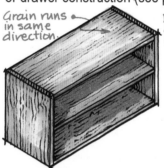

Grain runs in same direction.

Battens run contrary to grain.

Consistent movement
Movement can occur without restriction provided the wood grain of every component runs in the same direction.

Differential movement
Rigidly fixed battens running across the grain will promote splitting.

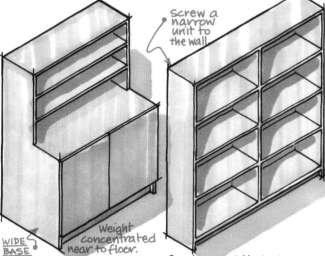

Screw a narrow unit to the wall

Weight concentrated near to floor.

WIDE BASE

Low centre of gravity
Concentrate the weight close to the floor to maintain equilibrium.

Securing an unstable structure
Storage cabinets with a relatively narrow base should be screwed to the wall or anchored to the floor.

Avoiding instability

Large storage units, which frequently carry very heavy loads, are potentially hazardous unless they are prevented from toppling. It pays to concentrate most of the weight as close to the floor as possible. This is especially important if your plan includes a fall flap or a deep drawer that could act as a lever when extended. Avoid attaching heavy mirrors to hinged doors – use sliding doors instead.

Framed doors are designed to allow inset panels to move freely

DOORS AND LIDS

Weigh up the benefits and disadvantages of different doors, flaps and lids to determine which will work best for the cupboard or box you have in mind.

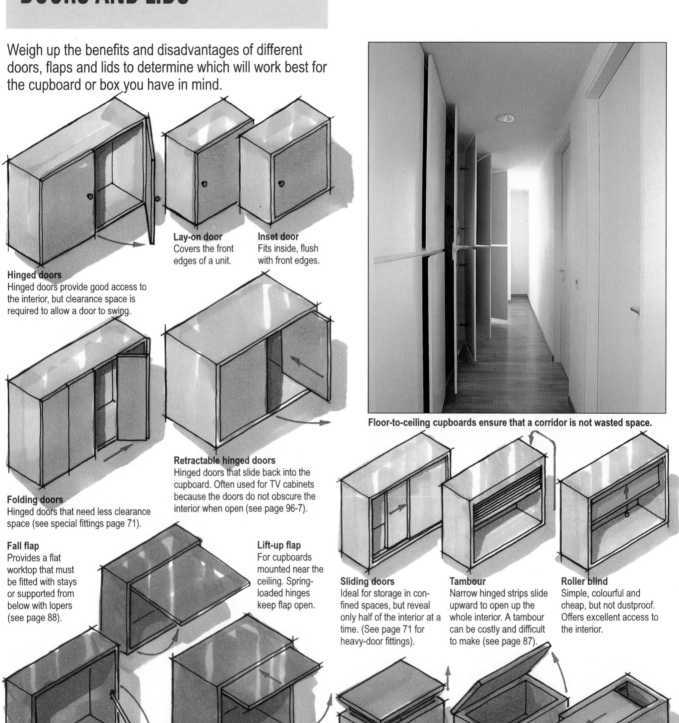

Lay-on door
Covers the front edges of a unit.

Inset door
Fits inside, flush with front edges.

Hinged doors
Hinged doors provide good access to the interior, but clearance space is required to allow a door to swing.

Retractable hinged doors
Hinged doors that slide back into the cupboard. Often used for TV cabinets because the doors do not obscure the interior when open (see page 96-7).

Folding doors
Hinged doors that need less clearance space (see special fittings page 71).

Fall flap
Provides a flat worktop that must be fitted with stays or supported from below with lopers (see page 88).

Lift-up flap
For cupboards mounted near the ceiling. Spring-loaded hinges keep flap open.

Retractable lift-up flap
Lifts and slides back. Special tracks and rollers are required (see page 27).

Floor-to-ceiling cupboards ensure that a corridor is not wasted space.

Sliding doors
Ideal for storage in confined spaces, but reveal only half of the interior at a time. (See page 71 for heavy-door fittings).

Tambour
Narrow hinged strips slide upward to open up the whole interior. A tambour can be costly and difficult to make (see page 87).

Roller blind
Simple, colourful and cheap, but not dustproof. Offers excellent access to the interior.

Lift-off lid
For small boxes only – must be lightweight.

Hinged lid
Hinges help support the weight of a heavy lid.

Sliding lid
Sliding lids require high level of craftsmanship.

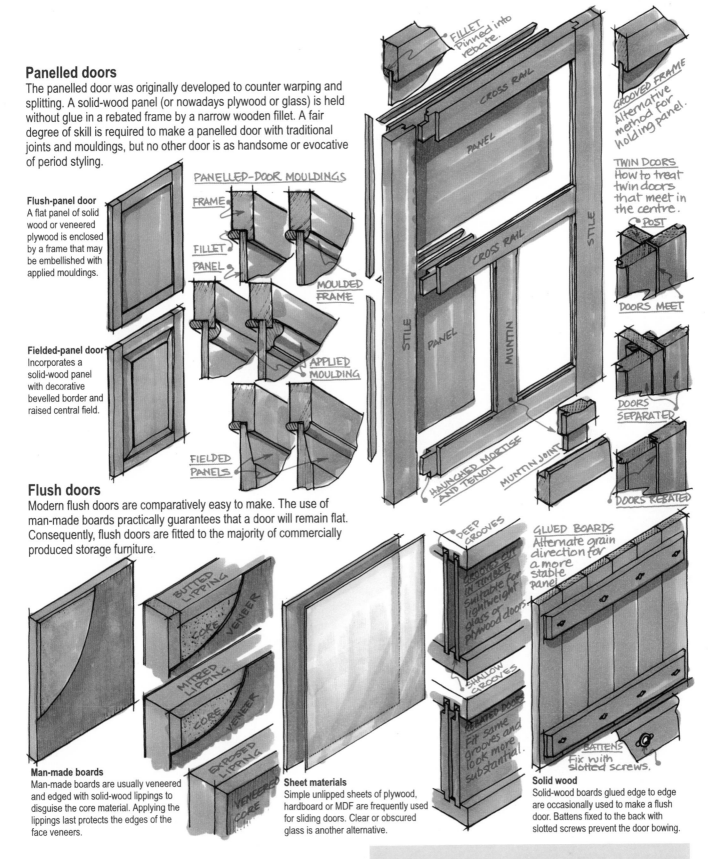

Panelled doors

The panelled door was originally developed to counter warping and splitting. A solid-wood panel (or nowadays plywood or glass) is held without glue in a rebated frame by a narrow wooden fillet. A fair degree of skill is required to make a panelled door with traditional joints and mouldings, but no other door is as handsome or evocative of period styling.

Flush-panel door
A flat panel of solid wood or veneered plywood is enclosed by a frame that may be embellished with applied mouldings.

Fielded-panel door
Incorporates a solid-wood panel with decorative bevelled border and raised central field.

FILLET Pinned into rebate.

CROSS RAIL

PANEL

GROOVED FRAME Alternative method for holding panel.

TWIN DOORS How to treat twin doors that meet in the centre.

POST

STILE

CROSS RAIL

PANEL

MUNTIN

STILE

DOORS MEET

DOORS SEPARATED

PANELLED-DOOR MOULDINGS

FRAME

FILLET

PANEL

MOULDED FRAME

APPLIED MOULDING

FIELDED PANELS

HAUNCHED MORTISE AND TENON

MUNTIN JOINT

DOORS REBATED

Flush doors

Modern flush doors are comparatively easy to make. The use of man-made boards practically guarantees that a door will remain flat. Consequently, flush doors are fitted to the majority of commercially produced storage furniture.

BUTTED LIPPING

CORE

VENEER

MITRED LIPPING

CORE

VENEER

EXPOSED LIPPING

VENEERED CORE

DEEP GROOVES

GROOVES CUT IN TIMBER Suitable for lightweight glass or plywood doors.

SHALLOW GROOVES

REBATED DOORS Fit same grooves and look more substantial.

GLUED BOARDS Alternate grain direction for a more stable panel.

BATTENS Fix with slotted screws.

Man-made boards
Man-made boards are usually veneered and edged with solid-wood lippings to disguise the core material. Applying the lippings last protects the edges of the face veneers.

Sheet materials
Simple unlipped sheets of plywood, hardboard or MDF are frequently used for sliding doors. Clear or obscured glass is another alternative.

Solid wood
Solid-wood boards glued edge to edge are occasionally used to make a flush door. Battens fixed to the back with slotted screws prevent the door bowing.

ACCESSING THE INTERIOR

Cupboard space is often divided with shelving, but storage units can also be fitted out in various ways to make them more accessible. Drawers or trays, for example, give better access to the contents of deep cupboards, and large trunks or chests can be subdivided with sliding or lift-out trays.

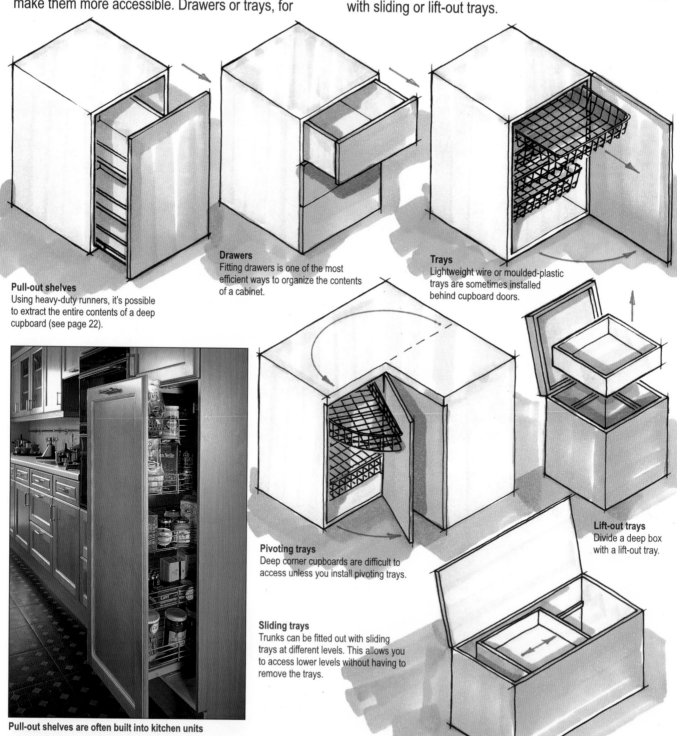

Pull-out shelves
Using heavy-duty runners, it's possible to extract the entire contents of a deep cupboard (see page 22).

Drawers
Fitting drawers is one of the most efficient ways to organize the contents of a cabinet.

Trays
Lightweight wire or moulded-plastic trays are sometimes installed behind cupboard doors.

Pivoting trays
Deep corner cupboards are difficult to access unless you install pivoting trays.

Sliding trays
Trunks can be fitted out with sliding trays at different levels. This allows you to access lower levels without having to remove the trays.

Lift-out trays
Divide a deep box with a lift-out tray.

Pull-out shelves are often built into kitchen units

Drawer construction

Drawers are sometimes made from softwoods, but hardwoods are more hard-wearing. Use inexpensive wood for backs and sides, reserving costly show woods for drawer fronts only. Nowadays, plywood or hardboard is invariably used for drawer bottoms. Dovetails are the strongest joints for drawer construction, but modern adhesives are so good you can rely on much simpler joints.

Bottom-run drawer
The drawer slides on battens, known as runners, fixed inside a carcass. Runners also act as 'kickers' to prevent the drawer below tipping when pulled out.

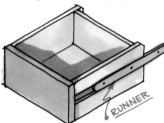

Side-run drawer
A stopped groove cut in each drawer side slides on a single batten that acts as both runner and kicker.

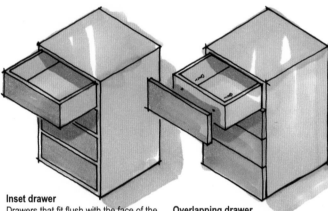

Inset drawer
Drawers that fit flush with the face of the carcass need to fit snugly.

Overlapping drawer
The simplest way to achieve an overlapping drawer (the equivalent of a lay-on door) is to screw an oversize false front onto an inset drawer.

Lapped-and-housed drawer

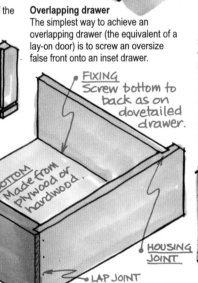

GROOVES
Bottom fits in groove in front and sides.

FIXING
Screw bottom to back as on dovetailed drawer.

BOTTOM
Made from plywood or hardwood.

HOUSING JOINT

LAP JOINT

Dovetailed drawer

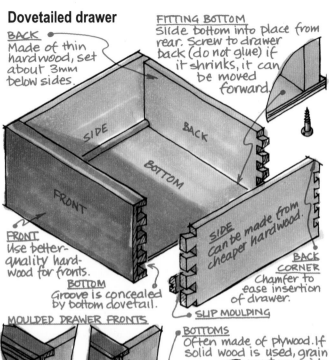

BACK
Made of thin hardwood, set about 3mm below sides.

SIDE

BACK

BOTTOM

FRONT
Use better-quality hardwood for fronts.

BOTTOM
Groove is concealed by bottom dovetail.

FITTING BOTTOM
Slide bottom into place from rear. Screw to drawer back (do not glue) if it shrinks, it can be moved forward.

SIDE
Can be made from cheaper hardwood.

BACK CORNER
Chamfer to ease insertion of drawer.

SLIP MOULDING

MOULDED DRAWER FRONTS

Applied moulding
Mitred moulding enriches drawer.

Cocked bead
Set in rebate at end of drawer front.

BOTTOMS
Often made of plywood. If solid wood is used, grain must run side to side.

SLIP MOULDING
Glued to each drawer side. End is notched to allow it to run under drawer back.

WIDER RUNNING SURFACE

Strengthening a wide drawer bottom
Use a hardwood muntin to divide and support the two halves of a wide drawer bottom.

MUNTIN

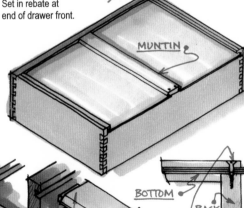

BOTTOM

BACK

MUNTIN
Screw to drawer back.

MUNTIN
Dovetail into front or tongue into groove.

SHELVING

Whether it be rough-sawn planks for the garage or an adjustable system for the lounge, putting up shelving is a job practically anyone can do. You can hardly go wrong, especially with manufactured systems, provided you make strong wall fixings and don't try to economise by reducing the number of shelf supports below a safe limit.

Shelving materials

Erecting shelving could hardly be easier thanks to the extensive range of ready-made shelves and adjustable wall-hanging systems now on the market. However, you might prefer to custom-build shelves, perhaps to fit an alcove precisely, and that will probably entail using ordinary planed softwood or cutting the shelves from standard sheets of man-made board.

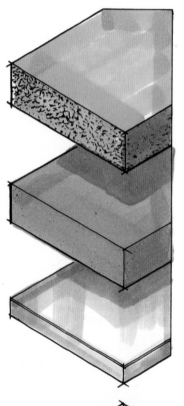

Solid wood
Although they are used to edge cheaper materials, hardwoods have become too expensive for shelving. However, softwoods make excellent shelves, being tough, easy to work, relatively lightweight, and not too expensive. Softwood with a clear finish is an attractive and hardwearing material. Most people cut their own shelves from stock sections, but there is also a limited range of ready-made prefinished softwood shelves.

Blockboard
Blockboard is made by sandwiching strips of glued softwood between thin sheets of plywood. Blockboard is as strong as solid wood, provided you cut shelves with the core strips running lengthwise, and it is unlikely to warp. But, you will need to lip the front edges with iron-on veneer or solid-wood.

Chipboard
Chipboard is the cheapest material to use for shelving, but it is also likely to bend under even moderately heavy loads unless the shelves are well supported (see below). There are a great many ready-made chipboard shelves to choose from. They are usually coated with coloured plastic or, alternatively, covered with genuine or simulated wood veneers.

Medium-density fibreboard
Medium-density fibreboard (MDF) is a tough, dense, stable material. MDF can be machined or even planed by hand to such a smooth finish that it does not require edging in any way to hide the core. However, somewhat smarter plastic-covered and pre-veneered MDF shelves are also available.

Glass
Plate glass makes surprisingly robust shelving provided you don't overload it. Glass 6mm thick is adequate for relatively short spans, but 9mm glass is safer for longer shelves. Toughened glass is stronger still, but is only available to special order. Use glass for light loads only.

Stiffening long shelves

Prevent a shelf bending under load by supporting its front edge with a wooden batten or metal extrusion. Alternatively, rest its back edge on a horizontal wall-fixed batten; or use cross-halving joints to fix the shelf to vertically-mounted wooden posts.

METAL FRONT-EDGE SUPPORTS

SUPPORTING BACK EDGES WITH WALL-FIXED POSTS

WOODEN FRONT-EDGE SUPPORTS

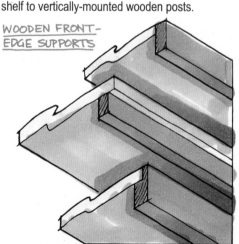

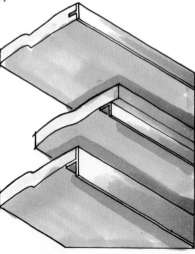

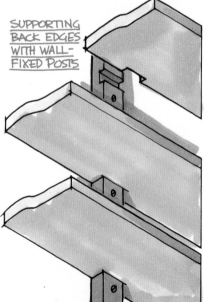

Supporting shelves in a cupboard

Installing the occasional shelf with fixed joints helps stop the sides of a carcass bowing outwards, but it is simpler to support most of your cupboard shelving on small plug-in studs.

Fixing shelves to the wall

Screw a wooden batten or a metal extrusion to the wall to support each end of a shelf spanning an alcove. Using a masonry drill, insert wall plugs to take large countersunk screws which will penetrate the wall by at least 38mm (1.5in). See BOOKS AND MAGAZINES for proprietary wall-fixed brackets.

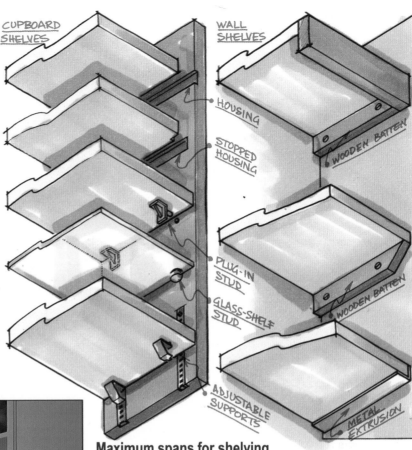

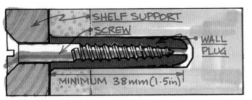

A wall plug expands as you insert the screw.

Framing conceals housing joints between shelves and wall-fixed vertical planks

Maximum spans for shelving

It can be difficult to anticipate future storage requirements with any accuracy. Consequently, it is easy to overload shelving as you gradually acquire more and more belongings. It therefore makes sense to provide for the possibility of additional loading by making shelves as short as practicable and to provide more wall-mounted supports than absolutely necessary.

The chart below lists recommended maximum spans for shelves made from different materials under various loads. As a rough guide, objects such as fine china or glassware constitute a light load; pots and pans constitute a medium load; and books or long-playing records a heavy load. If you wish to increase the span of any shelf, either use thicker material or support its edges to prevent it bending. Take care not to reduce the number of adjustable wall-fixed shelf supports below their manufacturer's recommendations.

RECOMMENDED SHELF SPANS

Material	Thickness	Light load	Medium load	Heavy load
Solid wood	18mm	800mm (2ft 8in)	750mm (2ft 6in)	700mm (2ft 4in)
Blockboard	18mm	800mm (2ft 8in)	750mm (2ft 6in)	700mm (2ft 4in)
Chipboard	16mm	750mm (2ft 6in)	600mm (2ft)	450mm (1ft 6in)
MDF	18mm	800mm (2ft 8in)	750mm (2ft 6in)	700mm (2ft 4in)
Glass	6mm	700mm (2ft 4in)	Not applicable	Not applicable

DETAILING YOUR PLANS

To plan a simple storage scheme such as a bank of wall-hung shelving, you probably need to do little more than take a few measurements to determine the number of shelves, uprights and brackets you require. For anything more complicated, it pays to make simple measured drawings to finalize your plans.

Sketching first ideas

Most designers begin to explore an idea with sketches that become more and more detailed as they begin to focus on the best solution. It is easiest to use some sort of graph paper printed with a grid or, better still, overlay the grid with tracing paper. The drawings in this book were made using an 'isometric' grid to create a three-dimensional effect. Adding colour with large felt-tipped pens helps to clarify a drawing.

Making scale drawings

There are advantages to be gained from making a full-size drawing on the wall to plot the main elements of built-in storage; and you can stretch lengths of string across a room to determine how much floor space it will occupy. These procedures will ensure you can reach the highest shelves and that there will be sufficient room to accommodate the unit comfortably. Nevertheless, most people find that it is useful to make a scale drawing in order to work out the construction in detail.

For large built-in projects, use 1:20 scale – 10mm on your drawing represents 200mm full size. (You will find it easier to adopt 1:24 scale when working with imperial measurements.) For smaller freestanding units, you can use 1:5 scale for metric dimensions and a 1:4 scale for imperial ones. Conventionally, a scale drawing includes a plan, elevations and at least one section.

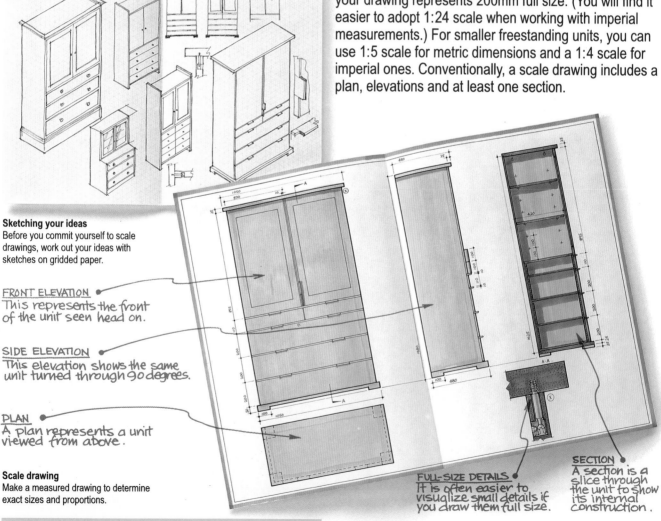

Sketching your ideas
Before you commit yourself to scale drawings, work out your ideas with sketches on gridded paper.

FRONT ELEVATION
This represents the front of the unit seen head on.

SIDE ELEVATION
This elevation shows the same unit turned through 90 degrees.

PLAN
A plan represents a unit viewed from above.

Scale drawing
Make a measured drawing to determine exact sizes and proportions.

FULL-SIZE DETAILS
It is often easier to visualize small details if you draw them full size.

SECTION
A section is a slice through the unit to show its internal construction.

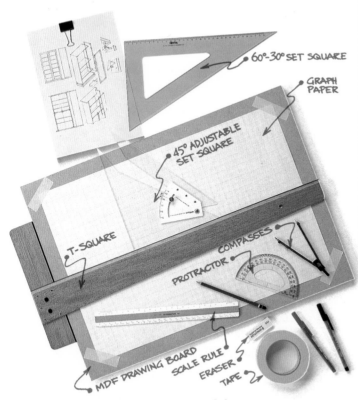

Woodworkers sometimes make small boxes, primarily as exercises in marquetry or to demonstrate their skills in cutting fine joints, but most storage is designed for fairly specific contents – objects which to a large extent determine its size and shape – and it also has to be accessible. Pertinent dimensions are provided throughout the book as a guide to overall proportions.

Constructing rectangles

It is sometimes argued that anything designed on purely functional grounds is automatically pleasing in appearance. However, having plotted all the essential dimensions, you will still often need to decide the exact proportions of the various elements of a design. Your own opinion is perfectly valid, and you should feel free to exercise your own judgement. But as storage is so often rectilinear in nature, you can also rely on certain 'classical' proportions as a basis for your decisions.

Drawing equipment and materials

A ready-made drawing board will be expensive, but an accurately cut sheet of MDF will do just as well. However, there is no alternative to buying a T-square for drawing horizontal lines, a plastic set square for drawing vertical ones, and a cheap protractor for measuring angles. An adjustable square combines the functions of protractor and set square. A special scale rule marked in the appropriate increments is also essential. You can make your drawings on any suitable-size paper, but tracing paper is useful when you want to change your plans. Use relatively hard pencils that will not blunt quickly.

Scale models

People who are not used to working with scale drawings sometimes find it difficult to visualize what a finished storage unit will look like in three dimensions. Before committing yourself to expensive materials, make a simple model to the same scale as the drawing. Cut components from balsa wood or cardboard, and glue them together neatly with balsa cement, smoothing any rough edges with fine sandpaper.

Root rectangles

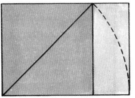
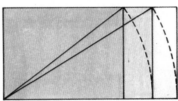

Use the diagonal of a square to determine the long side of a rectangle. This is the basis for preferred international paper sizes (see page 85).

To create a series of related shapes, use the diagonal of each rectangle to determine the proportion of the next.

Golden rectangles

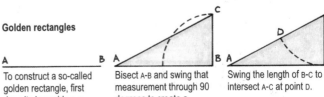

To construct a so-called golden rectangle, first draw its long side A-B.

Bisect A-B and swing that measurement through 90 degrees to create a vertical line B-C, completing the triangle A-B-C.

Swing the length of B-C to intersect A-C at point D.

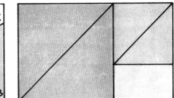

Swing A-D to the vertical to determine the short side of the golden rectangle.

If the square of the short side is removed from the rectangle, another golden rectangle remains. This is a property of every golden rectangle.

Chapter 2

KITCHENWARE

With a few exceptions, such as a wall-hung knife rack or a cutlery drawer, it pays not to overdesign kitchen storage. Instead, provide cupboards and drawers that are adaptable, so they can be used for whatever items are required in a particular area of the kitchen and accommodate new appliances and utensils as they are acquired. You might, however, take advantage of interior fittings that make it easier to retrieve items from deep cupboards, especially if the kitchen will be used by a physically handicapped or elderly person.

The kitchen is one of those areas of the home where storage units are expected to do more than simply house and protect their contents. Base units in particular double as worktops, and often accommodate appliances such as cookers, sinks and fridges. Consequently, there is general agreement between the various manufacturers on the dimensions they adopt. Standard sizes are derived from the optimum dimensions that, for example, enable an adult of average build to reach a top shelf without having to overstretch or prepare a meal on a work surface without stooping. Exceptionally tall or short people may want to tinker with these dimensions, but the human frame is so adaptable that most of us can operate quite satisfactorily with standard-size kitchen units.

Activity areas

Plan your kitchen storage to service specific zones or activity areas. Utensils, small electrical appliances and the majority of your groceries should be stored conveniently close to the preparation zone where you will be chopping, slicing and mixing ingredients. Naturally, the washing zone is centred on the sink, and this is where you should store all the products and equipment required for washing-up and for cleaning vegetables and salads. Facilities for waste disposal should also be located in this zone. The cooking zone, which incorporates the hob and oven, requires ample storage for pots and pans, baking trays, and so on.

Safety in the kitchen

Accidents are far more likely to occur in a kitchen that is poorly planned, with insufficient room to carry out the necessary activities safely. When planning a kitchen, it is therefore worth making sure

Work triangle
Traffic between zones describes what is known as 'the work triangle'. Reduce fatigue by keeping the length of each side of the work triangle to a minimum, but, if the three sides total less than 4.5m (15ft), you may find your kitchen cramped for space.

that storage will be accessible without having to lean across a cooker, for example, and without hindering the passage of another person through any part of the kitchen.

Good lighting
Poor lighting that throws your own shadow onto a counter top increases the risk of accidents. Either mount a ceiling light directly above the work surface or install strip lights under wall cupboards.

Head room
To avoid bumping your head while reaching to the back of a worktop, never make wall cupboards deeper than 300mm (1ft).

Worktop depth
600mm (2ft)
Major electrical appliances such as dishwashers and refrigerators will fit beneath a worktop of this depth.

Standard worktop height
900mm (3ft) from the floor
Most people are reasonably comfortable preparing food on a surface mounted at this height.

Maximum reach above a worktop
1.05m (3ft 6in) from the work surface
An adult can just reach this shelf while having to lean across a base unit. Don't store heavy objects at this height.

Optimum reach above a worktop
900mm (3ft) from the work surface
Items you need regularly should never be stored higher than this shelf.

Eye-level shelf
1.5m to 1.7m (5ft to 5ft 8in) from the floor
This is the optimum height for items you want to scan easily.

Lowest shelf above a worktop
450mm (1ft 6in) from the work surface
Shelves and wall-hung cupboards mounted lower than this begin to obscure your view of the back of the counter top. They also obstruct the use of food processors and similar appliances.

Safe passage
Allow for a corridor at least 900mm (3ft) wide for safe passage through a kitchen. Allow an extra 450mm (1ft 6in) for someone standing at a worktop.

KITCHEN STORAGE UNITS

Manufacturers of built-in kitchen units produce a wide range of fitments based on standard modules so that it is possible to assemble a run of storage that fills a wall space with little or no wasted space. A typical range of factory-made floor units is shown below. To expand your options still further, you can make your own matching fitments, such as mobile storage units, double-sided cupboards or special-purpose counter tops.

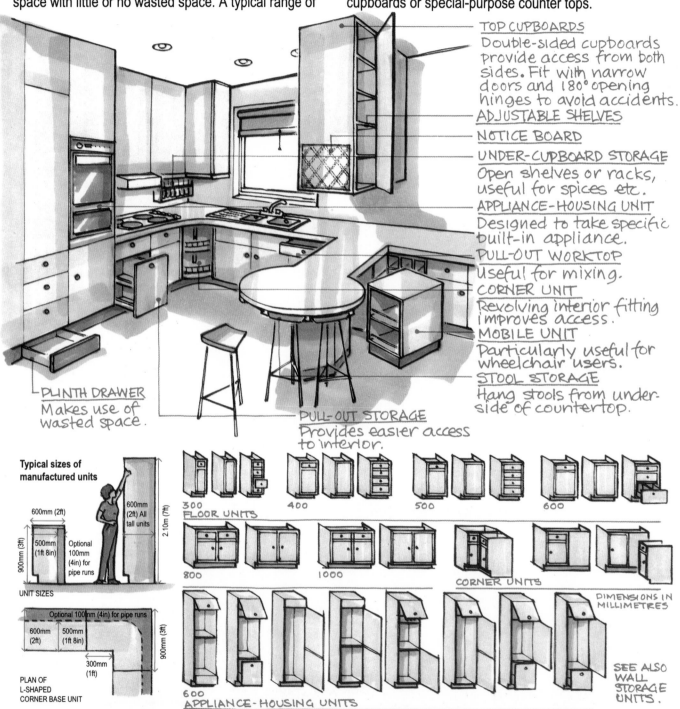

TOP CUPBOARDS
Double-sided cupboards provide access from both sides. Fit with narrow doors and 180° opening hinges to avoid accidents.

ADJUSTABLE SHELVES

NOTICE BOARD

UNDER-CUPBOARD STORAGE
Open shelves or racks, useful for spices etc.

APPLIANCE-HOUSING UNIT
Designed to take specific built-in appliance.

PULL-OUT WORKTOP
Useful for mixing.

CORNER UNIT
Revolving interior fitting improves access.

MOBILE UNIT
Particularly useful for wheelchair users.

STOOL STORAGE
Hang stools from underside of countertop.

PLINTH DRAWER
Makes use of wasted space.

PULL-OUT STORAGE
Provides easier access to interior.

Typical sizes of manufactured units

600mm (2ft)
500mm (1ft 8in)
900mm (3ft)
Optional 100mm (4in) for pipe runs
600mm (2ft) All tall units
2.10m (7ft)

UNIT SIZES

Optional 100mm (4in) for pipe runs
600mm (2ft)
500mm (1ft 8in)
300mm (1ft)
900mm (3ft)

PLAN OF L-SHAPED CORNER BASE UNIT

300
400
500
600
FLOOR UNITS

800
1000

CORNER UNITS

600
APPLIANCE-HOUSING UNITS

DIMENSIONS IN MILLIMETRES

SEE ALSO WALL STORAGE UNITS.

Fitted kitchens are normally constructed from a range of standard carcass units made with different styles of conventionally hinged doors, sliding doors or, in specific locations, special bi-fold doors. Drawers are ideal for storing smaller items and a pull-out interior makes it easier to retrieve items stored in a low cupboard.

Access to floor units

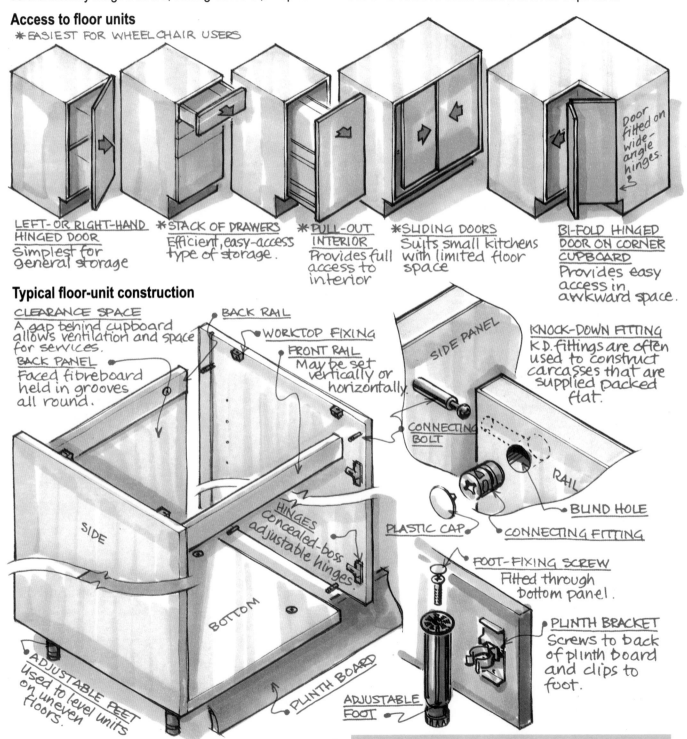

✴ EASIEST FOR WHEELCHAIR USERS

LEFT- OR RIGHT-HAND HINGED DOOR
Simplest for general storage

✴ STACK OF DRAWERS
Efficient, easy-access type of storage.

✴ PULL-OUT INTERIOR
Provides full access to interior

✴ SLIDING DOORS
Suits small kitchens with limited floor space

BI-FOLD HINGED DOOR ON CORNER CUPBOARD
Provides easy access in awkward space.

Door fitted on wide-angle hinges.

Typical floor-unit construction

CLEARANCE SPACE
A gap behind cupboard allows ventilation and space for services.

BACK PANEL
Faced fibreboard held in grooves all round.

BACK RAIL

WORKTOP FIXING

FRONT RAIL
May be set vertically or horizontally.

SIDE PANEL

KNOCK-DOWN FITTING
K.D. fittings are often used to construct carcasses that are supplied packed flat.

CONNECTING BOLT

RAIL

BLIND HOLE

SIDE

HINGES
Concealed-boss adjustable hinges.

PLASTIC CAP

CONNECTING FITTING

BOTTOM

FOOT-FIXING SCREW
Fitted through bottom panel.

PLINTH BRACKET
Screws to back of plinth board and clips to foot.

ADJUSTABLE FEET
Used to level units on uneven floors.

PLINTH BOARD

ADJUSTABLE FOOT

BUILT-IN KITCHEN FITTINGS

To avoid the inconvenience of having to rummage in the back of deep floor units, kitchen designers have come up with a number of ingenious fittings. They are available for self-assembly and installation, and are designed to fit standard-size kitchen cupboards. Such fittings are particularly suitable for the elderly or people with physical disabilities because they can be operated with the minimum of effort.

Fold-away fitting

Pull-out storage

Revolving units for corner cupboards

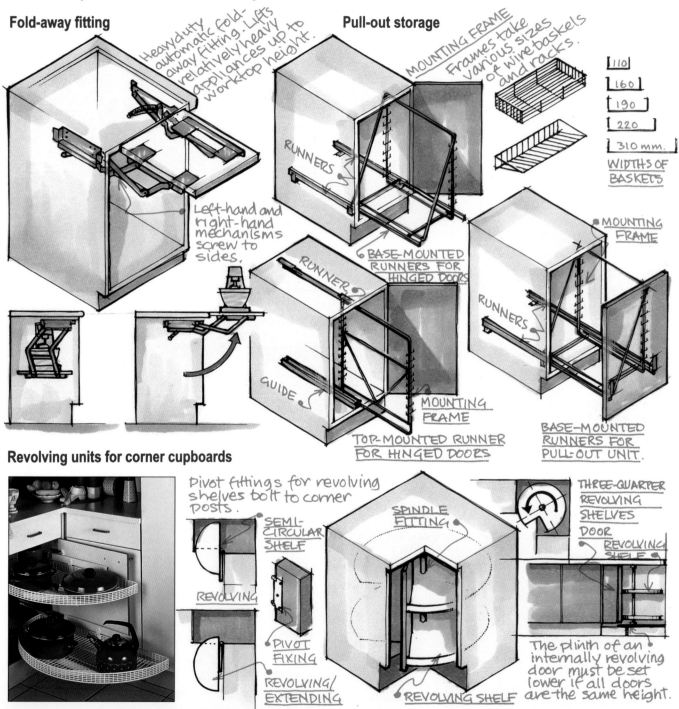

Heavyduty automatic fold-away fitting. Lifts relatively heavy appliances up to worktop height.

Left-hand and right-hand mechanisms screw to sides.

MOUNTING FRAME
Frames take various sizes of wire baskets and racks.

| 110 |
| 160 |
| 190 |
| 220 |
| 310 mm. |

WIDTHS OF BASKETS

RUNNERS

BASE-MOUNTED RUNNERS FOR HINGED DOORS

RUNNER

GUIDE

MOUNTING FRAME

TOP-MOUNTED RUNNER FOR HINGED DOORS

MOUNTING FRAME

RUNNERS

BASE-MOUNTED RUNNERS FOR PULL-OUT UNIT.

Pivot fittings for revolving shelves bolt to corner posts.

SEMI-CIRCULAR SHELF

REVOLVING

PIVOT FIXING

REVOLVING/EXTENDING

SPINDLE FITTING

REVOLVING SHELF

THREE-QUARTER REVOLVING SHELVES

DOOR

REVOLVING SHELF

The plinth of an internally revolving door must be set lower if all doors are the same height.

Waste bins

Packaged goods have contributed significantly to the amount of kitchen waste we have to deal with on a daily basis. It's not the sort of storage we want on view and a unit that discreetly houses a waste bin provides a valuable service in a modern kitchen, especially when the bin lid is lifted automatically as the door is opened.

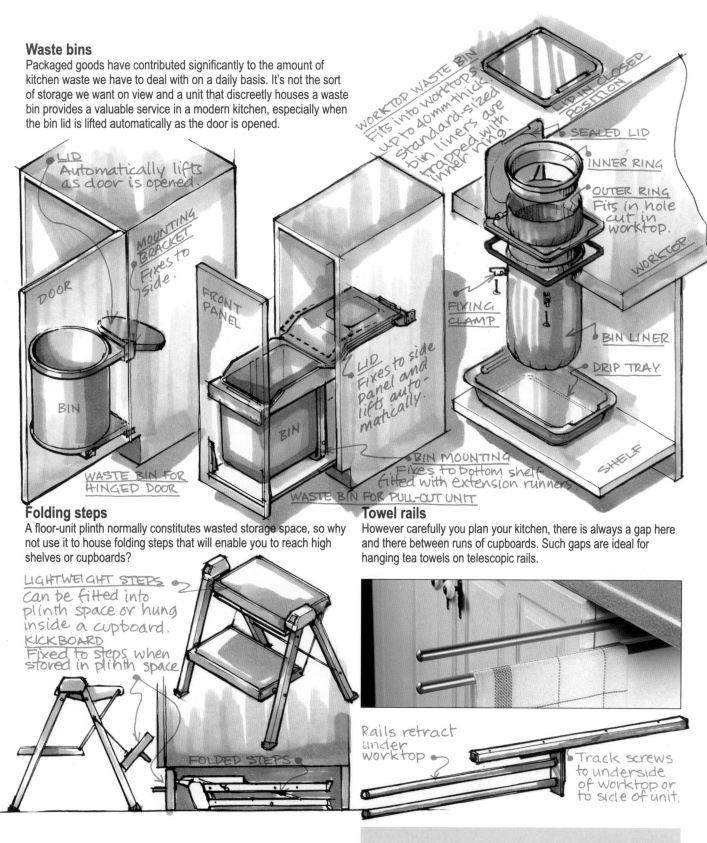

LID Automatically lifts as door is opened.

MOUNTING BRACKET Fixes to side.

DOOR

BIN

WASTE BIN FOR HINGED DOOR

FRONT PANEL

BIN

LID Fixes to side panel and lifts automatically.

BIN MOUNTING Fixes to bottom shelf fitted with extension runners.

WASTE BIN FOR PULL-OUT UNIT

WORKTOP WASTE BIN Fits into worktops up to 40mm thick. Standard-sized bin liners are trapped with inner ring.

LID IN CLOSED POSITION

SEALED LID

INNER RING

OUTER RING Fits in hole cut in worktop.

WORKTOP

FIXING CLAMP

BIN LINER

DRIP TRAY

SHELF

Folding steps

A floor-unit plinth normally constitutes wasted storage space, so why not use it to house folding steps that will enable you to reach high shelves or cupboards?

LIGHTWEIGHT STEPS Can be fitted into plinth space or hung inside a cupboard.

KICKBOARD Fixed to steps when stored in plinth space

FOLDED STEPS

Towel rails

However carefully you plan your kitchen, there is always a gap here and there between runs of cupboards. Such gaps are ideal for hanging tea towels on telescopic rails.

Rails retract under worktop

Track screws to underside of worktop or to side of unit.

SINK UNITS

Tasks such as preparing the raw ingredients for a meal or washing up afterwards are still often carried out at the kitchen sink. Until the introduction of the modern integrated sink unit, kitchens were fitted with a metal-lined or heavy ceramic sink supported on a wooden stand. Apart from a draining board and perhaps a shelf unit close by, there was little else in the way of storage. Many of these sinks have been replaced with modern versions, but the trend for characterful restoration of houses has led to an appreciation of the original fittings. The addition of shelving, racks or cupboards can make an attractive and functional period-style sink unit.

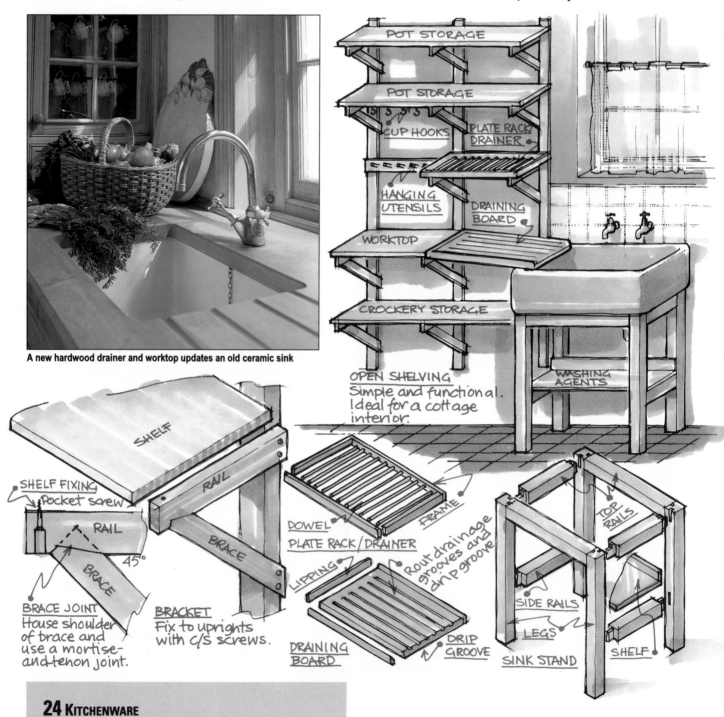

A new hardwood drainer and worktop updates an old ceramic sink

POT STORAGE

POT STORAGE

CUP HOOKS

PLATE RACK DRAINER

HANGING UTENSILS

DRAINING BOARD

WORKTOP

CROCKERY STORAGE

WASHING AGENTS

OPEN SHELVING
Simple and functional. Ideal for a cottage interior.

SHELF

RAIL

RAIL

BRACE

45°

SHELF FIXING
Pocket screw

BRACE JOINT
House shoulder of brace and use a mortise-and-tenon joint.

BRACKET
Fix to uprights with c/s screws.

DOWEL
PLATE RACK / DRAINER

FRAME

LIPPING

DRAINING BOARD

DRIP GROOVE

Rout drainage grooves and drip groove

TOP RAILS

SIDE RAILS

LEGS

SINK STAND

SHELF

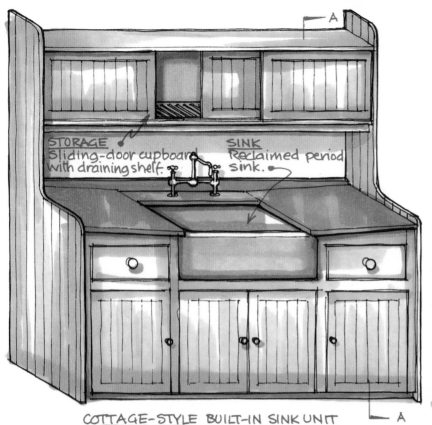

STORAGE Sliding-door cupboard with draining shelf.

SINK Reclaimed period sink.

COTTAGE-STYLE BUILT-IN SINK UNIT

A — A

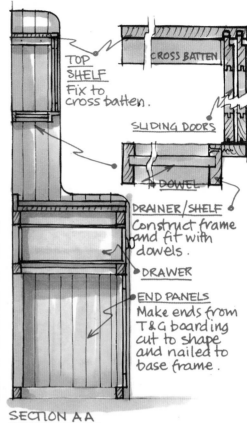

TOP SHELF Fix to cross batten.

CROSS BATTEN

SLIDING DOORS

DOWEL

DRAINER/SHELF Construct frame and fit with dowels.

DRAWER

END PANELS Make ends from T&G boarding cut to shape and nailed to base frame.

SECTION AA

CUPBOARD DOORS Make framed doors with panels of T&G boarding to match ends. Fit with butt hinges and knobs or latches according to period style.

DRAINER TOP Hardwood drainer screwed to frame using shrinkage plates.

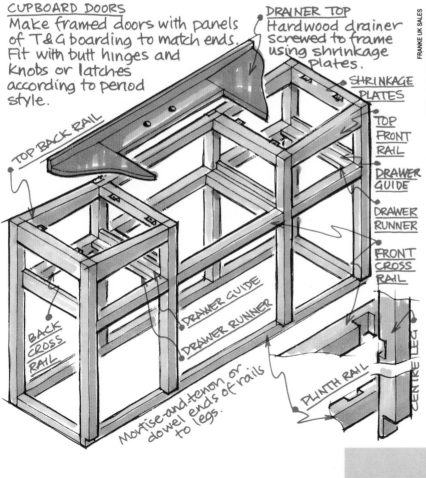

TOP BACK RAIL

SHRINKAGE PLATES

TOP FRONT RAIL

DRAWER GUIDE

DRAWER RUNNER

FRONT CROSS RAIL

BACK CROSS RAIL

DRAWER GUIDE

DRAWER RUNNER

CENTRE LEG

PLINTH RAIL

Mortise-and-tenon or dowel ends of rails to legs.

Workcentre sinks

Fitted in a continuous worktop, modern multi-bowl inset sinks are designed to function as adaptable workcentres. They are provided with drop-in baskets, chopping boards and drainer trays for preparing food and washing utensils.

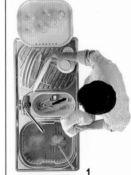

1 Washing china and utensils

2 Rinsing and peeling food

3 Cutting and chopping

WALL STORAGE

To complement standard floor units, kitchen-unit manufacturers also produce a range of wall-hung cabinets that are usually available in two heights. The taller ones are designed to fit up against the ceiling of an average modern home. Special display units are also made for some ranges. As heavy loads are involved, it is essential that all wall-hung cabinets are fixed securely. Alignment is easier if you use proprietary suspension fittings.

Glazed wall cabinets are a handsome alternative to standard wall cupboards

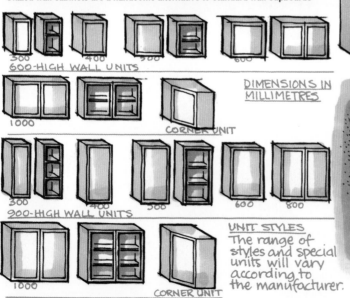

300 400 500
600-HIGH WALL UNITS

600

1000

DIMENSIONS IN MILLIMETRES

CORNER UNIT

300 400 500 600 800
900-HIGH WALL UNITS

UNIT STYLES
The range of styles and special units will vary according to the manufacturer.

1000

CORNER UNIT

Typical wall cupboard

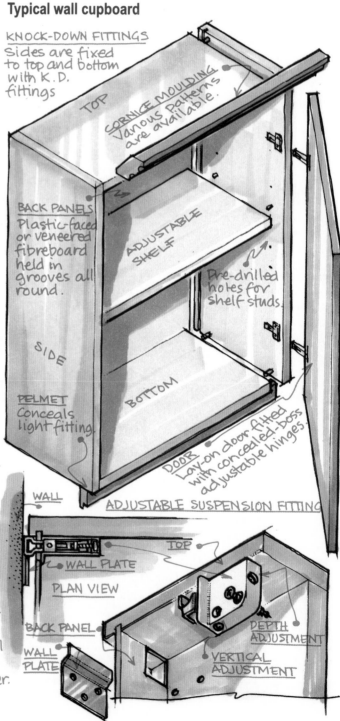

KNOCK-DOWN FITTINGS
Sides are fixed to top and bottom with K.D. fittings

TOP

CORNICE MOULDING
Various patterns are available.

BACK PANELS
Plastic-faced or veneered fibreboard held in grooves all round.

ADJUSTABLE SHELF

Pre-drilled holes for shelf studs.

SIDE

BOTTOM

PELMET
Conceals light fitting.

DOOR
Lay-on door fitted with concealed-boss adjustable hinges.

WALL

ADJUSTABLE SUSPENSION FITTING

WALL PLATE

TOP

PLAN VIEW

BACK PANEL

WALL PLATE

DEPTH ADJUSTMENT

VERTICAL ADJUSTMENT

Door mechanisms

Side-hinged doors are frequently fitted to wall-hung cupboards, but sliding doors, tambour shutters or lift-up flaps are more convenient in a compact kitchen.

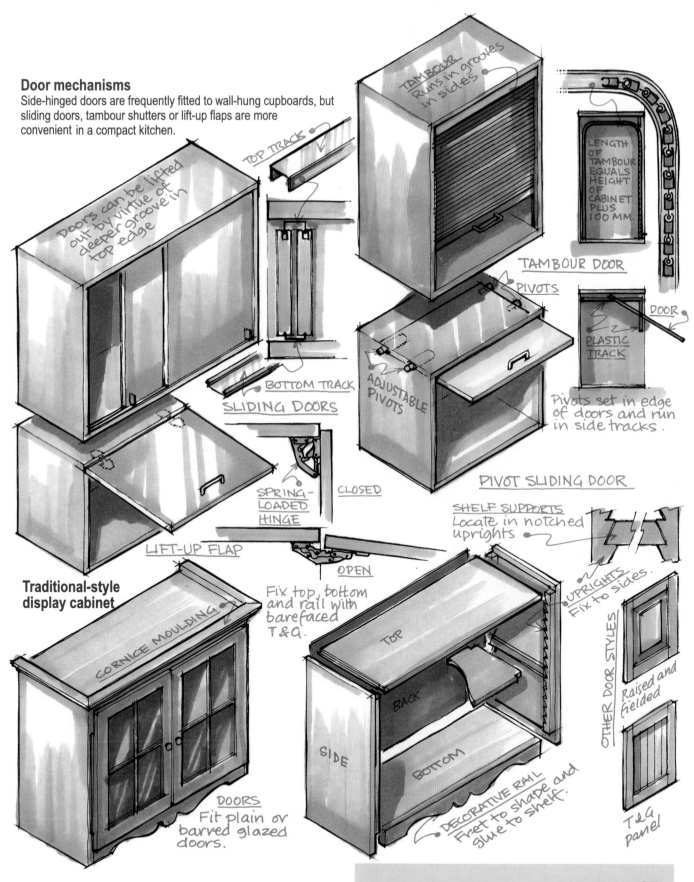

Doors can be lifted out by virtue of deeper groove in top edge

TOP TRACK

TAMBOUR Runs in grooves in sides

LENGTH OF TAMBOUR EQUALS HEIGHT OF CABINET PLUS 100 MM.

TAMBOUR DOOR

PIVOTS

BOTTOM TRACK

SLIDING DOORS

ADJUSTABLE PIVOTS

PLASTIC TRACK

DOOR

Pivots set in edge of doors and run in side tracks.

SPRING-LOADED HINGE

CLOSED

LIFT-UP FLAP

OPEN

Fix top, bottom and rail with barefaced T&G.

PIVOT SLIDING DOOR

SHELF SUPPORTS Locate in notched uprights

UPRIGHTS Fix to sides.

OTHER DOOR STYLES

Traditional-style display cabinet

CORNICE MOULDING

TOP

BACK

SIDE

BOTTOM

DOORS Fit plain or barred glazed doors.

DECORATIVE RAIL Fret to shape and glue to shelf.

Raised and fielded

T&G panel

CUTLERY AND UTENSILS

Kitchens in old houses were usually very basic, with a pantry or ventilated cupboard for perishable foodstuffs, and little more than shelves and racks for everything else. By today's standards, a modern streamlined kitchen seems more appealing, but a row of hanging utensils or a spice or wine rack still makes the room more homely. A rack also provides a simple but effective means of stowing awkwardly shaped utensils. Racks can be hung from the ceiling, fixed under an eye-level cupboard or attached to any convenient wall.

Suspended racks

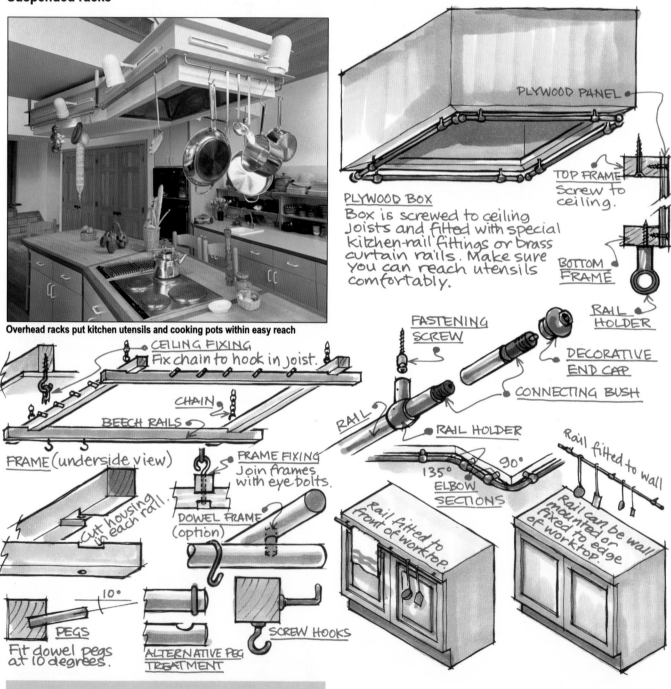

Overhead racks put kitchen utensils and cooking pots within easy reach

PLYWOOD PANEL

PLYWOOD BOX
Box is screwed to ceiling joists and fitted with special kitchen-rail fittings or brass curtain rails. Make sure you can reach utensils comfortably.

TOP FRAME
Screw to ceiling.

BOTTOM FRAME

RAIL HOLDER

CEILING FIXING
Fix chain to hook in joist.

CHAIN

BEECH RAILS

FRAME (underside view)

FRAME FIXING
Join frames with eye bolts.

Cut housing in each rail.

DOWEL FRAME (option)

FASTENING SCREW

RAIL

DECORATIVE END CAP

CONNECTING BUSH

RAIL HOLDER

135°   90°
ELBOW SECTIONS

Rail fitted to wall

Rail fitted to front of worktop.

Rail can be wall mounted or fixed to edge of worktop.

10°

PEGS
Fit dowel pegs at 10 degrees.

ALTERNATIVE PEG TREATMENT

SCREW HOOKS

Wall racks

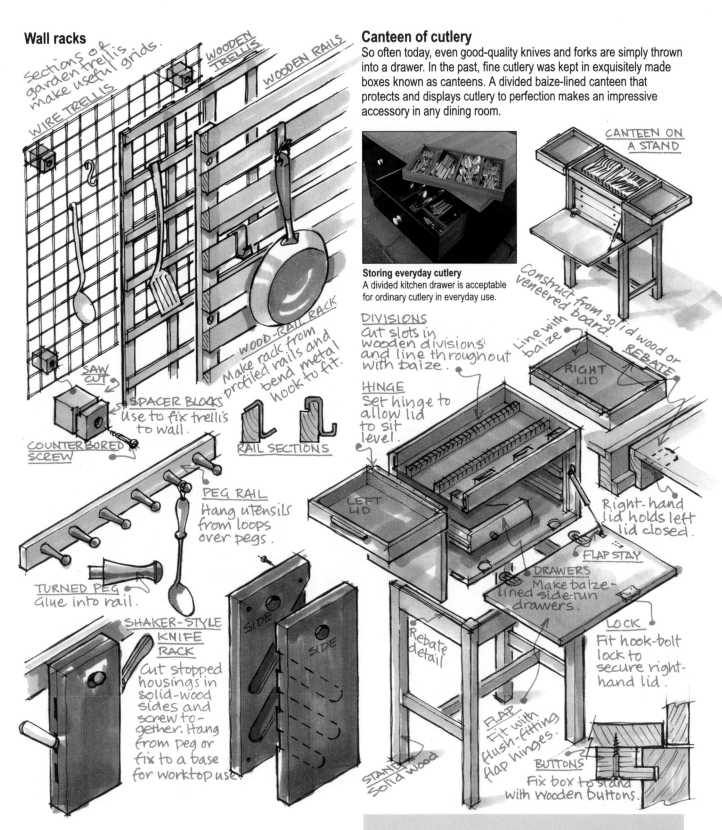

Sections of garden trellis make useful grids.

WIRE TRELLIS

WOODEN TRELLIS

WOODEN RAILS

WOOD-RAIL RACK
Make rack from profiled rails and bend metal hook to fit.

SAW CUT

SPACER BLOCKS
Use to fix trellis to wall.

COUNTER-BORED SCREW

RAIL SECTIONS

PEG RAIL
Hang utensils from loops over pegs.

TURNED PEG
Glue into rail.

SHAKER-STYLE KNIFE RACK
Cut stopped housings in solid-wood sides and screw together. Hang from peg or fix to a base for worktop use.

SIDE

SIDE

Canteen of cutlery

So often today, even good-quality knives and forks are simply thrown into a drawer. In the past, fine cutlery was kept in exquisitely made boxes known as canteens. A divided baize-lined canteen that protects and displays cutlery to perfection makes an impressive accessory in any dining room.

Storing everyday cutlery
A divided kitchen drawer is acceptable for ordinary cutlery in everyday use.

CANTEEN ON A STAND

Construct from solid wood or veneered board.

DIVISIONS
Cut slots in wooden divisions and line throughout with baize.

HINGE
Set hinge to allow lid to sit level.

Line with baize

RIGHT LID

REBATE

LEFT LID

Right-hand lid holds left lid closed.

FLAP STAY

DRAWERS
Make baize-lined side-run drawers.

LOCK
Fit hook-bolt lock to secure right-hand lid.

Rebate detail

STAND
Solid wood

FLAP
Fit with flush-fitting flap hinges.

BUTTONS
Fix box to stand with wooden buttons.

3

FOOD AND DRINK

Most of us store our groceries in the refrigerator, the freezer or kitchen cupboards, depending on the nature of the food. Special provision is therefore not essential unless you want to reproduce the conditions afforded by the old-fashioned larder. If you plan to store wine for more than a couple of weeks, it should be kept at a constant, fairly cool temperature – the kitchen is far from ideal. Bottles should be stored on their sides to keep the corks moist, with labels upwards so you know where the sediment has gathered when you come to pour the wine.

SPICE RACKS

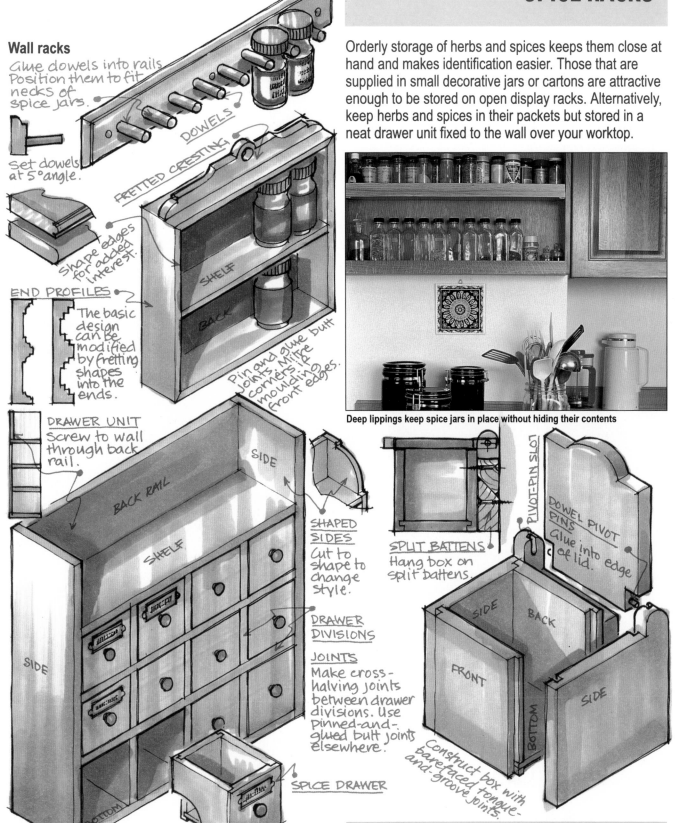

Orderly storage of herbs and spices keeps them close at hand and makes identification easier. Those that are supplied in small decorative jars or cartons are attractive enough to be stored on open display racks. Alternatively, keep herbs and spices in their packets but stored in a neat drawer unit fixed to the wall over your worktop.

Wall racks

Glue dowels into rails. Position them to fit necks of spice jars.

Set dowels at 5° angle.

FRETTED CRESTING

DOWELS

Shape edges for added interest.

END PROFILES

The basic design can be modified by fretting shapes into the ends.

SHELF

BACK

Pin and glue butt joints. Mitre corners if moulding front edges.

Deep lippings keep spice jars in place without hiding their contents

DRAWER UNIT
Screw to wall through back rail.

BACK RAIL

SIDE

SHELF

SHAPED SIDES
Cut to shape to change style.

DRAWER DIVISIONS

JOINTS
Make cross-halving joints between drawer divisions. Use pinned-and-glued butt joints elsewhere.

SIDE

BOTTOM

SPICE DRAWER

SPLIT BATTENS
Hang box on split battens.

PIVOT-PIN SLOT

DOWEL PIVOT PINS
Glue into edge of lid.

SIDE

BACK

FRONT

SIDE

BOTTOM

Construct box with barefaced tongue-and-groove joints.

LARDER CUPBOARDS

The traditional larder where people used to keep perishable food and dairy produce has been rendered practically obsolete by the widespread use of refrigeration and prepacked frozen food. However, certain foods lose their flavour if kept at fridge temperature, and it still pays to store them in a naturally cool ventilated cupboard.

MARTIN MOORE & CO

Hand-crafted ventilated cupboards recreate the advantages of larder storage

Modern-style vented cupboard

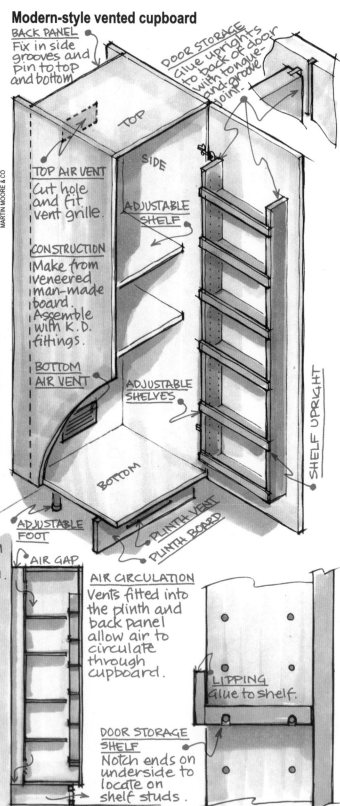

BACK PANEL
Fix in side grooves and pin to top and bottom

DOOR STORAGE
Glue uprights to back of door with tongue-and-groove joint.

TOP

SIDE

TOP AIR VENT
Cut hole and fit vent grille.

ADJUSTABLE SHELF

CONSTRUCTION
Make from veneered man-made board. Assemble with K.D. fittings.

BOTTOM AIR VENT

ADJUSTABLE SHELVES

SHELF UPRIGHT

BOTTOM

ADJUSTABLE FOOT

AIR GAP

PLINTH VENT
PLINTH BOARD

Traditional-style built-in larder

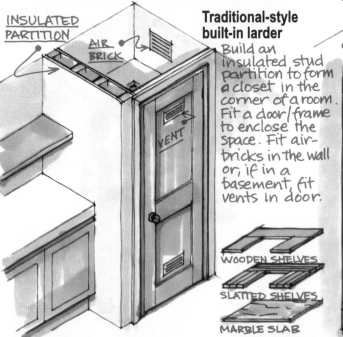

INSULATED PARTITION

AIR BRICK

VENT

Build an insulated stud partition to form a closet in the corner of a room. Fit a door/frame to enclose the space. Fit air-bricks in the wall or, if in a basement, fit vents in door.

WOODEN SHELVES

SLATTED SHELVES

MARBLE SLAB

AIR CIRCULATION
Vents fitted into the plinth and back panel allow air to circulate through cupboard.

LIPPING
Glue to shelf.

DOOR STORAGE SHELF
Notch ends on underside to locate on shelf studs.

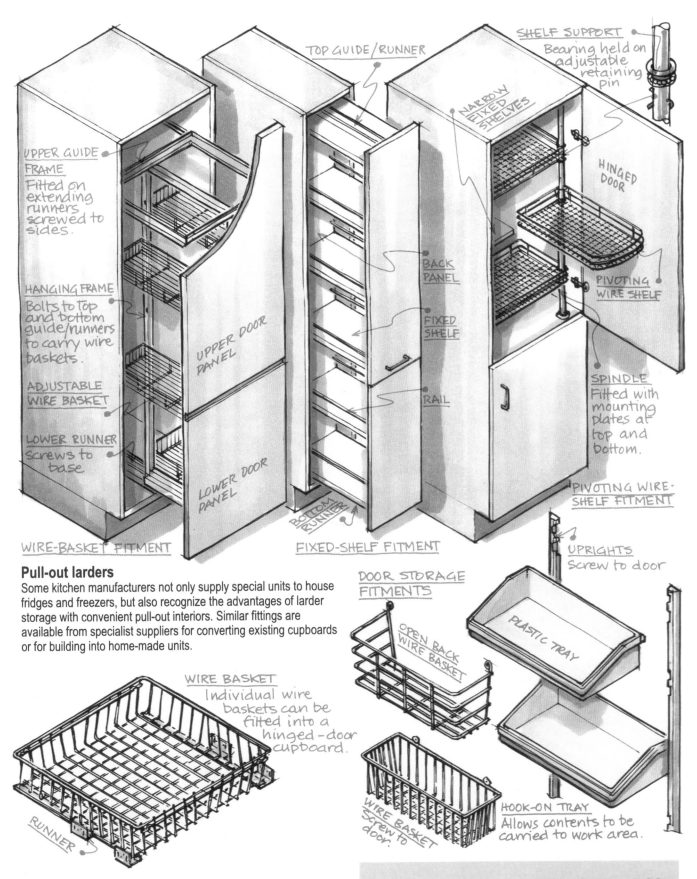

TOP GUIDE/RUNNER

SHELF SUPPORT
Bearing held on adjustable retaining pin

UPPER GUIDE FRAME
Fitted on extending runners screwed to sides.

NARROW FIXED SHELVES

HINGED DOOR

HANGING FRAME
Bolts to top and bottom guide/runners to carry wire baskets.

UPPER DOOR PANEL

BACK PANEL

FIXED SHELF

PIVOTING WIRE SHELF

ADJUSTABLE WIRE BASKET

RAIL

LOWER RUNNER
screws to base

SPINDLE
Fitted with mounting plates at top and bottom.

LOWER DOOR PANEL

BOTTOM RUNNER

PIVOTING WIRE-SHELF FITMENT

WIRE-BASKET FITMENT

FIXED-SHELF FITMENT

Pull-out larders

Some kitchen manufacturers not only supply special units to house fridges and freezers, but also recognize the advantages of larder storage with convenient pull-out interiors. Similar fittings are available from specialist suppliers for converting existing cupboards or for building into home-made units.

DOOR STORAGE FITMENTS

UPRIGHTS
Screw to door

OPEN BACK WIRE BASKET

PLASTIC TRAY

WIRE BASKET
Individual wire baskets can be fitted into a hinged-door cupboard.

HOOK-ON TRAY
Allows contents to be carried to work area.

WIRE BASKET
Screw to door

RUNNER

WINE RACKS

Thanks to the ever increasing popularity for wine and wine making, nowadays most people need to store more than the occasional bottle. There are considerable savings to be made by buying wine young and keeping it until it matures, or perhaps you just want to buy wine in bulk to take advantage of bargain rates. Provided you have a cool cellar or some similar location, you can simply store bottles of wine in the boxes in which they are supplied, but for accessibility and to keep the wine in top condition a rack is definitely preferable.

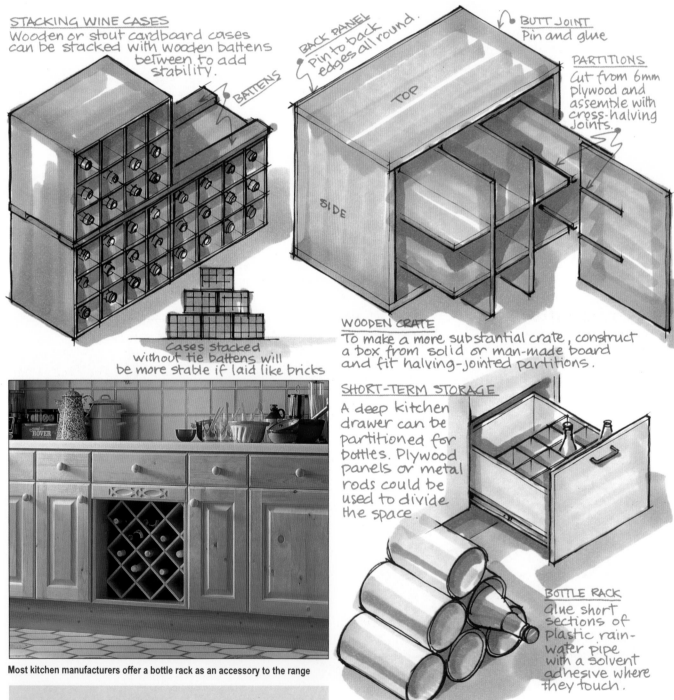

STACKING WINE CASES
Wooden or stout cardboard cases can be stacked with wooden battens between to add stability.

BATTENS

Cases stacked without tie battens will be more stable if laid like bricks

BACK PANEL
Pin to back edges all round.

TOP

SIDE

BUTT JOINT
Pin and glue

PARTITIONS
Cut from 6mm plywood and assemble with cross-halving joints.

WOODEN CRATE
To make a more substantial crate, construct a box from solid or man-made board and fit halving-jointed partitions.

SHORT-TERM STORAGE
A deep kitchen drawer can be partitioned for bottles. Plywood panels or metal rods could be used to divide the space.

BOTTLE RACK
Glue short sections of plastic rainwater pipe with a solvent adhesive where they touch.

Most kitchen manufacturers offer a bottle rack as an accessory to the range

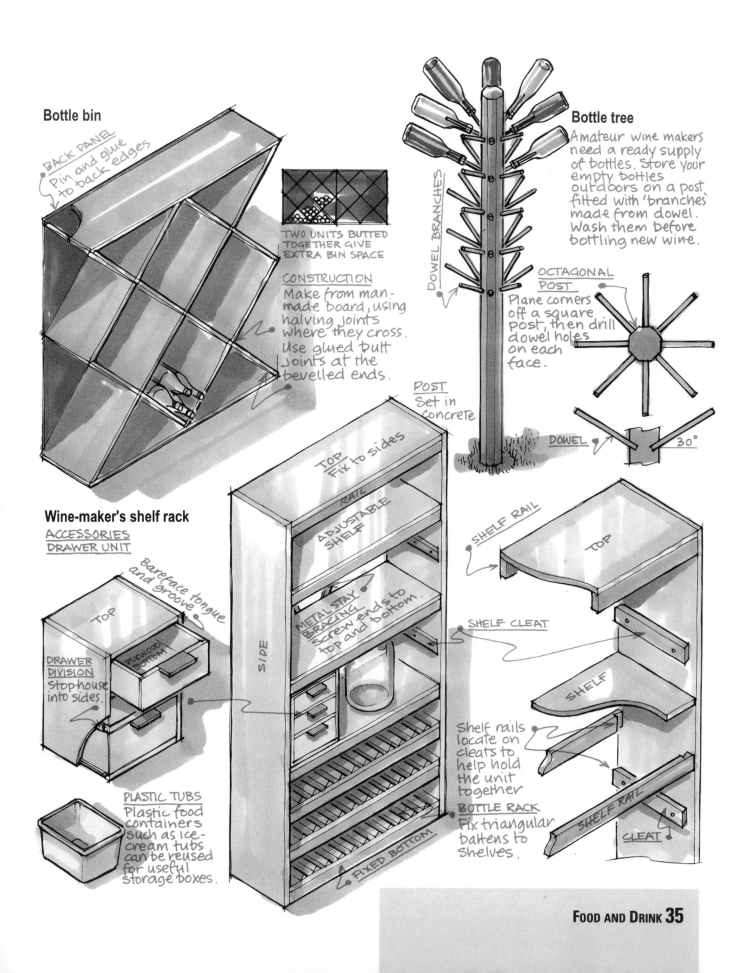

Bottle bin

BACK PANEL
Pin and glue to back edges

TWO UNITS BUTTED TOGETHER GIVE EXTRA BIN SPACE

CONSTRUCTION
Make from man-made board, using halving joints where they cross. Use glued butt joints at the bevelled ends.

Bottle tree

Amateur wine makers need a ready supply of bottles. Store your empty bottles outdoors on a post fitted with 'branches' made from dowel. Wash them before bottling new wine.

DOWEL BRANCHES

OCTAGONAL POST
Plane corners off a square post, then drill dowel holes on each face.

POST
Set in concrete

DOWEL

30°

Wine-maker's shelf rack

ACCESSORIES DRAWER UNIT

Bareface tongue and groove

TOP

PLYWOOD BOTTOM

DRAWER DIVISION
Stop house into sides.

PLASTIC TUBS
Plastic food containers such as ice-cream tubs can be reused for useful storage boxes.

TOP
Fix to sides

RAIL

ADJUSTABLE SHELF

METAL STAY BRACING
Screw ends to top and bottom.

SIDE

FIXED BOTTOM

SHELF RAIL

TOP

SHELF CLEAT

SHELF

Shelf rails locate on cleats to help hold the unit together

BOTTLE RACK
Fix triangular battens to shelves.

SHELF RAIL

CLEAT

DRINKS UNITS

The provision of alcohol is more or less *de rigueur* at most social gatherings, and to be able to serve drinks from a stylish cabinet or trolley adds to the sense of occasion. The ideal unit houses bottles, glasses and necessary accoutrements, and serves as a convenient surface on which to mix and pour the drinks.

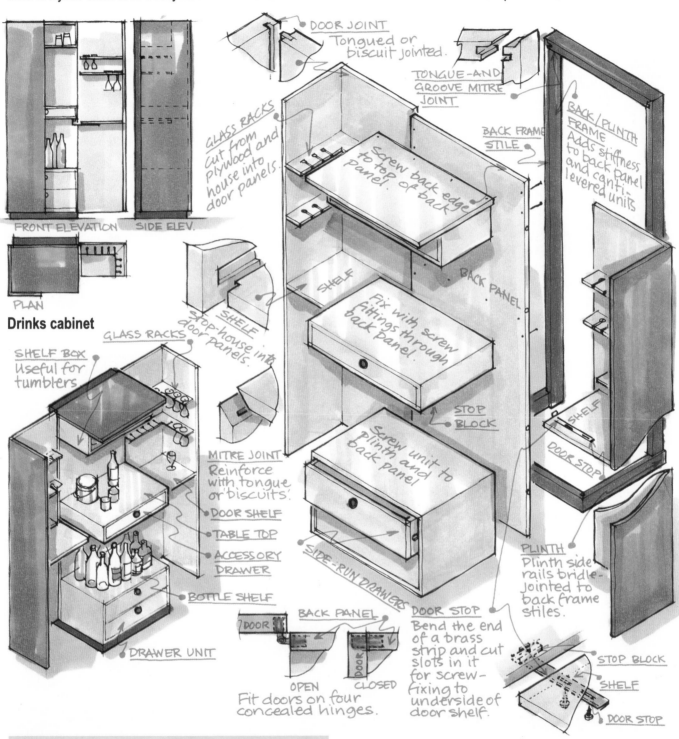

FRONT ELEVATION   SIDE ELEV.

PLAN

Drinks cabinet

GLASS RACKS Cut from plywood and house into door panels.

DOOR JOINT
Tongued or biscuit jointed.

TONGUE-AND-GROOVE MITRE JOINT

Screw back edge to top of back panel.

BACK FRAME STILE

BACK/PLINTH FRAME
Adds stiffness to back panel and cantilevered units

SHELF

BACK PANEL

SHELF
Stop-house into door panels.

Fix with screw fittings through back panel.

SHELF

DOOR STOP

STOP BLOCK

Screw unit to plinth and back panel

SHELF BOX
Useful for tumblers

GLASS RACKS

MITRE JOINT
Reinforce with tongue or 'biscuits'.

DOOR SHELF

TABLE TOP

ACCESSORY DRAWER

BOTTLE SHELF

DRAWER UNIT

SIDE-RUN DRAWERS

DOOR

BACK PANEL

OPEN   CLOSED

Fit doors on four concealed hinges.

DOOR STOP
Bend the end of a brass strip and cut slots in it for screw-fixing to underside of door shelf.

PLINTH
Plinth side rails bridle-jointed to back frame stiles.

STOP BLOCK

SHELF

DOOR STOP

Fall-flap unit

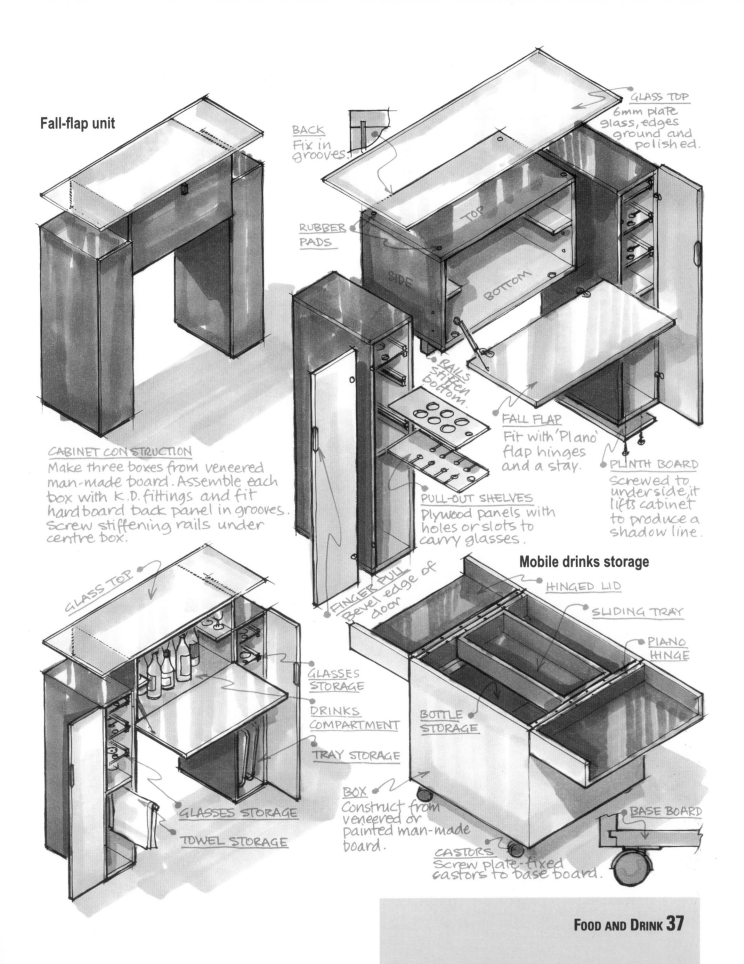

GLASS TOP
6mm plate
glass, edges
ground and
polished.

BACK
Fix in
grooves.

TOP

RUBBER
PADS

SIDE

BOTTOM

RAILS
Stiffen
bottom.

CABINET CONSTRUCTION
Make three boxes from veneered
man-made board. Assemble each
box with K.D. fittings and fit
hardboard back panel in grooves.
Screw stiffening rails under
centre box.

PULL-OUT SHELVES
Plywood panels with
holes or slots to
carry glasses.

FALL FLAP
Fit with 'Plano'
flap hinges
and a stay.

PLINTH BOARD
Screwed to
underside, it
lifts cabinet
to produce a
shadow line.

FINGER PULL
Bevel edge of
door

GLASS TOP

Mobile drinks storage

HINGED LID

SLIDING TRAY

PIANO
HINGE

GLASSES
STORAGE

DRINKS
COMPARTMENT

TRAY STORAGE

BOTTLE
STORAGE

GLASSES STORAGE

TOWEL STORAGE

BOX
Construct from
veneered or
painted man-made
board.

CASTORS
Screw plate-fixed
castors to base board.

BASE BOARD

4 CLEANING EQUIPMENT

The broom cupboard was traditionally the place where housemaids kept all the brushes and buckets, mops and dusters, polishes and detergents, often stored one on top of the other with barely enough room to close the door. Those essential but not particularly attractive bits and pieces we all need to keep our homes clean still need to be stored out of sight, but in an organized manner so that one can find and retrieve equipment with ease and tell in advance when essential materials need replenishing.

Cleaning equipment and materials

It is surprising how many items you need to accommodate. Below is a typical list of materials and equipment you should consider:

Broom	Paint cleaner
Carpet-shampoo	Paper towels
dispenser	Plastic bowl
Chamois leather	Plastic bucket
Dishcloths	Rubber gloves
Dustpan	Scouring pads
Duster cloths	Scrubbing brush
Feather or nylon-	Soft-bristle
fibre duster	handbrush
Floor polish	Solvents
Floor sealer	Stiff-bristle
Foam or cotton mop	handbrush
Furniture polish	Tea towels
Knee pads	Vacuum cleaner
Metal polish	Window cleaner

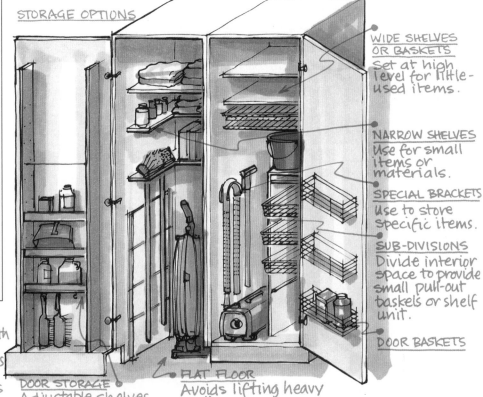

STORAGE OPTIONS

WIDE SHELVES OR BASKETS set at high level for little-used items.

NARROW SHELVES Use for small items or materials.

SPECIAL BRACKETS Use to store specific items.

SUB-DIVISIONS Divide interior space to provide small pull-out baskets or shelf unit.

DOOR BASKETS

PULL-OUT INTERIOR Can be fitted with wire baskets and/or racks for brooms etc.

DOOR STORAGE Adjustable shelves fitted between uprights.

FLAT FLOOR Avoids lifting heavy appliances.

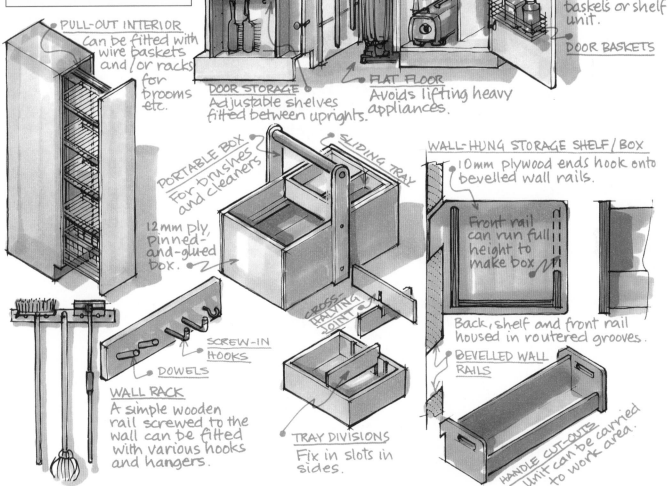

PORTABLE BOX For brushes and cleaners

12mm ply, pinned-and-glued box.

SLIDING TRAY

CROSS-HALVING JOINT

TRAY DIVISIONS Fix in slots in sides.

WALL-HUNG STORAGE SHELF/BOX 10mm plywood ends hook onto bevelled wall rails.

Front rail can run full height to make box

Back, shelf and front rail housed in routered grooves.

BEVELLED WALL RAILS

HANDLE CUT-OUTS Unit can be carried to work area.

SCREW-IN HOOKS

DOWELS

WALL RACK A simple wooden rail screwed to the wall can be fitted with various hooks and hangers.

UNDERSTAIRS STORAGE

The triangular space below a flight of stairs is an ideal place for storing cleaning equipment. In many cases it is already enclosed to form a deep cupboard that needs little more than a bank of narrow shelving for your various bottles and aerosols. There's plenty of scope for remodelling an understairs cupboard to suit your particular needs, but take care not to remove any loadbearing elements of the staircase in the process.

This mahogany staircase is not just an impressive flight of steps

A sliding panel reveals cavernous understairs storage

LADDER RACK
Fit a lightweight step ladder on a pair of racks screwed to the stair risers. Make bottom hooks larger for ease of removal and replacement

BACK BOARD

12mm PLYWOOD HOOKS

TROLLEY BOX
Make simple wooden boxes mounted on castors for ease of storage in awkward spaces.

ADJUSTABLE SHELVES
Fit an adjustable bracket system to provide for changing needs. Make upper shelves narrow so that all objects are visible.

BROOM RACK
Notch shelf to receive broom handles.

SCREW-IN HOOKS

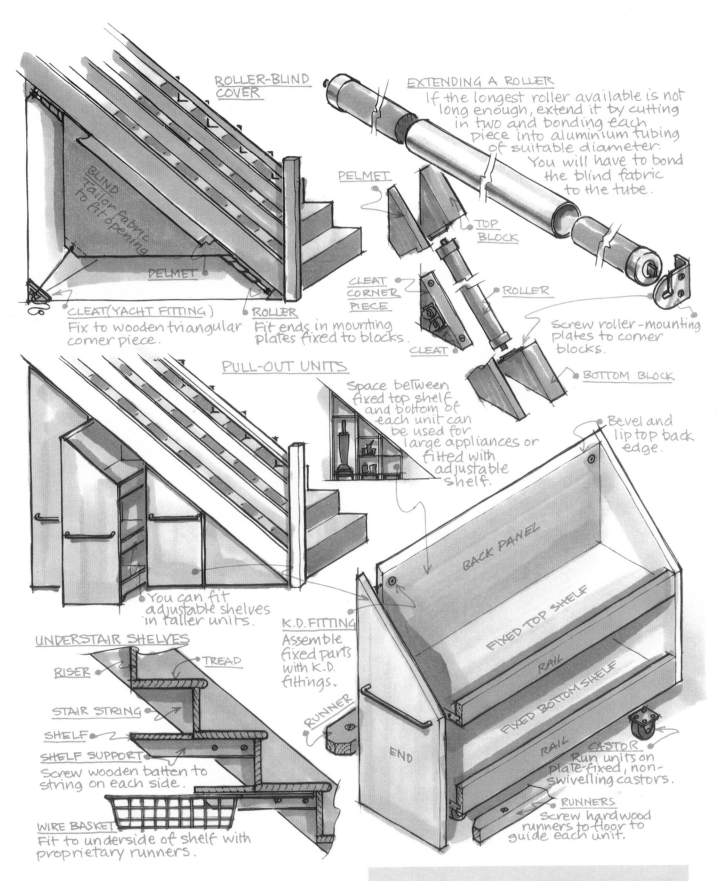

ROLLER-BLIND COVER

BLIND
Tailor fabric to fit opening

PELMET

CLEAT (YACHT FITTING)
Fix to wooden triangular corner piece.

ROLLER
Fit ends in mounting plates fixed to blocks.

EXTENDING A ROLLER
If the longest roller available is not long enough, extend it by cutting in two and bonding each piece into aluminium tubing of suitable diameter. You will have to bond the blind fabric to the tube.

PELMET

TOP BLOCK

CLEAT CORNER PIECE

CLEAT

ROLLER

Screw roller-mounting plates to corner blocks.

BOTTOM BLOCK

PULL-OUT UNITS

Space between fixed top shelf and bottom of each unit can be used for large appliances or fitted with adjustable shelf.

You can fit adjustable shelves in taller units.

Bevel and lip top back edge.

BACK PANEL

FIXED TOP SHELF

RAIL

FIXED BOTTOM SHELF

RAIL

UNDERSTAIR SHELVES

RISER

TREAD

STAIR STRING

SHELF

SHELF SUPPORT
Screw wooden batten to string on each side.

WIRE BASKET
Fit to underside of shelf with proprietary runners.

K.D. FITTING
Assemble fixed parts with K.D. fittings.

RUNNER

END

CASTOR
Run units on plate-fixed, non-swivelling castors.

RUNNERS
Screw hardwood runners to floor to guide each unit.

LAUNDRY AND LINEN

Chapter 5

Most of us have no choice but to combine laundry and kitchen in one space; consequently, washing machines and dryers are designed to fit under or beside standard kitchen units. But ideally a laundry should be situated elsewhere, perhaps in a basement or scullery, to prevent clean linen becoming contaminated with kitchen smells and grease. Position your appliances where they can be plumbed and wired conveniently, make separate provision for dirty and clean laundry, and plan adaptable storage for all the materials and equipment you need for washing, ironing and mending clothes and linen.

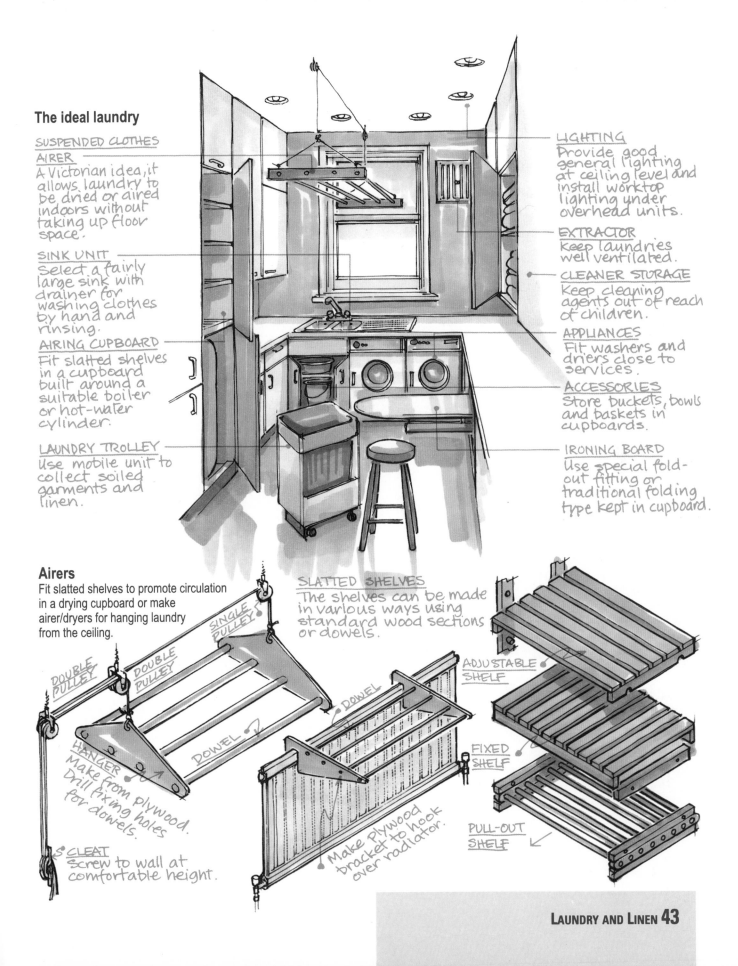

The ideal laundry

SUSPENDED CLOTHES AIRER
A Victorian idea, it allows laundry to be dried or aired indoors without taking up floor space.

SINK UNIT
Select a fairly large sink with drainer for washing clothes by hand and rinsing.

AIRING CUPBOARD
Fit slatted shelves in a cupboard built around a suitable boiler or hot-water cylinder.

LAUNDRY TROLLEY
Use mobile unit to collect soiled garments and linen.

LIGHTING
Provide good general lighting at ceiling level and install worktop lighting under overhead units.

EXTRACTOR
Keep laundries well ventilated.

CLEANER STORAGE
Keep cleaning agents out of reach of children.

APPLIANCES
Fit washers and driers close to services.

ACCESSORIES
Store buckets, bowls and baskets in cupboards.

IRONING BOARD
Use special fold-out fitting or traditional folding type kept in cupboard.

Airers

Fit slatted shelves to promote circulation in a drying cupboard or make airer/dryers for hanging laundry from the ceiling.

SLATTED SHELVES
The shelves can be made in various ways using standard wood sections or dowels.

DOUBLE PULLEY

SINGLE PULLEY

DOUBLE PULLEY

DOWEL

HANGER
Make from plywood. Drill fixing holes for dowels.

CLEAT
Screw to wall at comfortable height.

DOWEL

Make plywood bracket to hook over radiator.

ADJUSTABLE SHELF

FIXED SHELF

PULL-OUT SHELF

IRONING AND SEWING

Ironing is a time-consuming, often tedious, aspect of laundering. However, a stout ironing board at a comfortable height with ample worktop space nearby helps to reduce backache and fatigue. Most ironing boards are portable and are simply stowed away in a cupboard, but you might consider a factory-made fitting that slides out from beneath a worktop. A similar fitment can be used to support a sewing machine.

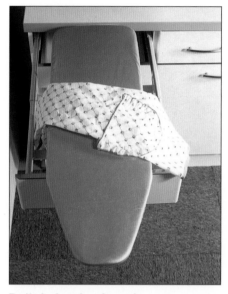

Built-in ironing board
When deployed, the ironing board automatically rises to a comfortable worktop height.

Pull-out table
When there's no option but to locate the laundry in the kitchen, this fitting can double as a breakfast bar and sewing worktop.

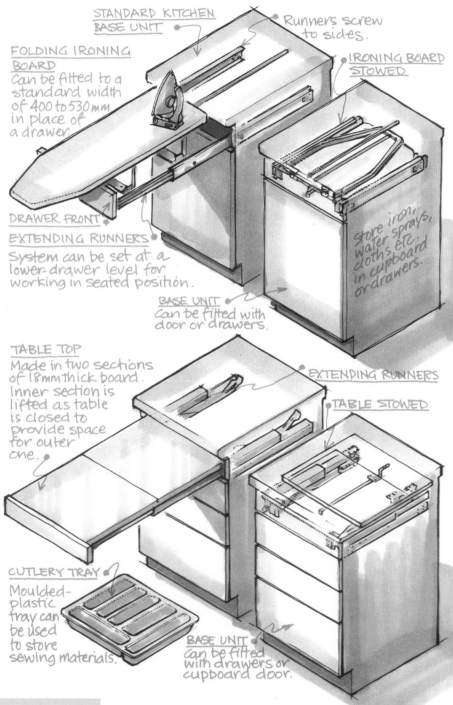

STANDARD KITCHEN BASE UNIT

Runners screw to sides.

IRONING BOARD STOWED

FOLDING IRONING BOARD
Can be fitted to a standard width of 400 to 530mm in place of a drawer.

DRAWER FRONT

EXTENDING RUNNERS
System can be set at a lower-drawer level for working in seated position.

Store iron, water sprays, cloths etc. in cupboard or drawers.

BASE UNIT
Can be fitted with door or drawers.

TABLE TOP
Made in two sections of 18mm thick board. Inner section is lifted as table is closed to provide space for outer one.

EXTENDING RUNNERS

TABLE STOWED

CUTLERY TRAY
Moulded-plastic tray can be used to store sewing materials.

BASE UNIT
Can be fitted with drawers or cupboard door.

OVERHEAD STORAGE

Spare sheets, blankets, duvets and pillows are bulky items that can occupy valuable storage space for months on end. Place those that are not required regularly in long-term overhead storage. Guest rooms and landings are possible locations, and you need nothing more than a step ladder to gain access.

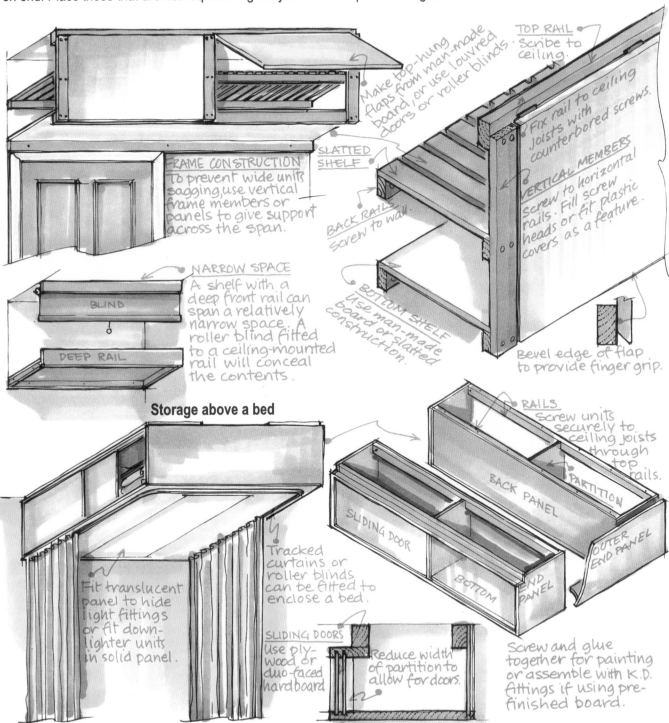

Make top-hung flaps from man-made board, or use louvred doors or roller blinds.

TOP RAIL Scribe to ceiling.

Fix rail to ceiling joists with counterbored screws.

VERTICAL MEMBERS Screw to horizontal rails. Fill screw heads or fit plastic covers as a feature.

SLATTED SHELF

FRAME CONSTRUCTION To prevent wide units sagging, use vertical frame members or panels to give support across the span.

BACK RAILS Screw to wall.

BOTTOM SHELF Use man-made board or slatted construction.

Bevel edge of flap to provide finger grip.

NARROW SPACE A shelf with a deep front rail can span a relatively narrow space. A roller blind fitted to a ceiling-mounted rail will conceal the contents.

BLIND

DEEP RAIL

Storage above a bed

Fit translucent panel to hide light fittings or fit down-lighter units in solid panel.

Tracked curtains or roller blinds can be fitted to enclose a bed.

SLIDING DOORS Use ply-wood or duo-faced hardboard

Reduce width of partition to allow for doors.

RAILS Screw units securely to ceiling joists through top rails.

BACK PANEL

PARTITION

SLIDING DOOR

END PANEL

BOTTOM

OUTER END PANEL

Screw and glue together for painting or assemble with K.D. fittings if using pre-finished board.

LINEN CHESTS

Crude wooden chests hewn from logs or made from solid-wood planks were among the earliest forms of storage. Despite their undoubted charm, these rudimentary chests were prone to warping and splitting, and were eventually outmoded by a more sophisticated frame-and-panel construction. Instead of the massive single boards that had been used previously, comparatively lightweight frames were employed, incorporating small wooden panels that, though held in grooves, were free to expand or contract with changes in humidity. Thanks to superior glues and modern methods of drying timber, it is possible nowadays to make solid-wood chests that remain relatively stable, and it's feasible to make a traditional-style framed chest with veneered plywood panels.

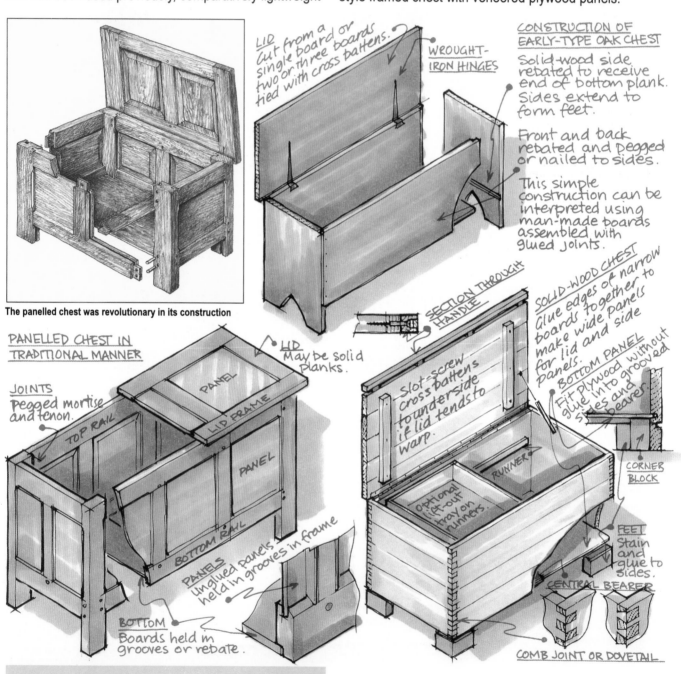

The panelled chest was revolutionary in its construction

LID
Cut from a single board or two or three boards tied with cross battens.

WROUGHT-IRON HINGES

CONSTRUCTION OF EARLY-TYPE OAK CHEST
Solid-wood side rebated to receive end of bottom plank. Sides extend to form feet.

Front and back rebated and pegged or nailed to sides.

This simple construction can be interpreted using man-made boards assembled with glued joints.

SECTION THROUGH HANDLE

SOLID-WOOD CHEST
Glue edges of narrow boards together to make wide panels for lid and side panels.

BOTTOM PANEL
Fit plywood without glue into grooved sides and bearer.

Slot-screw cross battens to underside if lid tends to warp.

PANELLED CHEST IN TRADITIONAL MANNER

LID
May be solid planks.

JOINTS
Pegged mortise and tenon.

TOP RAIL

PANEL

LID FRAME

PANEL

BOTTOM RAIL

PANELS
Unglued panels held in grooves in frame

BOTTOM
Boards held in grooves or rebate.

Optional lift-out tray on runners.

RUNNER

CORNER BLOCK

FEET
Stain and glue to sides.

CENTRAL BEARER

COMB JOINT OR DOVETAIL

LINEN PRESSES

Handsome antique linen presses are now highly prized for their exquisite materials and craftsmanship. The press, which usually stood on another low cupboard or chest of drawers, was the wardrobe of the day. Clothes were not hung, but folded and placed on pull-out trays that were sometimes made from scented cedar wood and provided with baize covers to protect the contents from dust. In Victorian times the press was frequently combined with a hanging wardrobe in what today seems like an inordinately bulky piece of furniture.

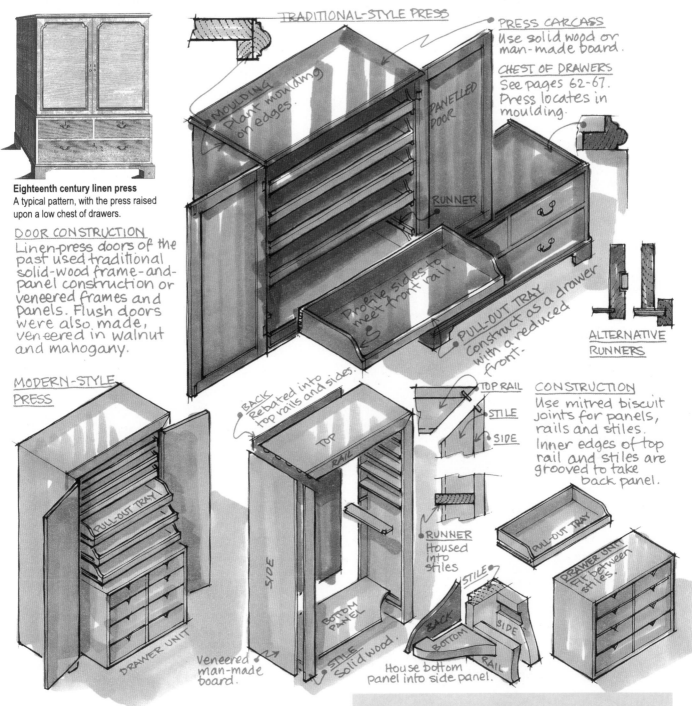

Eighteenth century linen press
A typical pattern, with the press raised upon a low chest of drawers.

DOOR CONSTRUCTION
Linen-press doors of the past used traditional solid-wood frame-and-panel construction or veneered frames and panels. Flush doors were also made, veneered in walnut and mahogany.

MODERN-STYLE PRESS

TRADITIONAL-STYLE PRESS

PRESS CARCASS
Use solid wood or man-made board.

CHEST OF DRAWERS
See pages 62-67. Press locates in moulding.

MOULDING
Plant moulding on edges.

PANELLED DOOR

RUNNER

PULL-OUT TRAY
Construct as a drawer with a reduced front.

Profile sides to meet front rail.

ALTERNATIVE RUNNERS

BACK
Rebated into top rails and sides.

TOP RAIL

STILE

SIDE

CONSTRUCTION
Use mitred biscuit joints for panels, rails and stiles. Inner edges of top rail and stiles are grooved to take back panel.

TOP RAIL

SIDE

RUNNER
Housed into stiles

PULL-OUT TRAY

DRAWER UNIT
Fit between stiles.

STILE

BACK

BOTTOM

SIDE

RAIL

BOTTOM PANEL

PULL-OUT TRAY

DRAWER UNIT

STILE
Solid wood.

Veneered man-made board.

House bottom panel into side panel.

Chapter 6

CHINA AND GLASS

With china and glass we are talking about two distinctly different forms of storage. All of us have the everyday crockery and glassware that we tend to keep in our kitchen cupboards or on a dresser, while the best dinner service is perhaps put away in a sideboard. However, china and glass is much admired by collectors who aspire to special cabinets or shelving that will display their treasures to best advantage.

A drainage rack alongside the kitchen sink provides convenient storage for crockery in regular use. Manufactured moulded-plastic or plastic-coated-wire racks are plainly functional; a rack made from wood is equally useful and much more attractive.

A continuous narrow shelf running round a room or an entrance hall is a charming way to display a collection of plates or other small items. This was a feature of many Victorian and Edwardian homes and looks especially good at about picture-rail height.

Plate racks

Machine-cut transverse and longitudinal grooves in opposite faces of a hardwood board. Cut the width or angle of the top transverse grooves to suit your plates. Thoroughly seal wood with yacht varnish.

Drain holes formed by crossed grooves

DOWELS
Drill rails and insert glued dowel-posts, spaced to suit your plates.

RAIL
CROSS RAIL

Construct entirely from dowel.

Set out rails to suit sizes of plates.

Turn ends of legs to shape.

Reduce diameter of rails on a lathe to make joints.

LEG
RAIL

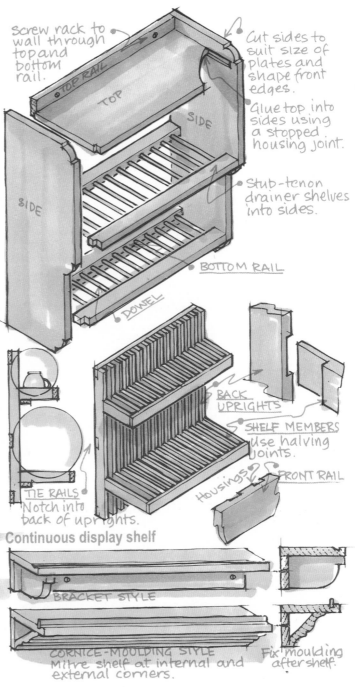

Screw rack to wall through top and bottom rail.

TOP RAIL
TOP
SIDE

Cut sides to suit size of plates and shape front edges.

Glue top into sides using a stopped housing joint.

Stub-tenon drainer shelves into sides.

SIDE

BOTTOM RAIL

DOWEL

TIE RAILS
Notch into back of uprights.

BACK UPRIGHTS

SHELF MEMBERS
Use halving joints.

HOUSINGS
FRONT RAIL

Continuous display shelf

BRACKET STYLE

CORNICE-MOULDING STYLE
Mitre shelf at internal and external corners.

Fix moulding after shelf.

DRESSERS

The traditional floor-to-ceiling kitchen dresser has remained a cherished piece of furniture since Georgian times. It was an impressive sight, with its broad open shelves for platters and jugs, its ample drawers for cutlery and other utensils, and deep cupboards that swallowed up all manner of pots and pans. Most dressers were made from cheap native timbers, using local forms of construction and restrained decoration that owed more to custom and practice than formal design. Sadly many dressers were ripped out when kitchens were modernized, but they are now appreciated for their admirable combination of display and storage space.

18th century domestic interior with a dresser

Early Victorian built-in pine dresser with open pot board at floor level

Typical traditional dresser

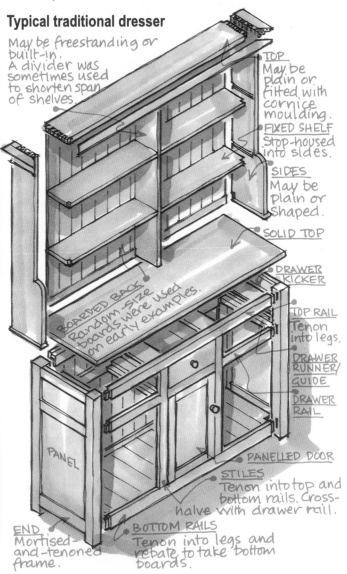

May be freestanding or built-in. A divider was sometimes used to shorten span of shelves.

TOP
May be plain or fitted with cornice moulding.

FIXED SHELF
Stop-housed into sides.

SIDES
May be plain or shaped.

SOLID TOP

DRAWER KICKER

BOARDED BACK
Random-size boards were used on early examples.

TOP RAIL
Tenon into legs.

DRAWER RUNNER/GUIDE

DRAWER RAIL

PANEL

PANELLED DOOR

STILES
Tenon into top and bottom rails. Cross-halve with drawer rail.

END
Mortised-and-tenoned frame.

BOTTOM RAILS
Tenon into legs and rebate to take bottom boards.

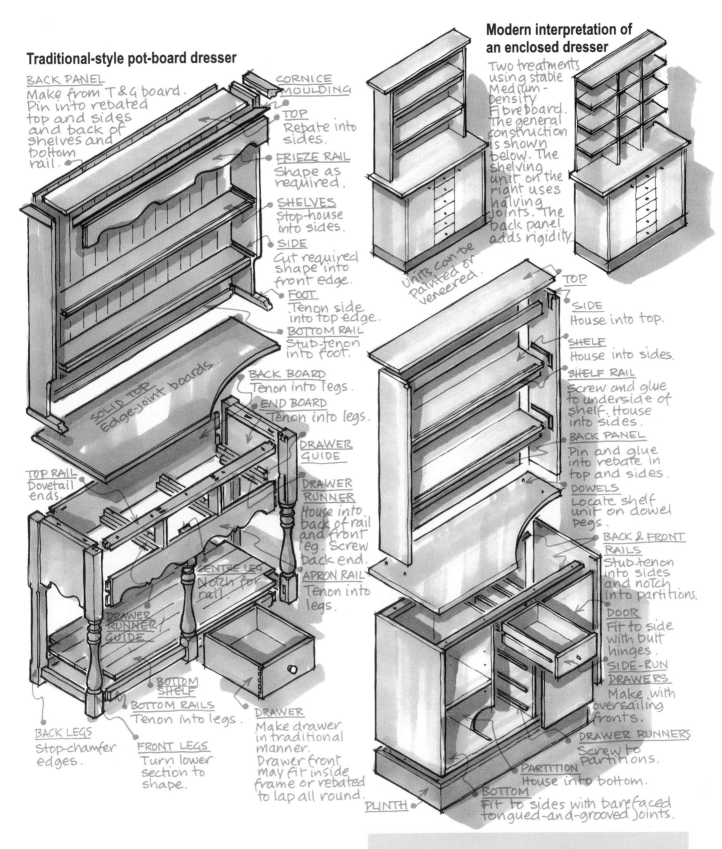

Traditional-style pot-board dresser

BACK PANEL
Make from T&G board. Pin into rebated top and sides and back of shelves and bottom rail.

CORNICE MOULDING

TOP
Rebate into sides.

FRIEZE RAIL
Shape as required.

SHELVES
Stop-house into sides.

SIDE
Cut required shape into front edge.

FOOT
Tenon side into top edge.

BOTTOM RAIL
Stub-tenon into foot.

SOLID TOP
Edge-joint boards.

BACK BOARD
Tenon into legs.

END BOARD
Tenon into legs.

DRAWER GUIDE

DRAWER RUNNER
House into back of rail and front leg. Screw back end.

APRON RAIL
Tenon into legs.

TOP RAIL
Dovetail ends.

CENTRE LEG
Notch for rail.

DRAWER RUNNER GUIDE

BOTTOM SHELF

BOTTOM RAILS
Tenon into legs.

DRAWER
Make drawer in traditional manner. Drawer front may fit inside frame or rebated to lap all round.

BACK LEGS
Stop-chamfer edges.

FRONT LEGS
Turn lower section to shape.

Modern interpretation of an enclosed dresser

Two treatments using stable Medium-Density Fibreboard. The general construction is shown below. The shelving unit on the right uses halving joints. The back panel adds rigidity.

Units can be painted or veneered.

TOP

SIDE
House into top.

SHELF
House into sides.

SHELF RAIL
Screw and glue to underside of shelf. House into sides.

BACK PANEL
Pin and glue into rebate in top and sides.

DOWELS
Locate shelf unit on dowel pegs.

BACK & FRONT RAILS
Stub-tenon into sides and notch into partitions.

DOOR
Fit to side with butt hinges.

SIDE-RUN DRAWERS
Make with oversailing fronts.

DRAWER RUNNERS
Screw to partitions.

PARTITION
House into bottom.

BOTTOM
Fit to sides with barefaced tongued-and-grooved joints.

PLINTH

SIDEBOARDS

The sideboard evolved in the late eighteenth century from the simpler side table. Separate pedestal units were placed at each end of the table to serve as plate cupboards and 'cellarets' for wine bottles. Originally designed as long low pieces of furniture, Victorian sideboards became more upright and increasingly elaborate, with tall mirrors and ornamented shelving. The modern sideboard has simpler lines, more in character with eighteenth century examples, to provide cupboard space and drawer storage for tableware and cutlery.

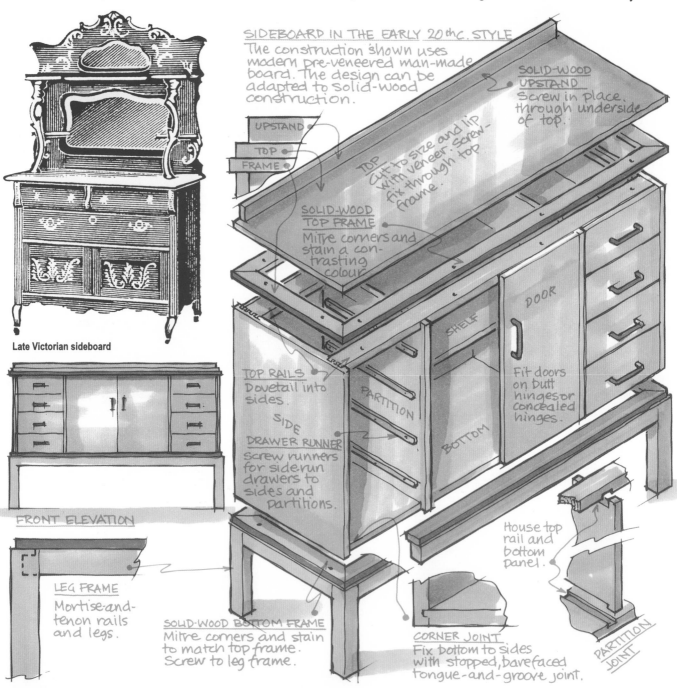

Late Victorian sideboard

SIDEBOARD IN THE EARLY 20th C. STYLE
The construction shown uses modern pre-veneered man-made board. The design can be adapted to solid-wood construction.

UPSTAND
TOP
FRAME

SOLID-WOOD UPSTAND
Screw in place through underside of top.

TOP
Cut to size and lip with veneer. Screw. Fix through top frame.

SOLID-WOOD TOP FRAME
Mitre corners and stain a contrasting colour.

SHELF

DOOR

Fit doors on butt hinges or concealed hinges.

TOP RAILS
Dovetail into sides.

PARTITION

BOTTOM

SIDE

DRAWER RUNNER
Screw runners for side-run drawers to sides and partitions.

FRONT ELEVATION

LEG FRAME
Mortise-and-tenon rails and legs.

SOLID-WOOD BOTTOM FRAME
Mitre corners and stain to match top frame. Screw to leg frame.

CORNER JOINT
Fix bottom to sides with stopped, barefaced tongue-and-groove joint.

House top rail and bottom panel.

PARTITION JOINT

Small solid-wood sideboard

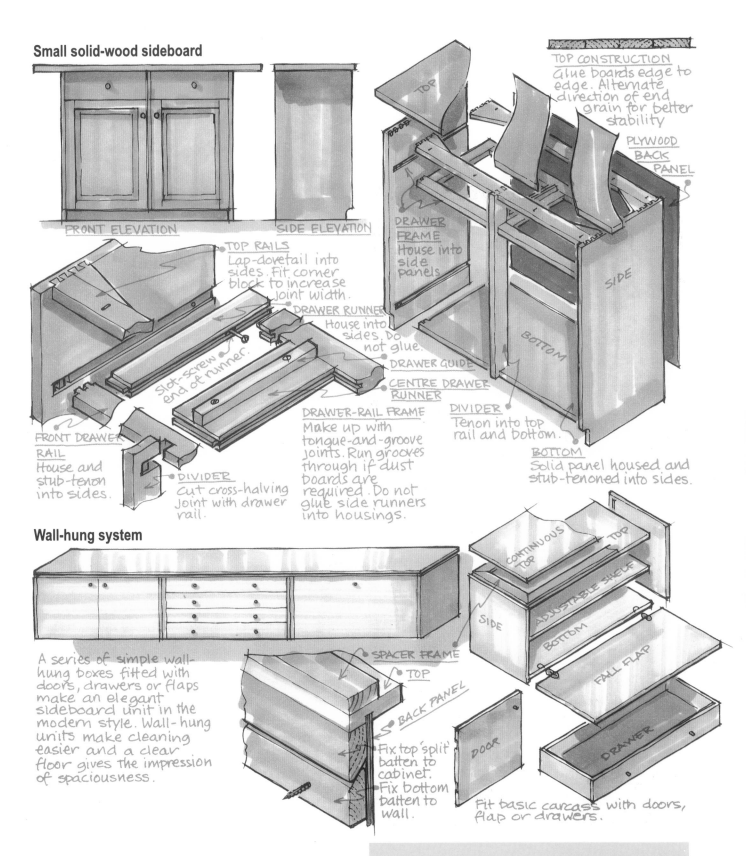

FRONT ELEVATION

SIDE ELEVATION

TOP CONSTRUCTION
Glue boards edge to edge. Alternate direction of end grain for better stability

PLYWOOD BACK PANEL

TOP

DRAWER FRAME
House into side panels

SIDE

BOTTOM

TOP RAILS
Lap-dovetail into sides. Fit corner block to increase joint width.

DRAWER RUNNER
House into sides. Do not glue.

Slot-screw end of runner.

DRAWER GUIDE

CENTRE DRAWER RUNNER

DRAWER-RAIL FRAME
Make up with tongue-and-groove joints. Run grooves through if dust boards are required. Do not glue side runners into housings.

DIVIDER
Tenon into top rail and bottom.

BOTTOM
Solid panel housed and stub-tenoned into sides.

FRONT DRAWER RAIL
House and stub-tenon into sides.

DIVIDER
Cut cross-halving joint with drawer rail.

Wall-hung system

A series of simple wall-hung boxes fitted with doors, drawers or flaps make an elegant sideboard unit in the modern style. Wall-hung units make cleaning easier and a clear floor gives the impression of spaciousness.

SPACER FRAME

TOP

BACK PANEL

Fix top 'split' batten to cabinet. Fix bottom batten to wall.

CONTINUOUS TOP

TOP

ADJUSTABLE SHELF

SIDE

BOTTOM

FALL FLAP

DOOR

DRAWER

Fit basic carcass with doors, flap or drawers.

CORNER CUPBOARDS

Corner cupboards make use of space that might otherwise be redundant. Small glazed cupboards make ideal display cabinets, and many people use them for their finest glassware. Complete floor-to-ceiling units literally change the shape of the room, creating unconventional shapes and spaces.

Elaborate corner cupboard, incorporating a deep niche with open shelves

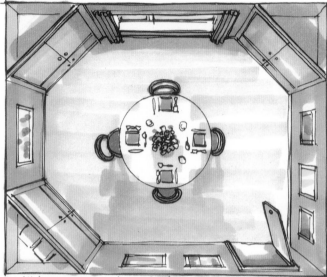

Built-in corner cupboards change a room dramatically

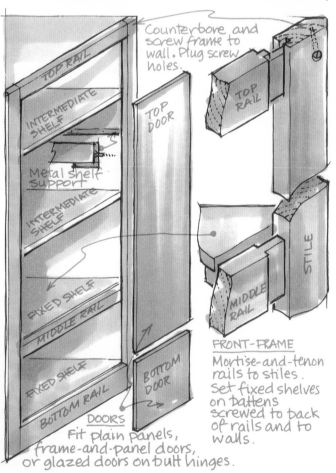

Counterbore and screw frame to wall. Plug screw holes.

TOP RAIL

INTERMEDIATE SHELF

TOP RAIL

TOP DOOR

Metal shelf support

INTERMEDIATE SHELF

STILE

FIXED SHELF

MIDDLE RAIL

MIDDLE RAIL

FIXED SHELF

BOTTOM RAIL

BOTTOM DOOR

FRONT-FRAME
Mortise-and-tenon rails to stiles. Set fixed shelves on battens screwed to back of rails and to walls.

DOORS
Fit plain panels, frame-and-panel doors, or glazed doors on butt hinges.

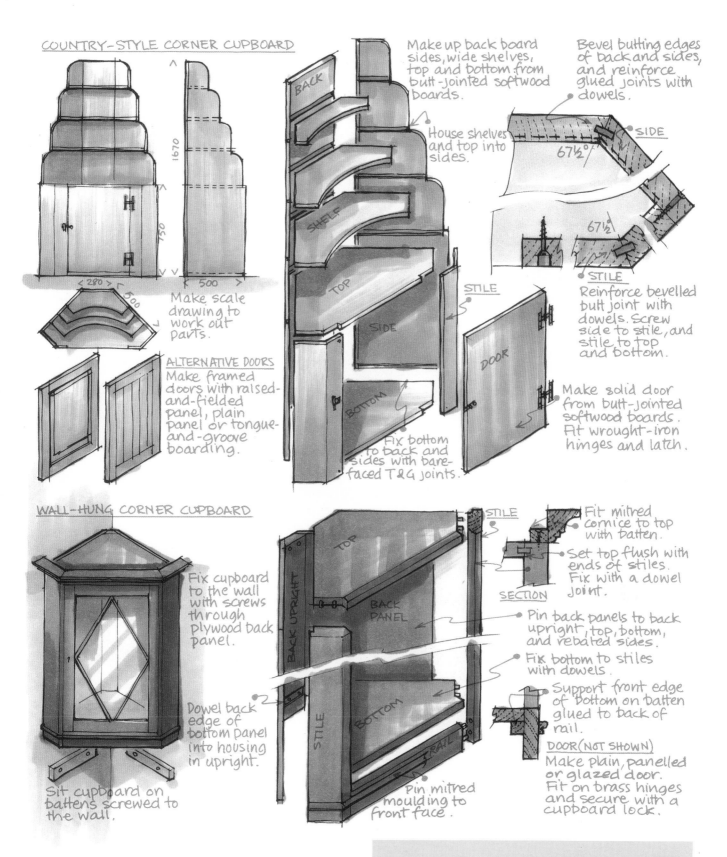

COUNTRY-STYLE CORNER CUPBOARD

1670

750

< 280 >

< 500 >

500

Make scale drawing to work out parts.

ALTERNATIVE DOORS
Make framed doors with raised-and-fielded panel, plain panel or tongue-and-groove boarding.

BACK

SHELF

TOP

SIDE

BOTTOM

Make up back board sides, wide shelves, top and bottom from butt-jointed softwood boards.

House shelves and top into sides.

Fix bottom to back and sides with bare-faced T&G joints.

STILE

DOOR

Bevel butting edges of back and sides, and reinforce glued joints with dowels.

SIDE

67½°

67½

STILE

Reinforce bevelled butt joint with dowels. Screw side to stile, and stile to top and bottom.

Make solid door from butt-jointed softwood boards. Fit wrought-iron hinges and latch.

WALL-HUNG CORNER CUPBOARD

Fix cupboard to the wall with screws through plywood back panel.

Dowel back edge of bottom panel into housing in upright.

Sit cupboard on battens screwed to the wall.

TOP

BACK UPRIGHT

BACK PANEL

STILE

BOTTOM

RAIL

Pin mitred moulding to front face.

STILE

SECTION

Fit mitred cornice to top with batten.

Set top flush with ends of stiles. Fix with a dowel joint.

Pin back panels to back upright, top, bottom, and rebated sides.

Fix bottom to stiles with dowels.

Support front edge of bottom on batten glued to back of rail.

DOOR (NOT SHOWN)
Make plain, panelled or glazed door. Fit on brass hinges and secure with a cupboard lock.

DISPLAY CABINETS

Antique cabinets, once made for wealthy collectors, were intended to be as impressive as their contents. They were often deliberately ostentatious, being exceedingly delicate and incorporating joints and other details that could only have been made by an accomplished craftsman. It's a tradition that continues to this day, and a woodworker will often set out to make a display cabinet as a *tour de force*.

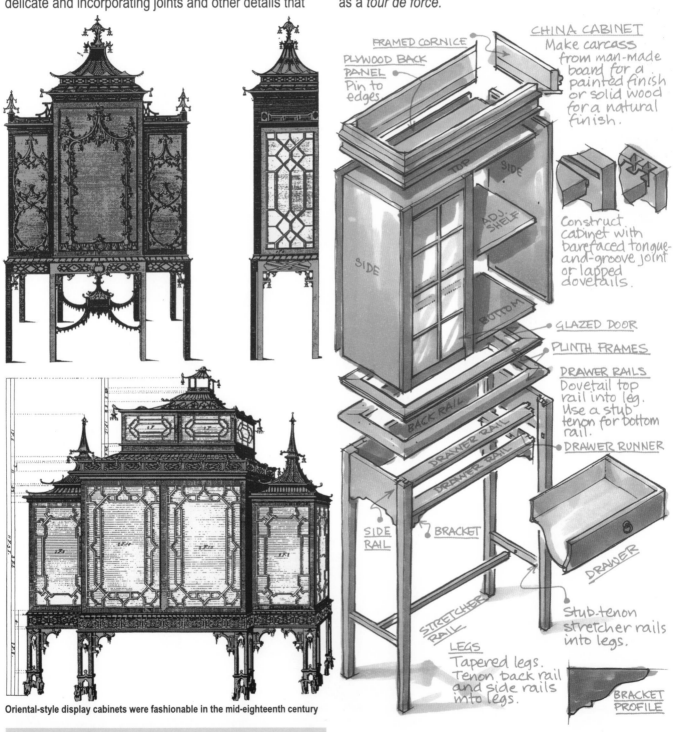

Oriental-style display cabinets were fashionable in the mid-eighteenth century

FRAMED CORNICE

PLYWOOD BACK PANEL Pin to edges.

CHINA CABINET Make carcass from man-made board for a painted finish or solid wood for a natural finish.

TOP

SIDE

SIDE

ADJ. SHELF

BOTTOM

Construct cabinet with barefaced tongue-and-groove joint or lapped dovetails.

GLAZED DOOR

PLINTH FRAMES

DRAWER RAILS Dovetail top rail into leg. Use a stub tenon for bottom rail.

BACK RAIL

DRAWER RAIL

DRAWER RAIL

DRAWER RUNNER

SIDE RAIL

BRACKET

DRAWER

STRETCHER RAIL

Stub-tenon stretcher rails into legs.

LEGS Tapered legs. Tenon back rail and side rails into legs.

BRACKET PROFILE

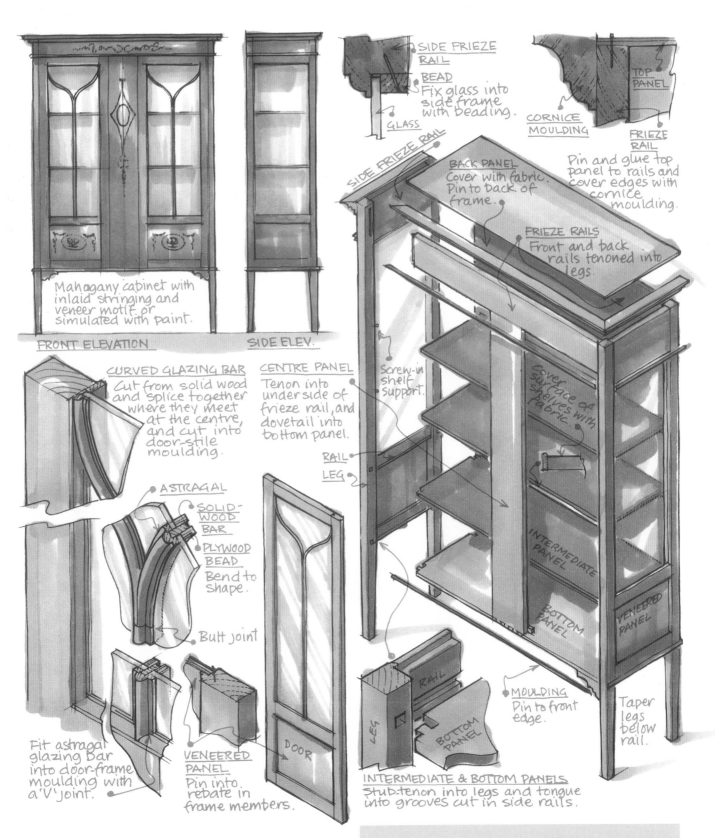

SIDE FRIEZE RAIL

BEAD
Fix glass into side frame with beading.

GLASS

TOP PANEL

CORNICE MOULDING

FRIEZE RAIL
Pin and glue top panel to rails and cover edges with cornice moulding.

BACK PANEL
Cover with fabric. Pin to back of frame.

SIDE FRIEZE RAIL

FRIEZE RAILS
Front and back rails tenoned into legs.

Screw-in shelf support.

Cover surface of shelves with fabric.

RAIL

LEG

INTERMEDIATE PANEL

BOTTOM PANEL

VENEERED PANEL

Mahogany cabinet with inlaid stringing and veneer motif, or simulated with paint.

FRONT ELEVATION

SIDE ELEV.

CURVED GLAZING BAR
Cut from solid wood and splice together where they meet at the centre, and cut into door-stile moulding.

CENTRE PANEL
Tenon into underside of frieze rail, and dovetail into bottom panel.

ASTRAGAL

SOLID-WOOD BAR

PLYWOOD BEAD
Bend to shape.

Butt joint

DOOR

Fit astragal glazing bar into door-frame moulding with a 'V' joint.

VENEERED PANEL
Pin into rebate in frame members.

LEG

RAIL

BOTTOM PANEL

MOULDING
Pin to front edge.

Taper legs below rail.

INTERMEDIATE & BOTTOM PANELS
Stub-tenon into legs and tongue into grooves cut in side rails.

INCONSPICUOUS CABINETS

The modern approach to displaying china and glass is to provide a protective case that is as inconspicuous as possible, putting all the emphasis on the collection itself.

We are aided in this respect by the easy availability of man-made boards, simple unobtrusive fittings, and sheets of plate glass for frameless doors.

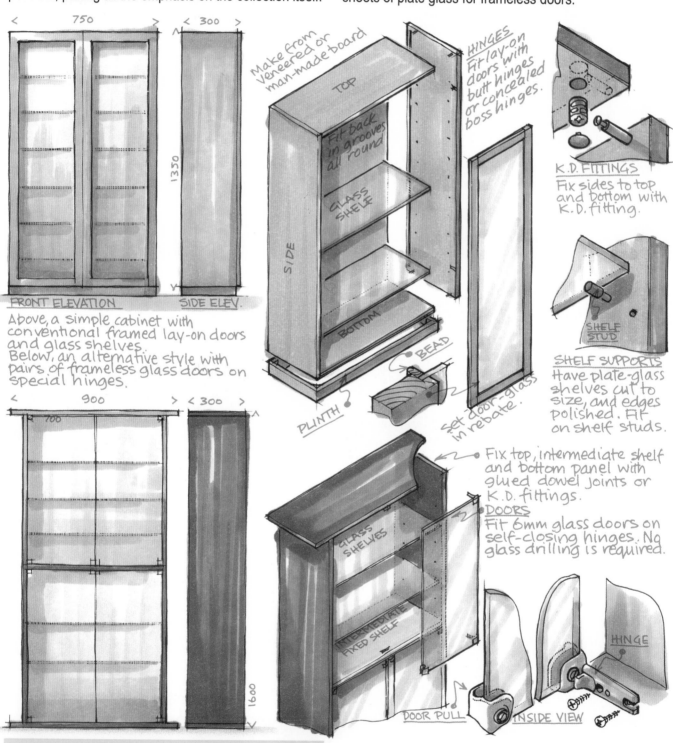

750

300

1350

FRONT ELEVATION

SIDE ELEV.

Above, a simple cabinet with conventional framed lay-on doors and glass shelves.
Below, an alternative style with pairs of frameless glass doors on special hinges.

Make from veneered or man-made board

TOP

Fit back in grooves all round

GLASS SHELF

SIDE

BOTTOM

PLINTH

BEAD

Set door-glass in rebate.

HINGES
Fit lay-on doors with butt hinges or concealed boss hinges.

K.D. FITTINGS
Fix sides to top and bottom with K.D. fitting.

SHELF STUD

SHELF SUPPORTS
Have plate-glass shelves cut to size, and edges polished. Fit on shelf studs.

900

300

700

1600

Fix top, intermediate shelf and bottom panel with glued dowel joints or K.D. fittings.

DOORS
Fit 6mm glass doors on self-closing hinges. No glass drilling is required.

GLASS SHELVES

INTERMEDIATE FIXED SHELF

DOOR PULL

INSIDE VIEW

HINGE

DISPLAY SHELVES

There's no need to make an expensive cabinet to house a small collection of glass or china. Provided you are prepared to dust your collection regularly, a bank of toughened-glass shelves will do just as well. One option is to adapt commercial shop-display fittings.

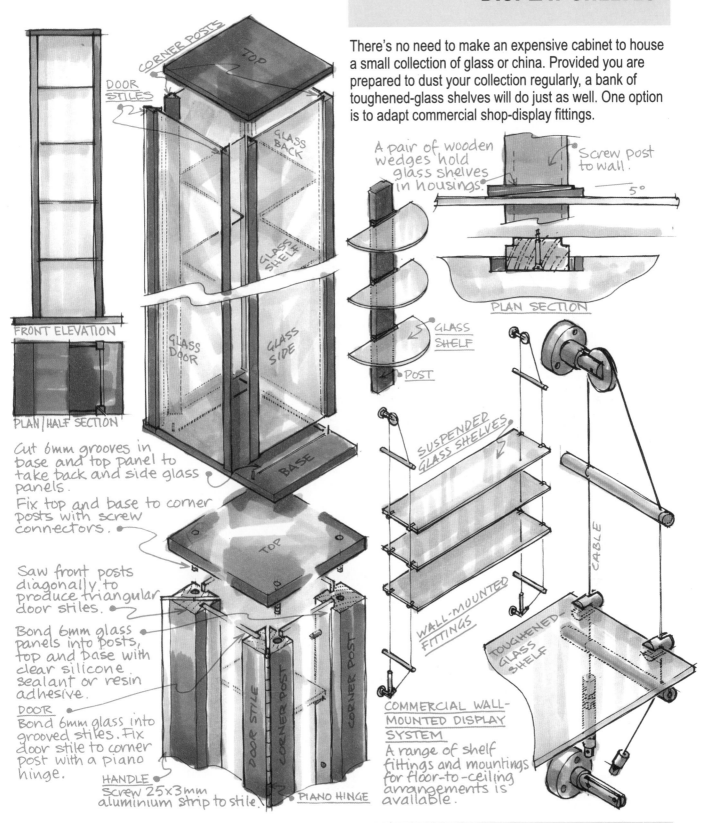

CORNER POSTS
TOP
DOOR STILES
GLASS BACK
GLASS SHELF
GLASS SIDE
GLASS DOOR
BASE

FRONT ELEVATION

PLAN / HALF SECTION

A pair of wooden wedges hold glass shelves in housings.

Screw post to wall.

5°

PLAN SECTION

GLASS SHELF

POST

SUSPENDED GLASS SHELVES

WALL-MOUNTED FITTINGS

CABLE

TOUGHENED-GLASS SHELF

Cut 6mm grooves in base and top panel to take back and side glass panels.
Fix top and base to corner posts with screw connectors.

Saw front posts diagonally to produce triangular door stiles.

Bond 6mm glass panels into posts, top and base with clear silicone sealant or resin adhesive.

DOOR
Bond 6mm glass into grooved stiles. Fix door stile to corner post with a piano hinge.

HANDLE
Screw 25x3mm aluminium strip to stile.

TOP

DOOR STILE
CORNER POST
CORNER POST

PIANO HINGE

COMMERCIAL WALL-MOUNTED DISPLAY SYSTEM
A range of shelf fittings and mountings for floor-to-ceiling arrangements is available.

7 CLOTHING

Adequate and appropriate storage extends the life of your clothing and keeps it fresh and crease-free. Large and relatively heavy garments such as coats, suits and dresses should be stored on coat hangers. People with enough space are inclined to hang shirts and blouses too – but, provided they are not squashed under a pile of bulky woollens, lightweight garments can be folded away in open wire trays or in a chest of drawers. If you have a lot of clothing, or space is very limited, it might pay to install a special compact-storage fitment.

When planning wardrobe storage, try to ensure there are enough drawers and that there's sufficient hanging space for your future needs. If you skimp on space now, you may find yourself spoiling expensive clothing by having to squeeze it into storage already crammed to capacity. Wardrobes and chests of drawers occupy a lot of floor area, so before you install your furniture, check that you will have enough room to open doors and drawers.

Hanging space

It is very easy to underestimate the amount of hanging space required for clothing. An internal front-to-back measurement of 600mm (2ft) is required for the average man's jacket or coat: This allows garments to hang edge-on to the door opening, making it easy to slide them from side to side and find a particular item. To reduce the depth of the carcass, a designer will occasionally opt for short rails mounted front-to-back in a wardrobe. However, unless the rails are designed to slide out of the wardrobe, clothing hung in this manner is difficult to access.

You should allow a drop of about 1.45m (4ft 10in) below the hanging rail for full-length coats and evening dresses; 900mm (3ft) is sufficient for most jackets. You can take advantage of the space below jacket-hanging space by installing a bank of open trays or lightweight drawers.

Drawer space

Drawers that measure 425 to 500m (1ft 5in to 1ft 8in) from front to back are adequate for folded clothing. Plan to incorporate at least one deep drawer for winter cardigans and sweaters. A heavy loose-knitted woollen garment may stretch if it is hung on a coat hanger for any length of time.

Access space

Leave enough space in front of a wardrobe for the swing of hinged doors – sliding doors might be a better option. If possible, allow a full 1.25m (4ft 2in) in front of a chest of drawers.

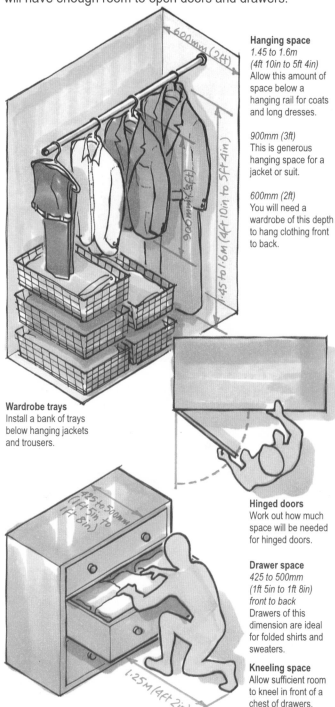

Hanging space
1.45 to 1.6m
(4ft 10in to 5ft 4in)
Allow this amount of space below a hanging rail for coats and long dresses.

900mm (3ft)
This is generous hanging space for a jacket or suit.

600mm (2ft)
You will need a wardrobe of this depth to hang clothing front to back.

Wardrobe trays
Install a bank of trays below hanging jackets and trousers.

Hinged doors
Work out how much space will be needed for hinged doors.

Drawer space
425 to 500mm
(1ft 5in to 1ft 8in)
front to back
Drawers of this dimension are ideal for folded shirts and sweaters.

Kneeling space
Allow sufficient room to kneel in front of a chest of drawers.

Shoe storage

Organize your shoe storage with a simple rack built into your wardrobe, using hanging-rail fittings and chromed-steel tubing.

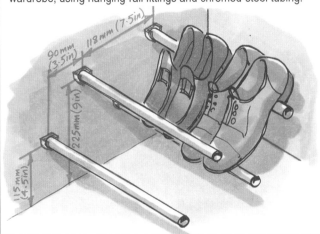

CHESTS OF DRAWERS

The traditional chest, comprising two small drawers over three or four deeper full-width drawers, took shape in the seventeenth and eighteenth centuries and remains a supremely functional piece of furniture for storing folded garments. It also demonstrates how two basic forms of construction evolved to compensate for the inevitable movement of solid-wood components that would otherwise distort or split.

Frame-and-panel construction

Relatively lightweight cabinets can be made using thin solid-wood panels housed in grooves cut on the inside of the end frames. Modern versions often include plywood panels.

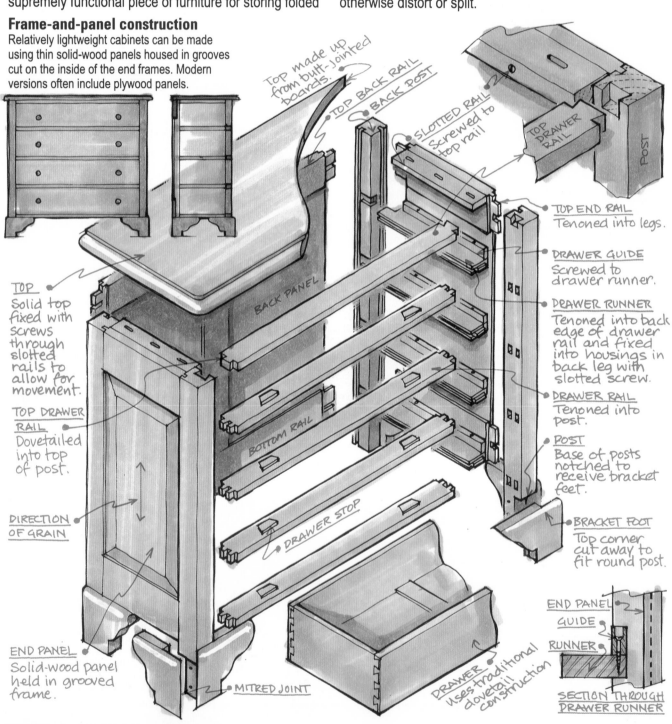

Top made up from butt-jointed boards.

TOP BACK RAIL

BACK POST

SLOTTED RAIL Screwed to top rail

TOP DRAWER RAIL

POST

TOP END RAIL Tenoned into legs.

DRAWER GUIDE Screwed to drawer runner.

DRAWER RUNNER Tenoned into back edge of drawer rail and fixed into housings in back leg with slotted screw.

DRAWER RAIL Tenoned into post.

POST Base of posts notched to receive bracket feet.

BRACKET FOOT Top corner cut away to fit round post.

BACK PANEL

TOP Solid top fixed with screws through slotted rails to allow for movement.

TOP DRAWER RAIL Dovetailed into top of post.

BOTTOM RAIL

DIRECTION OF GRAIN

DRAWER STOP

END PANEL Solid-wood panel held in grooved frame.

MITRED JOINT

DRAWER uses traditional dovetail construction

END PANEL

GUIDE

RUNNER

SECTION THROUGH DRAWER RUNNER

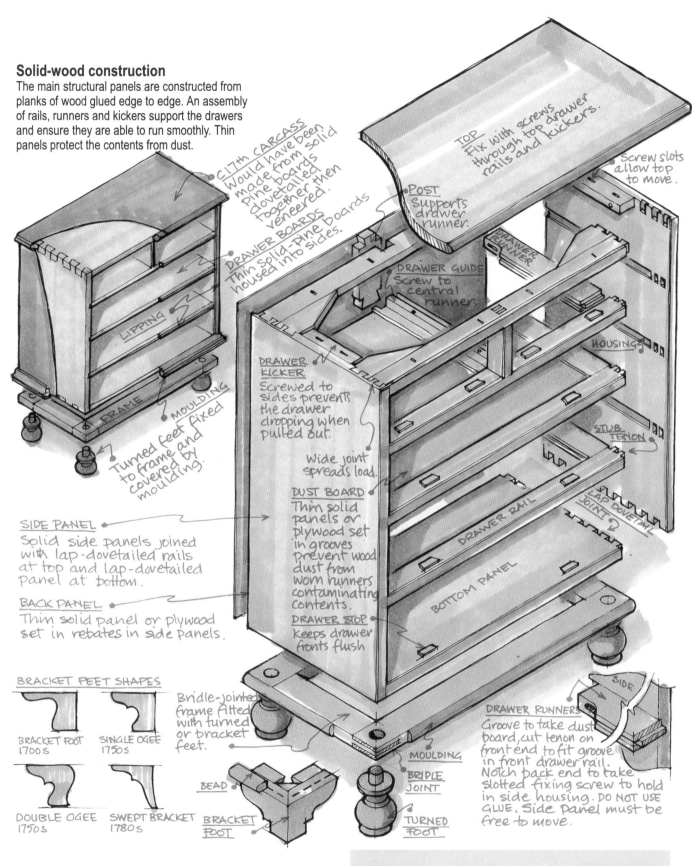

Solid-wood construction

The main structural panels are constructed from
planks of wood glued edge to edge. An assembly
of rails, runners and kickers support the drawers
and ensure they are able to run smoothly. Thin
panels protect the contents from dust.

C17th CARCASS
Would have been
made from solid
pine boards
dovetailed
together then
veneered.

DRAWER BOARDS
Thin solid-pine boards
housed into sides.

LIPPING

FRAME

MOULDING

Turned feet fixed
to frame and
covered by
moulding.

TOP
Fix with screws
through top drawer
rails and kickers.

Screw slots
allow top
to move.

POST
supports
drawer
runner.

DRAWER
RUNNER

DRAWER GUIDE
Screw to
central
runner.

HOUSING

DRAWER
KICKER
Screwed to
sides prevents
the drawer
dropping when
pulled out.

STUB
TENON

Wide joint
spreads load.

DUST BOARD
Thin solid
panels or
plywood set
in grooves
prevent wood
dust from
worn runners
contaminating
contents.

DRAWER RAIL

LAP DOVETAIL
JOINT

SIDE PANEL
Solid side panels joined
with lap-dovetailed rails
at top and lap-dovetailed
panel at bottom.

BACK PANEL
Thin solid panel or plywood
set in rebates in side panels.

BOTTOM PANEL

DRAWER STOP
Keeps drawer
fronts flush

BRACKET FEET SHAPES

BRACKET FOOT
1700s

SINGLE OGEE
1750s

DOUBLE OGEE
1750s

SWEPT BRACKET
1780s

Bridle-jointed
frame fitted
with turned
or bracket
feet.

BEAD

BRACKET
FOOT

SIDE

DRAWER RUNNERS
Groove to take dust
board, cut tenon on
front end to fit groove
in front drawer rail.
Notch back end to take
slotted fixing screw to hold
in side housing. DO NOT USE
GLUE. Side panel must be
free to move.

MOULDING

BRIDLE
JOINT

TURNED
FOOT

MODERN DRAWER UNITS

Man-made boards are available as large flat sheets that are much more stable than panels made from solid timber. Consequently they allow us to move away from traditional methods of construction and enable us to design and make furniture that is exceptionally simple in appearance. Modern styling requires an eye for good proportions and fine detailing, with an emphasis on the sensitive use and positioning of fittings.

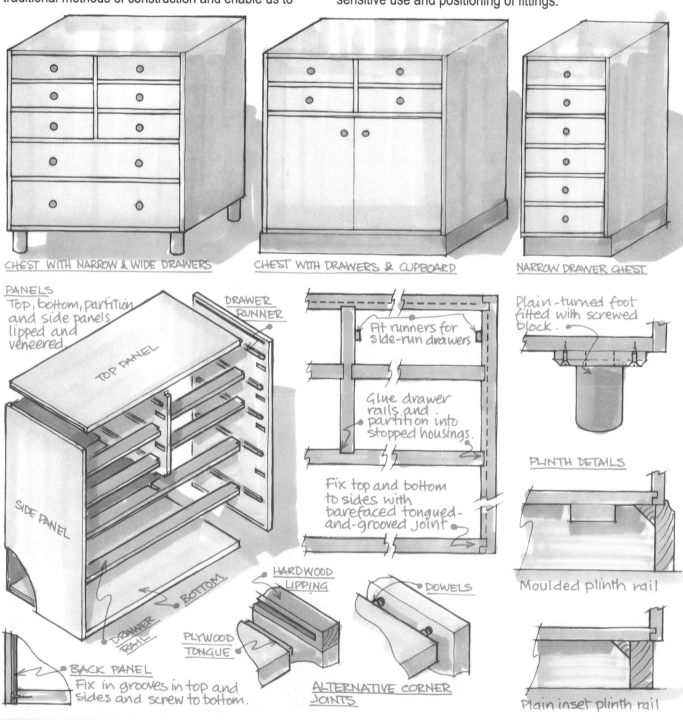

CHEST WITH NARROW & WIDE DRAWERS

CHEST WITH DRAWERS & CUPBOARD

NARROW DRAWER CHEST

PANELS
Top, bottom, partition and side panels lipped and veneered.

DRAWER RUNNER

TOP PANEL

SIDE PANEL

DRAWER RAIL

BACK PANEL
Fix in grooves in top and sides and screw to bottom.

BOTTOM

HARDWOOD LIPPING

PLYWOOD TONGUE

DOWELS

ALTERNATIVE CORNER JOINTS

Fit runners for side-run drawers

Glue drawer rails and partition into stopped housings.

Fix top and bottom to sides with barefaced tongued-and-grooved joint

Plain-turned foot fitted with screwed block.

PLINTH DETAILS

Moulded plinth rail

Plain inset plinth rail

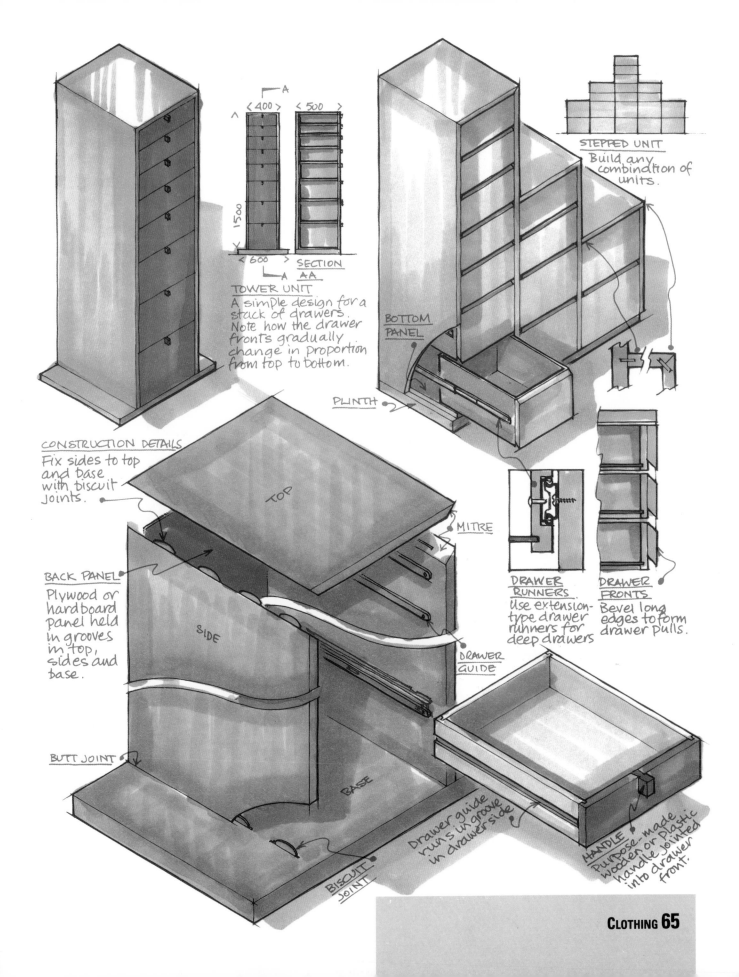

A

< 400 >   < 500 >

1500

< 600 >   SECTION
  A   AA

TOWER UNIT
A simple design for a
stack of drawers.
Note how the drawer
fronts gradually
change in proportion
from top to bottom.

STEPPED UNIT
Build any
combination of
units.

**BOTTOM
PANEL**

PLINTH

CONSTRUCTION DETAILS
Fix sides to top
and base
with biscuit
joints.

TOP

MITRE

BACK PANEL
Plywood or
hardboard
panel held
in grooves
in top,
sides and
base.

SIDE

**DRAWER
RUNNERS.**
Use extension-
type drawer
runners for
deep drawers

**DRAWER
FRONTS**
Bevel long
edges to form
drawer pulls.

**DRAWER
GUIDE**

BUTT JOINT

BASE

**BISCUIT
JOINT**

Drawer guide
runs in groove
in drawer side

HANDLE
Purpose-made
wooden or plastic
handle jointed
into drawer
front.

CHEST ON STAND

Late-seventeenth century elegance is typified by the characteristic chest on stand, originally designed to raise a chest of drawers to a height where it could be seen to advantage and admired for its fine proportions and costly veneers. This is storage of quality that will enhance a period interior while providing ample drawer space.

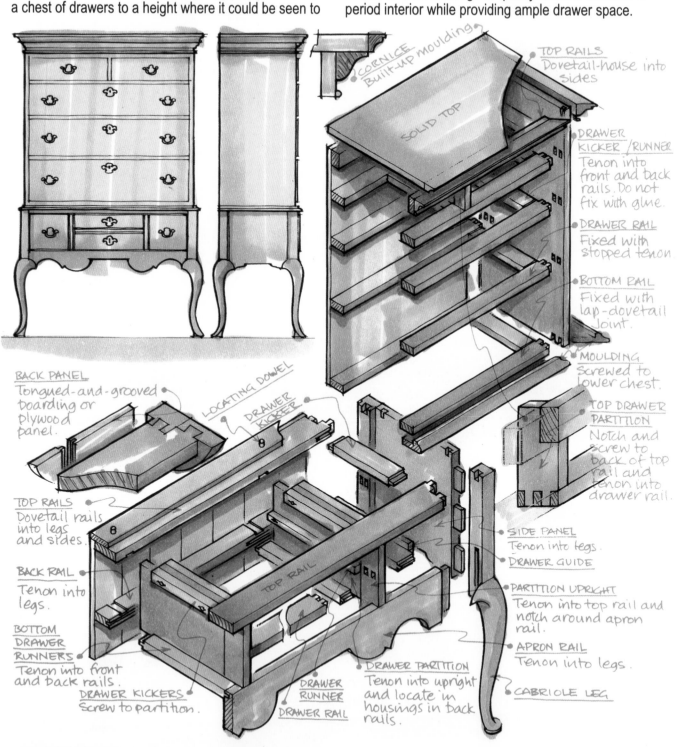

CORNICE
Built-up moulding

TOP RAILS
Dovetail-house into sides

SOLID TOP

DRAWER KICKER/RUNNER
Tenon into front and back rails. Do not fix with glue.

DRAWER RAIL
Fixed with stopped tenon

BOTTOM RAIL
Fixed with lap-dovetail joint.

MOULDING
Screwed to lower chest.

TOP DRAWER PARTITION
Notch and screw to back of top rail and tenon into drawer rail.

BACK PANEL
Tongued-and-grooved boarding or plywood panel.

LOCATING DOWEL

DRAWER KICKER

TOP RAILS
Dovetail rails into legs and sides.

BACK RAIL
Tenon into legs.

BOTTOM DRAWER RUNNERS
Tenon into front and back rails.

DRAWER KICKERS
Screw to partition.

TOP RAIL

DRAWER RUNNER

DRAWER RAIL

DRAWER PARTITION
Tenon into upright and locate in housings in back rails.

SIDE PANEL
Tenon into legs.

DRAWER GUIDE

PARTITION UPRIGHT
Tenon into top rail and notch around apron rail.

APRON RAIL
Tenon into legs.

CABRIOLE LEG

CHEST ON CHEST

A chest on chest, more commonly called a tallboy, is impressive for its sheer size, with a storage capacity that is double that of the average chest of drawers. However, the upper stack extends well above head height. The topmost drawers should therefore be reserved for items of clothing you rarely use.

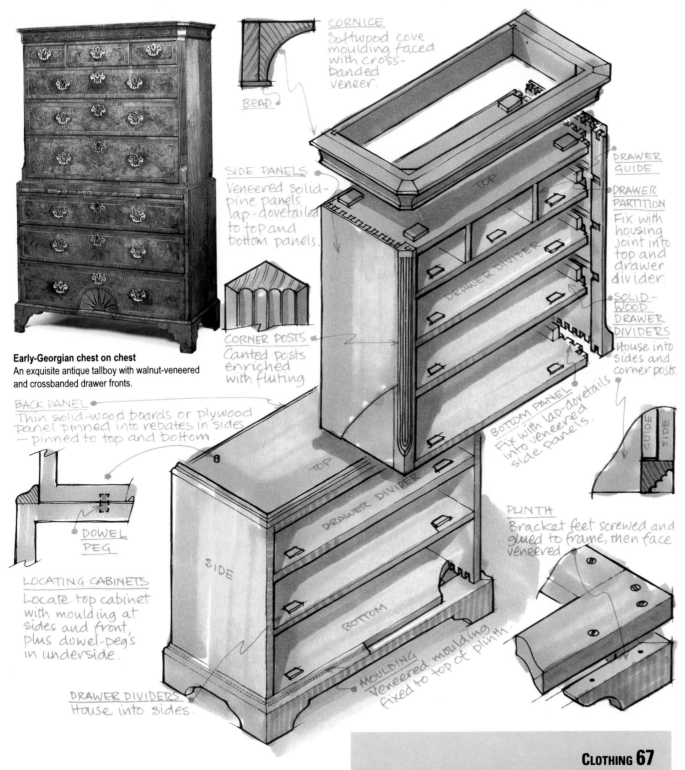

Early-Georgian chest on chest
An exquisite antique tallboy with walnut-veneered and crossbanded drawer fronts.

CORNICE
Softwood cove moulding faced with cross-banded veneer.

BEAD

SIDE PANELS
Veneered solid-pine panels lap-dovetailed to top and bottom panels.

DRAWER GUIDE

DRAWER PARTITION
Fix with housing joint into top and drawer divider.

SOLID-WOOD DRAWER DIVIDERS
House into sides and corner posts.

TOP

DRAWER DIVIDER

CORNER POSTS
Canted posts enriched with fluting

BOTTOM PANEL
Fix with lap-dovetails into veneered side panels.

GUIDE SIDE

BACK PANEL
Thin solid-wood boards or plywood panel pinned into rebates in sides — pinned to top and bottom.

DOWEL PEG

LOCATING CABINETS
Locate top cabinet with moulding at sides and front, plus dowel-pegs in underside.

TOP

SIDE

DRAWER DIVIDER

BOTTOM

PLINTH
Bracket feet screwed and glued to frame, then face veneered

MOULDING
Veneered moulding fixed to top of plinth.

DRAWER DIVIDERS
House into sides.

WARDROBES

Hanging clothes from a rail is in many ways much more practical than folding them away in a drawer. Garments keep their shape better, creases tend to drop out, and it is easier to sift through an assortment of clothes when you can see them at a glance. The traditional solution is a large freestanding cupboard or wardrobe, often made with lightweight framed panels to reduce the cost of materials. The modern method is to combine individual modular units that incorporate hanging rails, shelves and drawers.

Frame-and-panel wardrobe
The basic design can be modified by altering the proportions of the door panels, the method of hinging the doors and the style of plinth. Use veneered-plywood panels to blend with the framework or paint them to create a striking contrast.

Canvas wardrobe
Canvas coveralls suspended from a rail keep your clothes clean and organized. When you move house, just fold them up and take them with you.

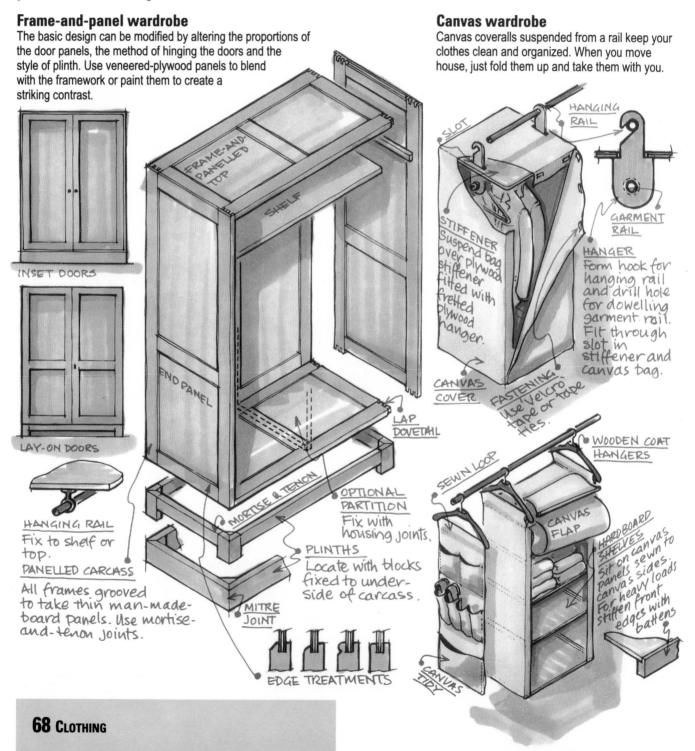

INSET DOORS

LAY-ON DOORS

FRAME-AND-PANELLED TOP

SHELF

END PANEL

LAP DOVETAIL

MORTISE & TENON

HANGING RAIL
Fix to shelf or top.

PANELLED CARCASS
All frames grooved to take thin man-made-board panels. Use mortise-and-tenon joints.

MITRE JOINT

EDGE TREATMENTS

OPTIONAL PARTITION
Fix with housing joints.

PLINTHS
Locate with blocks fixed to under-side of carcass.

SLOT

HANGING RAIL

GARMENT RAIL

STIFFENER
Suspend bag over plywood stiffener fitted with fretted plywood hanger.

HANGER
Form hook for hanging rail and drill hole for dowelling garment rail. Fit through slot in stiffener and canvas bag.

CANVAS COVER

FASTENING
Use velcro tape or tape ties.

SEWN LOOP

WOODEN COAT HANGERS

CANVAS FLAP

HARDBOARD SHELVES
sit on canvas panels sewn to canvas sides. For heavy loads stiffen front edges with battens

CANVAS TIDY

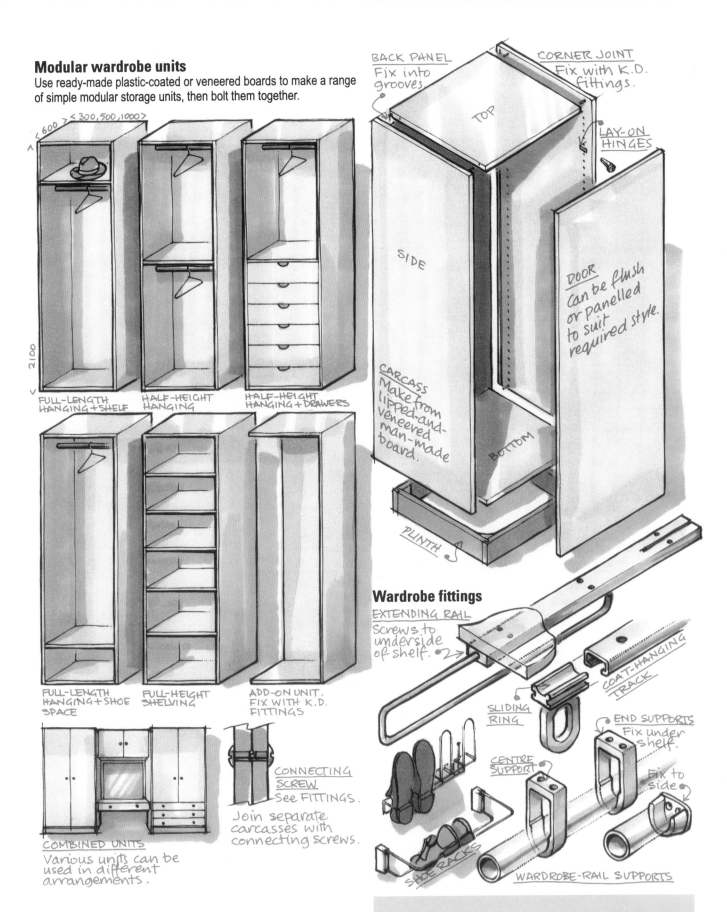

Modular wardrobe units

Use ready-made plastic-coated or veneered boards to make a range of simple modular storage units, then bolt them together.

< 600 >   < 300, 500, 1000 >

2100

FULL-LENGTH
HANGING + SHELF

HALF-HEIGHT
HANGING

HALF-HEIGHT
HANGING + DRAWERS

FULL-LENGTH
HANGING + SHOE
SPACE

FULL-HEIGHT
SHELVING

ADD-ON UNIT.
FIX WITH K.D.
FITTINGS

COMBINED UNITS
Various units can be
used in different
arrangements.

CONNECTING
SCREW
See FITTINGS.
Join separate
carcasses with
connecting screws.

BACK PANEL
Fix into
grooves.

CORNER JOINT
Fix with K.D.
fittings.

TOP

LAY-ON
HINGES

SIDE

DOOR
Can be flush
or panelled
to suit
required style.

CARCASS
Make from
lipped-and-
veneered
man-made
board.

BOTTOM

PLINTH

Wardrobe fittings

EXTENDING RAIL
Screws to
underside
of shelf.

COAT-HANGING
TRACK

SLIDING
RING

END SUPPORTS
Fix under
shelf.

CENTRE
SUPPORT

Fix to
side

SHOE RACKS

WARDROBE-RAIL SUPPORTS

BUILT-IN WARDROBES

Enclosing one end of a room with a relatively simple framework provides cost-effective floor-to-ceiling storage. Similarly, it pays to incorporate useful storage alcoves when dividing a large space with partition walls. It is then a simple step to complete the job with a pair of doors – or a roller blind instead.

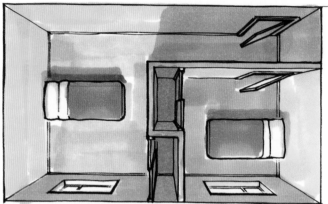

PARTITION WALL BUILT TO FORM ALCOVES

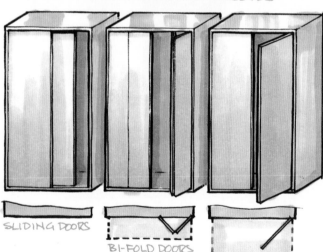

SLIDING DOORS

BI-FOLD DOORS

HINGED DOORS

SPACE REQUIREMENTS
Where space is limited use a sliding-door system or bi-fold doors in preference to hinged doors.

SCRIBING FILLETS

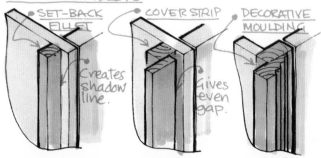

SET-BACK FILLET

COVER STRIP

DECORATIVE MOULDING

Creates shadow line.

Gives even gap.

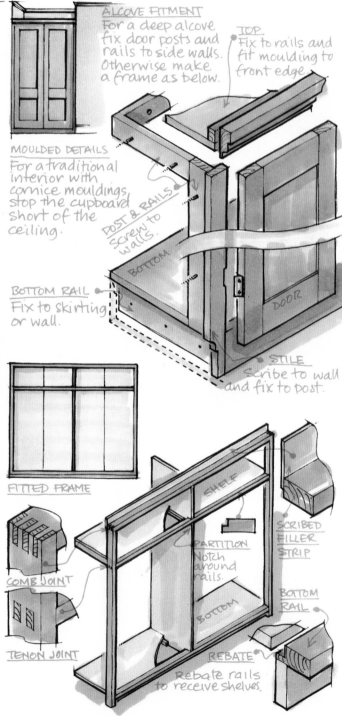

ALCOVE FITMENT
For a deep alcove fix door posts and rails to side walls. Otherwise make a frame as below.

TOP
Fix to rails and fit moulding to front edge.

MOULDED DETAILS
For a traditional interior with cornice mouldings, stop the cupboard short of the ceiling.

POST & RAILS screw to walls.

BOTTOM

BOTTOM RAIL
Fix to skirting or wall.

DOOR

STILE
Scribe to wall and fix to post.

FITTED FRAME

SHELF

SCRIBED FILLER STRIP

PARTITION
Notch around rails.

COMB JOINT

BOTTOM

BOTTOM RAIL

TENON JOINT

REBATE
Rebate rails to receive shelves.

SPACE-SAVING MECHANISMS

Doors that swing open on hinges require a clear space equal to their own width in front of the wardrobe. This may not be convenient in a small room. To overcome the problem, you could install a folding-door system that halves the clearance space or one of a variety of sliding-door mechanisms that offer different design solutions.

Sliding-door systems

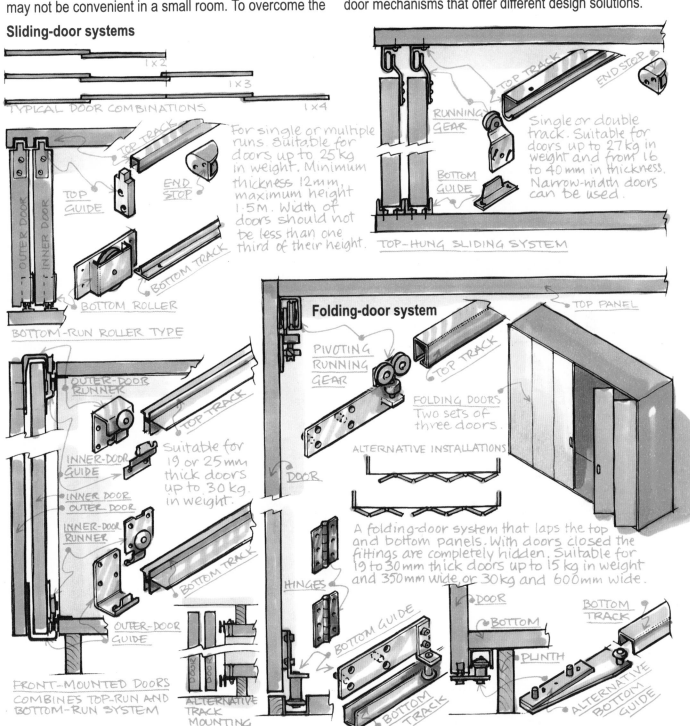

TYPICAL DOOR COMBINATIONS
1 x 2
1 x 3
1 x 4

TOP TRACK
OUTER DOOR
INNER DOOR
TOP GUIDE
END STOP
BOTTOM TRACK
BOTTOM ROLLER
BOTTOM-RUN ROLLER TYPE

For single or multiple runs. Suitable for doors up to 25kg in weight. Minimum thickness 12mm, maximum height 1.5M. Width of doors should not be less than one third of their height.

TOP TRACK
END STOP
RUNNING GEAR
BOTTOM GUIDE
Single or double track. Suitable for doors up to 27kg in weight and from 16 to 40mm in thickness. Narrow-width doors can be used.
TOP-HUNG SLIDING SYSTEM

OUTER-DOOR RUNNER
TOP TRACK
INNER-DOOR GUIDE
INNER DOOR
OUTER DOOR
INNER-DOOR RUNNER
BOTTOM TRACK
OUTER-DOOR GUIDE
Suitable for 19 or 25mm thick doors up to 30 kg. in weight.

FRONT-MOUNTED DOORS COMBINES TOP-RUN AND BOTTOM-RUN SYSTEM
ALTERNATIVE TRACK MOUNTING

Folding-door system

PIVOTING RUNNING GEAR
TOP TRACK
TOP PANEL
FOLDING DOORS Two sets of three doors.
ALTERNATIVE INSTALLATIONS
DOOR
HINGES
A folding-door system that laps the top and bottom panels. With doors closed the fittings are completely hidden. Suitable for 19 to 30mm thick doors up to 15 kg in weight and 350mm wide, or 30kg and 600mm wide.

BOTTOM GUIDE
BOTTOM TRACK
DOOR
BOTTOM
PLINTH
BOTTOM TRACK
ALTERNATIVE BOTTOM GUIDE

COMPACT STORAGE

When space is limited it may not be possible to accommodate all your clothing in a standard wardrobe that is designed for storing garments side by side. You may have to consider alternative arrangements that provide access to high-density storage. The systems shown below are available from specialist suppliers.

Automated carousel

A switch-controlled revolving carousel gradually presents the entire contents of your wardrobe to a single door.

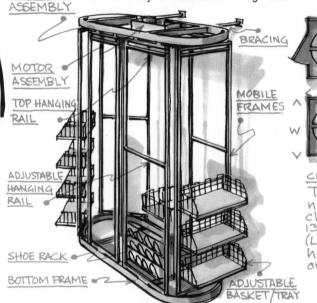

TOP-TRACK AND CHAIN ASSEMBLY

MOTOR ASSEMBLY

TOP HANGING RAIL

ADJUSTABLE HANGING RAIL

SHOE RACK

BOTTOM FRAME

BRACING

MOBILE FRAMES

ADJUSTABLE BASKET/TRAY

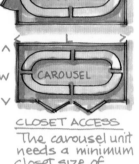

CAROUSEL

L

W

CAROUSEL

CLOSET ACCESS
The carousel unit needs a minimum closet size of 1370 mm (W) x 1830 mm (L), and a ceiling height of 2235 mm or 2310 mm.

Sliding cabinets

Double your storage space by mounting cabinets on a special sliding track in front of another bank of fixed storage. Sliding each cabinet sideways provides access to the clothing behind.

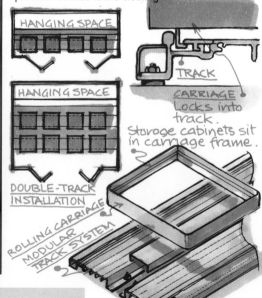

HANGING SPACE

HANGING SPACE

DOUBLE-TRACK INSTALLATION

ROLLING CARRIAGE MODULAR TRACK SYSTEM

TRACK

CARRIAGE locks into track. Storage cabinets sit in carriage frame.

WARDROBE LIFT
Screws to sides of cabinet.

Wardrobe lift

A pull-down hanging rail allows you to retrieve clothing that is otherwise out of reach.

The hats and coats we wear daily end up cluttering the hallway unless a convenient solution is provided. One simple answer is to screw ready-made coat hooks to the back of a door or to a wall-mounted board – and playful wall hooks may encourage children to hang up their coats. Perhaps the ultimate solution is a coat cupboard that incorporates a mirror to make sure you are presentable before you leave home.

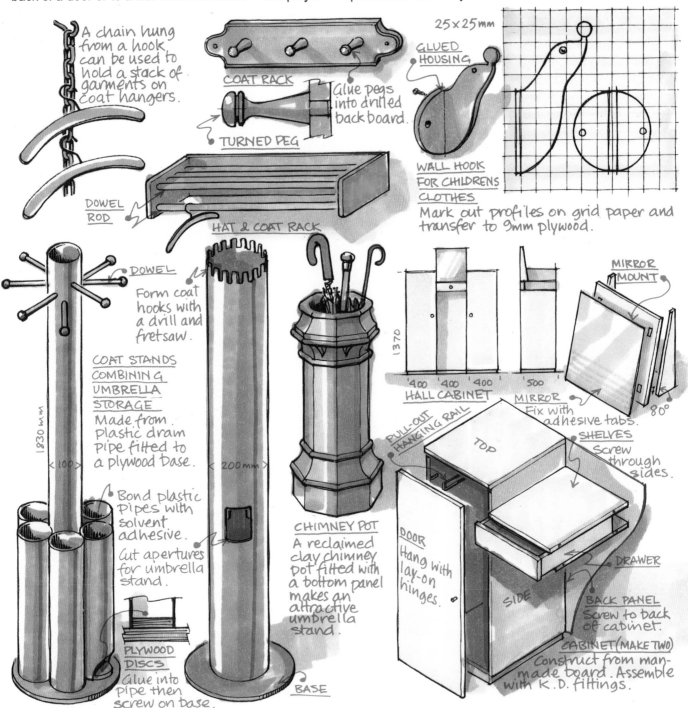

A chain hung from a hook can be used to hold a stack of garments on coat hangers.

COAT RACK

Glue pegs into drilled back board.

TURNED PEG

DOWEL ROD

HAT & COAT RACK

25 x 25 mm

GLUED HOUSING

WALL HOOK FOR CHILDRENS CLOTHES
Mark out profiles on grid paper and transfer to 9mm plywood.

DOWEL
Form coat hooks with a drill and fretsaw.

COAT STANDS COMBINING UMBRELLA STORAGE
Made from plastic drain pipe fitted to a plywood base.

Bond plastic pipes with solvent adhesive.

Cut apertures for umbrella stand.

1830 mm
100
200 mm

PLYWOOD DISCS
Glue into pipe then screw on base.

BASE

CHIMNEY POT
A reclaimed clay chimney pot fitted with a bottom panel makes an attractive umbrella stand.

1370
400 400 400 500
HALL CABINET

MIRROR MOUNT

MIRROR
Fix with adhesive tabs.

80°

PULL-OUT HANGING RAIL

TOP

SHELVES
Screw through sides.

DOOR
Hang with lay-on hinges.

SIDE

DRAWER

BACK PANEL
Screw to back of cabinet.

CABINET (MAKE TWO)
Construct from man-made board. Assemble with K.D. fittings.

Chapter 8 COSMETICS & TOILETRIES

In terms of priorities, the storage of cosmetics and toiletries no doubt comes fairly low down on most people's lists. Who needs to make special provision for items that are generally sold in such glamorous packages? But we tend to hang on to a great many half-used jars, tubes and bottles of make-up, creams and other toiletries that look anything but appealing and stain practically any surface they stand on. Some form of simple and practical storage is a small price to pay for tidy, attractive bathrooms and bedrooms.

Most families opt for a small wall cabinet for bathroom cosmetics, especially one that is fitted with a lock to keep harmful medicines out of the reach of children. However a bank of storage can meet all your needs, including a receptacle for dirty laundry. In a small bathroom you cannot afford to waste even the space occupied by the bathtub – there's plenty of room for cleaning materials behind a removable bath panel.

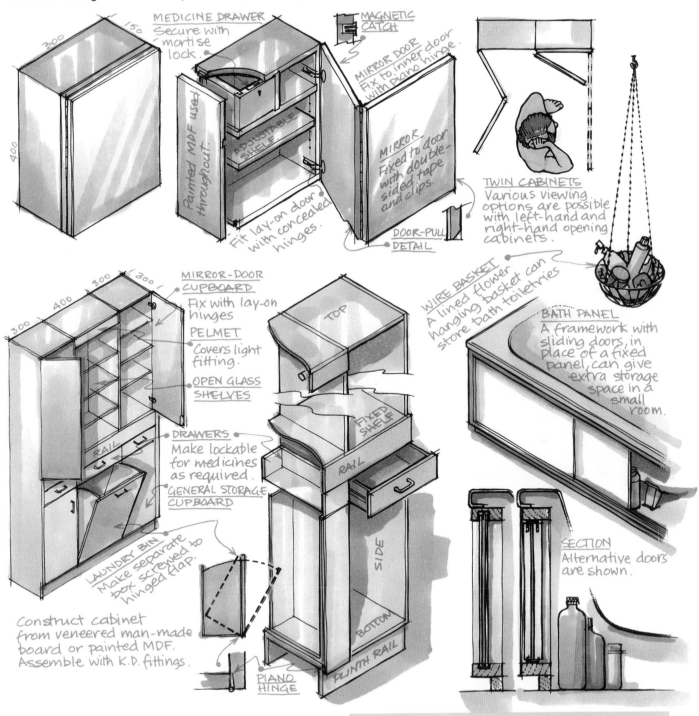

300
150
400

MEDICINE DRAWER Secure with mortise lock.

MAGNETIC CATCH

MIRROR DOOR Fix to inner door with piano hinge.

Painted MDF used throughout.

ADJUSTABLE SHELF

MIRROR Fixed to door with double-sided tape and clips.

Fit lay-on door with concealed hinges.

DOOR-PULL DETAIL

TWIN CABINETS Various viewing options are possible with left-hand and right-hand opening cabinets.

300 300 300
400
300

MIRROR-DOOR CUPBOARD Fix with lay-on hinges

PELMET Covers light fitting.

OPEN GLASS SHELVES

TOP

FIXED SHELF

RAIL

DRAWERS Make lockable for medicines as required.

GENERAL STORAGE CUPBOARD

RAIL

WIRE BASKET A lined flower hanging basket can store bath toiletries

BATH PANEL A framework with sliding doors, in place of a fixed panel, can give extra storage space in a small room.

SIDE

BOTTOM

PLINTH RAIL

LAUNDRY BIN Make separate box screwed to hinged flap.

Construct cabinet from veneered man-made board or painted MDF. Assemble with K.D. fittings.

PIANO HINGE

SECTION Alternative doors are shown.

DRESSING TABLES

A dressing table with mirror and cosmetics storage may be considered by some to be a trifle old-fashioned these days – but, as a principle, no one has yet come up with anything better. Good lighting is absolutely imperative; consequently, a freestanding dressing table is invariably placed in front of the bedroom window. A dressing table that is part of a modern built-in wardrobe system requires good artificial illumination.

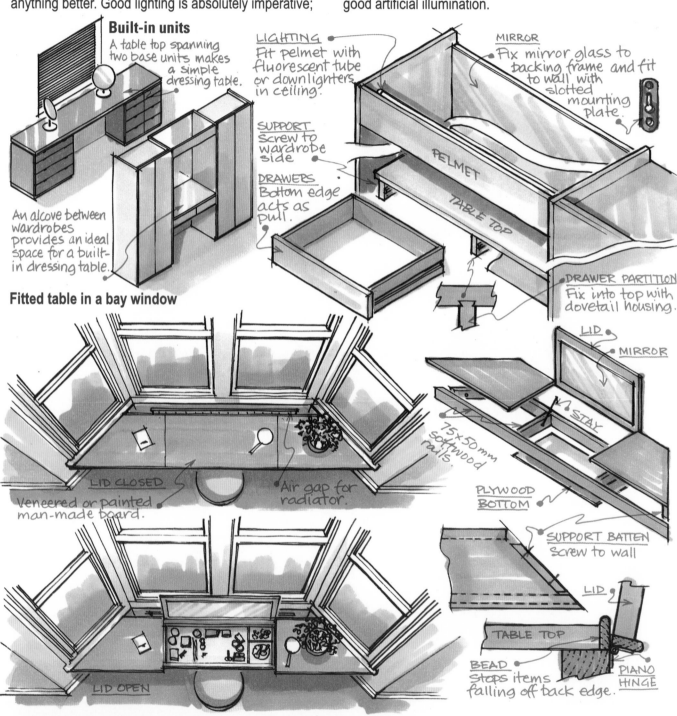

Built-in units

A table top spanning two base units makes a simple dressing table.

An alcove between wardrobes provides an ideal space for a built-in dressing table.

Fitted table in a bay window

LIGHTING
Fit pelmet with fluorescent tube or downlighters in ceiling.

SUPPORT
Screw to wardrobe side

DRAWERS
Bottom edge acts as pull.

MIRROR
Fix mirror glass to backing frame and fit to wall with slotted mounting plate.

PELMET

TABLE TOP

DRAWER PARTITION
Fix into top with dovetail housing.

LID CLOSED
Veneered or painted man-made board.

Air gap for radiator.

LID OPEN

75×50mm softwood rails

LID

MIRROR

STAY

PLYWOOD BOTTOM

SUPPORT BATTEN
Screw to wall

LID

TABLE TOP

BEAD
Stops items falling off back edge.

PIANO HINGE

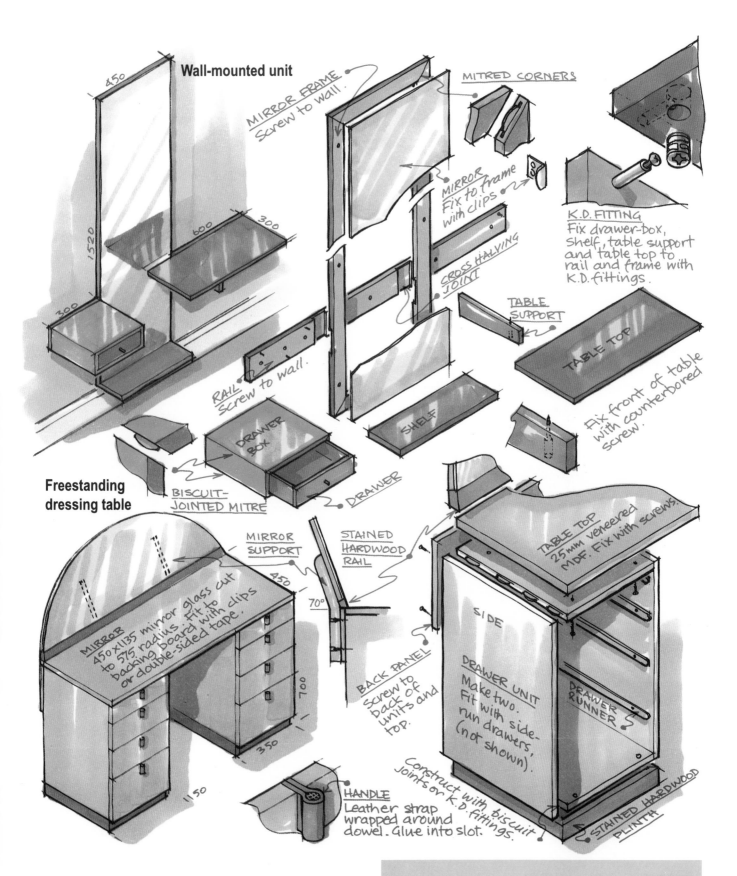

Wall-mounted unit

450

1520

600

300

300

MIRROR FRAME.
Screw to wall.

MITRED CORNERS

MIRROR
Fix to frame
with clips

K.D. FITTING
Fix drawer-box,
shelf, table support
and table top to
rail and frame with
K.D. fittings.

CROSS HALVING
JOINT

TABLE
SUPPORT

TABLE TOP

Fix front of table
with counterbored
screw.

RAIL
Screw to wall.

SHELF

**Freestanding
dressing table**

BISCUIT-
JOINTED MITRE

DRAWER
BOX

DRAWER

MIRROR
SUPPORT

450

70°

STAINED
HARDWOOD
RAIL

TABLE TOP
25mm veneered
MDF. Fix with screws.

MIRROR
450 x 1135 mirror glass cut
to 575 radius. Fit to
backing board with clips
or double-sided tape.

700

350

1150

SIDE

BACK PANEL
Screw to
back of
units and
top.

DRAWER UNIT
Make two.
Fit with side-
run drawers.
(not shown).

DRAWER
RUNNER

Construct with biscuit
joints or K.D. fittings.

HANDLE
Leather strap
wrapped around
dowel. Glue into slot.

STAINED HARDWOOD
PLINTH

9 BOOKS AND MAGAZINES

There is very little need to consider anything but open shelving for storing books, and the alcoves on either side of a fireplace make ideal locations for fully built-in shelves. Real book lovers, however, may want to keep their most treasured volumes behind doors and out of direct sunlight. Magazines are much more difficult to store. Most of us throw them away after a week or two, but if you intend to keep magazines for posterity it is probably best to store them in special-purpose binders and shelve them along with your books.

BOOK AND MAGAZINE RACKS

If your collection of books is small, it is a waste of time and space to erect a wall of shelving when a simple rack would suffice. A similar rack fixed above your desk or standing beside your favourite chair is ideal for housing a limited selection of books that you refer to frequently. Magazines which cannot be stored conveniently on edge need a rack of a different sort. Those shown below are meant to hold current periodicals for a short while.

Book racks

Magazine racks

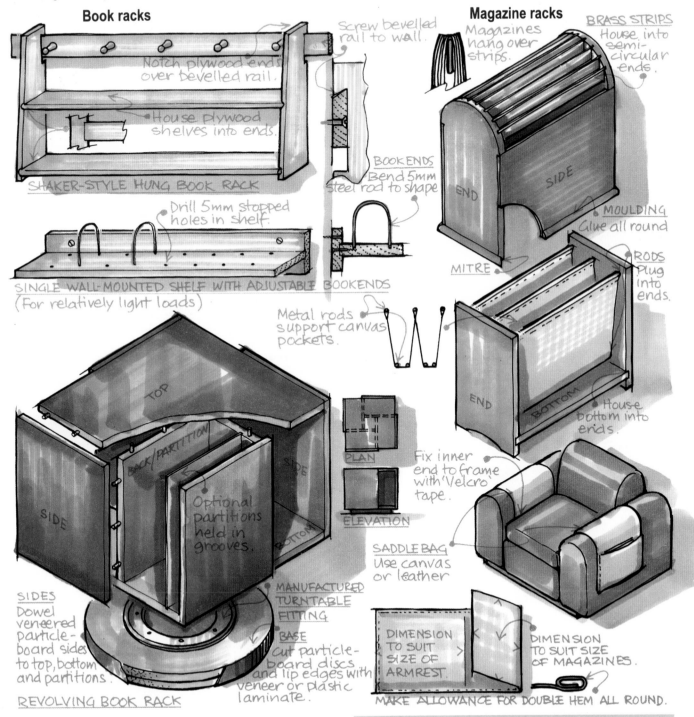

Notch plywood ends over bevelled rail.

House plywood shelves into ends.

SHAKER-STYLE HUNG BOOK RACK

Screw bevelled rail to wall.

BOOK ENDS
Bend 5mm steel rod to shape

Drill 5mm stopped holes in shelf.

SINGLE WALL-MOUNTED SHELF WITH ADJUSTABLE BOOKENDS
(For relatively light loads)

Metal rods support canvas pockets.

BRASS STRIPS
House into semi-circular ends.

Magazines hang over strips.

MOULDING
Glue all round

RODS
Plug into ends.

MITRE

House bottom into ends.

END   SIDE

END   BOTTOM

PLAN

ELEVATION

Fix inner end to frame with 'Velcro' tape.

TOP

BACK/PARTITION

SIDE

SIDE

Optional partitions held in grooves.

BOTTOM

SADDLE BAG
Use canvas or leather

SIDES
Dowel veneered particle-board sides to top, bottom and partitions.

MANUFACTURED TURNTABLE FITTING

BASE
Cut particle-board discs and lip edges with veneer or plastic laminate.

REVOLVING BOOK RACK

DIMENSION TO SUIT SIZE OF ARMREST.

DIMENSION TO SUIT SIZE OF MAGAZINES.

MAKE ALLOWANCE FOR DOUBLE HEM ALL ROUND.

SHELVING BRACKETS

Commercially available shelving systems are most people's first choice when it comes to storing a large number of books. However, books and magazines are surprisingly heavy and it would be a mistake to skimp on the number of wall-hung uprights and you should never use shelves that are so slim that they bend under the load. See DESIGNING AND PLANNING for recommended shelf dimensions.

Adjustable brackets
Fixed brackets
Hidden shelf supports

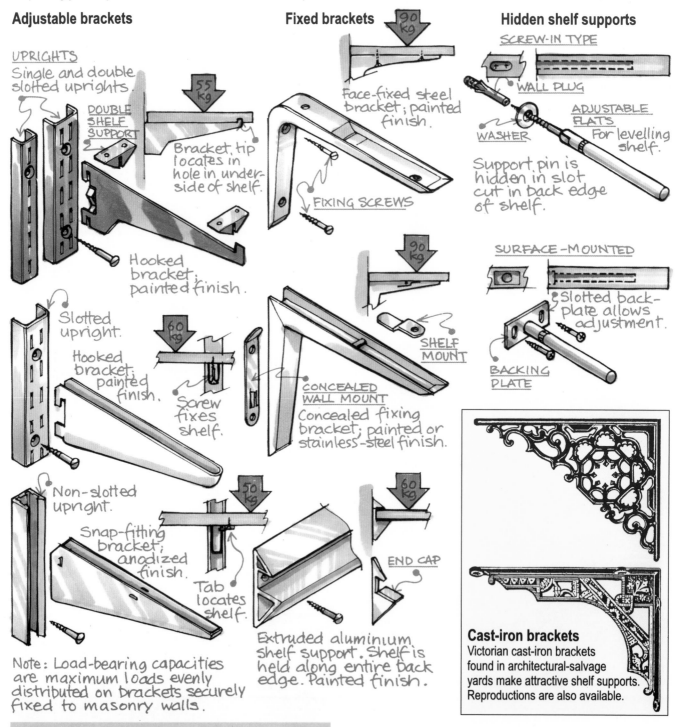

UPRIGHTS
Single and double slotted uprights.

DOUBLE SHELF SUPPORT

55 kg

Bracket tip locates in hole in underside of shelf.

Hooked bracket; painted finish.

Slotted upright.

Hooked bracket; painted finish.

60 kg

Screw fixes shelf.

Non-slotted upright.

Snap-fitting bracket; anodized finish.

50 kg

Tab locates shelf.

Extruded aluminium shelf support. Shelf is held along entire back edge. Painted finish.

Note: Load-bearing capacities are maximum loads evenly distributed on brackets securely fixed to masonry walls.

90 kg

Face-fixed steel bracket; painted finish.

FIXING SCREWS

90 kg

SHELF MOUNT

CONCEALED WALL MOUNT
Concealed fixing bracket; painted or stainless-steel finish.

60 kg

END CAP

SCREW-IN TYPE

WALL PLUG

WASHER

ADJUSTABLE FLATS
For levelling shelf.

Support pin is hidden in slot cut in back edge of shelf.

SURFACE-MOUNTED

Slotted back-plate allows adjustment.

BACKING PLATE

Cast-iron brackets
Victorian cast-iron brackets found in architectural-salvage yards make attractive shelf supports. Reproductions are also available.

BOOK SHELVES

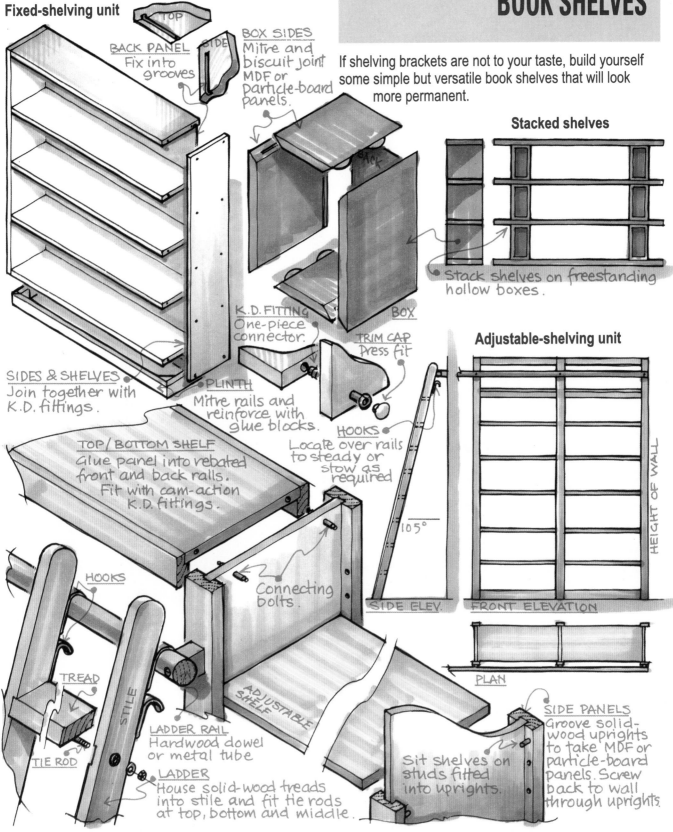

Fixed-shelving unit

TOP

BACK PANEL Fix into grooves

SIDE

BOX SIDES Mitre and biscuit joint MDF or particle-board panels.

If shelving brackets are not to your taste, build yourself some simple but versatile book shelves that will look more permanent.

Stacked shelves

Stack shelves on freestanding hollow boxes.

BOX

K.D. FITTING One-piece connector.

TRIM CAP Press fit

SIDES & SHELVES Join together with K.D. fittings.

PLINTH Mitre rails and reinforce with glue blocks.

HOOKS Locate over rails to steady or stow as required

Adjustable-shelving unit

TOP/ BOTTOM SHELF Glue panel into rebated front and back rails. Fit with cam-action K.D. fittings.

Connecting bolts.

ADJUSTABLE SHELF

105°

SIDE ELEV.

FRONT ELEVATION

HEIGHT OF WALL

PLAN

HOOKS

TREAD

STILE

LADDER RAIL Hardwood dowel or metal tube

TIE ROD

LADDER House solid-wood treads into stile and fit tie rods at top, bottom and middle.

Sit shelves on studs fitted into uprights.

SIDE PANELS Groove solid-wood uprights to take MDF or particle-board panels. Screw back to wall through uprights.

BOOKCASES

A bookcase is essentially a cabinet containing fixed or adjustable shelves, but it is usually fitted with sliding or hinged glass doors to protect the contents from dust. Although the majority of bookcases are designed to stand with their backs against a wall, there is no reason why a bookcase should not serve as a double-sided room divider or even be a freestanding unit with access from all four sides.

Bookcase

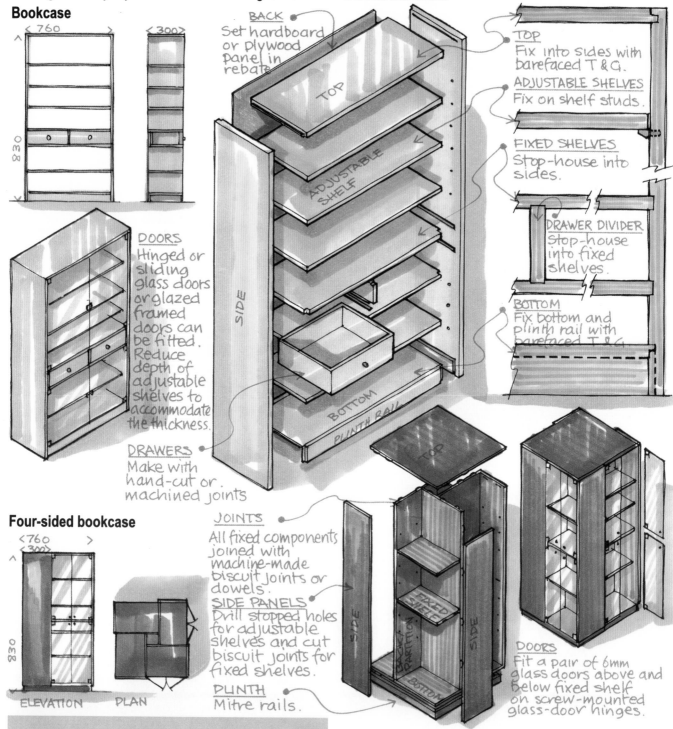

< 760 >

< 300 >

830

BACK
Set hardboard or plywood panel in rebate

TOP

ADJUSTABLE SHELF

SIDE

BOTTOM

PLINTH RAIL

TOP
Fix into sides with barefaced T & G.

ADJUSTABLE SHELVES
Fix on shelf studs.

FIXED SHELVES
Stop-house into sides.

DRAWER DIVIDER
Stop-house into fixed shelves.

BOTTOM
Fix bottom and plinth rail with barefaced T & G.

DOORS
Hinged or sliding glass doors or glazed framed doors can be fitted. Reduce depth of adjustable shelves to accommodate the thickness.

DRAWERS
Make with hand-cut or machined joints

Four-sided bookcase

< 760 >
< 300 >

830

ELEVATION   PLAN

TOP

SIDE

BACK PARTITION

FIXED SHELF

SIDE

BOTTOM

JOINTS
All fixed components joined with machine-made biscuit joints or dowels.

SIDE PANELS
Drill stopped holes for adjustable shelves and cut biscuit joints for fixed shelves.

PLINTH
Mitre rails.

DOORS
Fit a pair of 6mm glass doors above and below fixed shelf on screw-mounted glass-door hinges.

TRADITIONAL BOOKCASE

In the seventeenth and eighteenth centuries, bookcases were made on a lavish scale for the scholarly well-to-do. Designed in the classical style of the period, such bookcases were to establish a traditional pattern that is still reproduced today.

Traditional-style bookcase

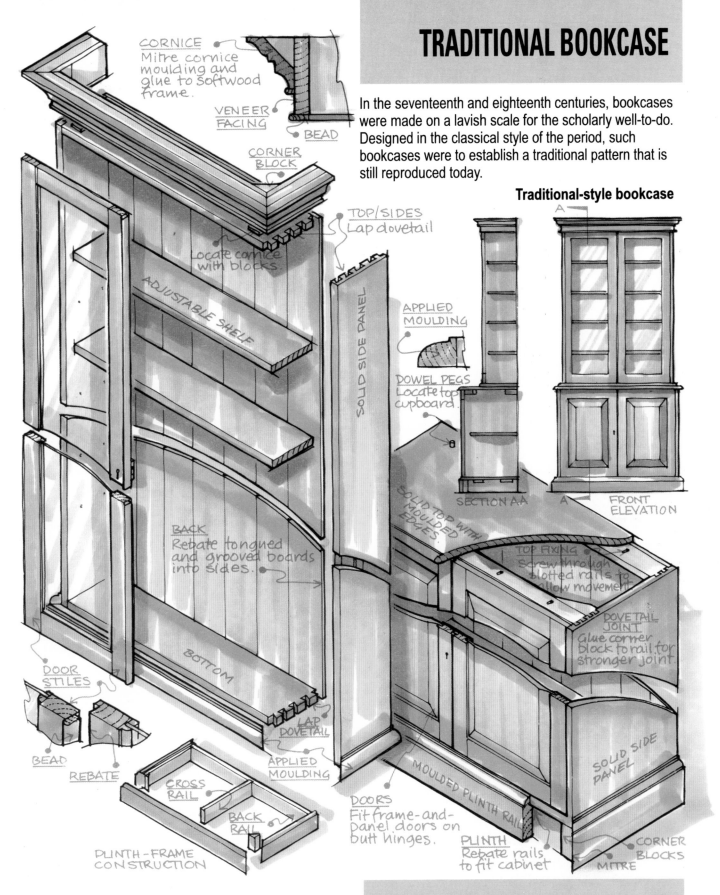

CORNICE
Mitre cornice moulding and glue to softwood frame.

VENEER FACING

BEAD

CORNER BLOCK

Locate cornice with blocks.

TOP/SIDES
Lap dovetail

ADJUSTABLE SHELF

SOLID SIDE PANEL

APPLIED MOULDING

DOWEL PEGS
Locate top cupboard.

BACK
Rebate tongued and grooved boards into sides.

SOLID TOP WITH MOULDED EDGES

SECTION AA

A

FRONT ELEVATION

TOP FIXING
Screw through slotted rails to allow movement

DOVETAIL JOINT
Glue corner block to rail for stronger joint

DOOR STILES

BEAD

REBATE

BOTTOM

LAP DOVETAIL

APPLIED MOULDING

CROSS RAIL

BACK RAIL

PLINTH-FRAME CONSTRUCTION

DOORS
Fit frame-and-panel doors on butt hinges.

MOULDED PLINTH RAIL

PLINTH
Rebate rails to fit cabinet

MITRE

SOLID SIDE PANEL

CORNER BLOCKS

Chapter 10

STATIONERY

Rather than submit to the rigours of modern-day commuting, many people prefer to work from home, at least on a part-time basis – a trend that has been accelerated by the widespread use of word processors and fax machines. Consequently, there's often a need to store a wider range of stationery and office equipment than was customary in the days when a simple letter rack was sufficient for people's needs.

INTERNATIONAL SIZES

In 1970, the British paper-manufacturing and printing industries adopted internationally agreed standards for paper sizes. Although some of the older, peculiarly British, paper sizes are still available, the majority of commercial and domestic stationery is now based on what is known as A-sizes.

Proportions and dimensions
Each A-size piece of paper is made to the same proportion – a rectangle with the longer side equal to the diagonal of a square on the shorter side. Each A-size is exactly half that of the preceding one in the series. Thus A2 is half A1, A3 is half A2, and so on. Typing paper, writing pads and notepaper are usually A4 (210 x 297mm) or A5 (148 x 210mm).

Many different-size envelopes exist, but four standard sizes (C4, C5, C6 and DL) are sufficient to accommodate the most common A-size writing papers.

A-size proportions

Each A-size is half the preceding one

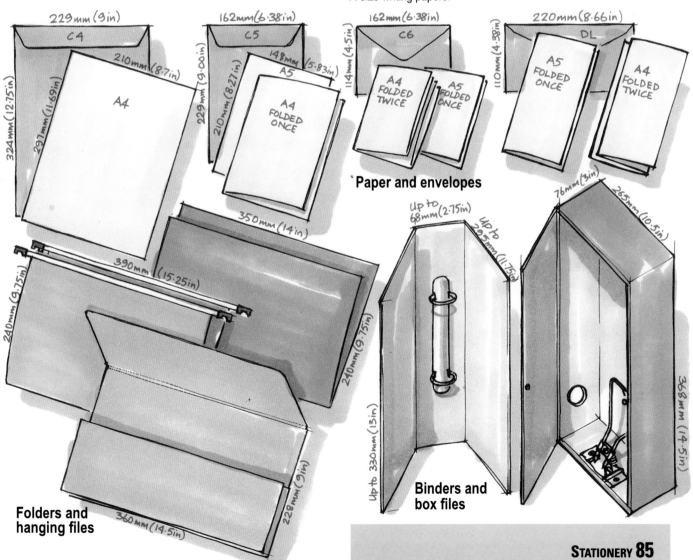

Paper and envelopes

Folders and hanging files

Binders and box files

LETTER RACKS AND BOXES

In a world where words are mostly generated and stored electronically, to many of us, the compact portable writing slope that houses paper, envelopes, pen and ink represents a more leisurely existence, with time to exchange personal handwritten notes and letters. And the object itself, with its semi-secret compartments, is a joy to use. Compartmentalized pencil boxes, though on a smaller scale, hold a similar fascination for children.

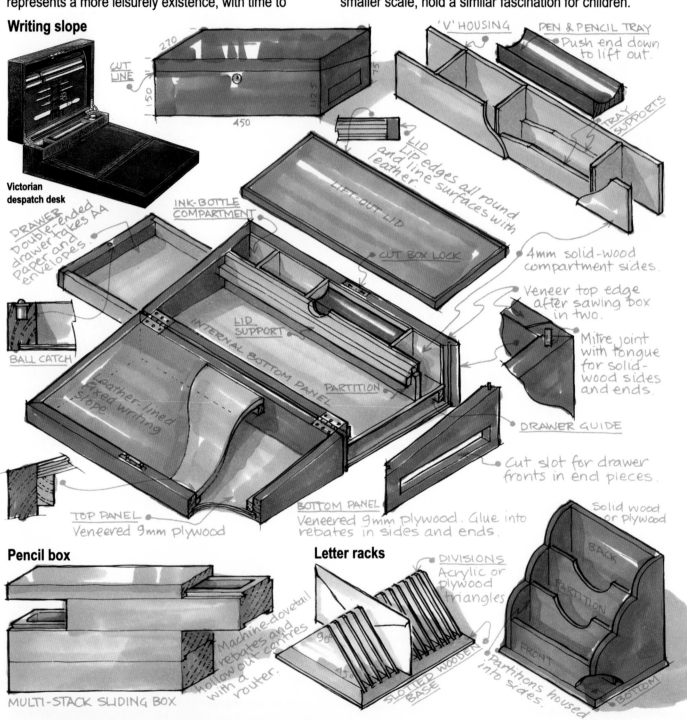

Writing slope

Victorian despatch desk

270
CUT LINE
150
112·5
450

'V' HOUSING

PEN & PENCIL TRAY
Push end down to lift out.

75

TRAY SUPPORTS

LID
Lip edges all round and line surfaces with leather.

DRAWER
Double-ended drawer takes A4 paper and envelopes.

INK-BOTTLE COMPARTMENT

LIFT-OUT LID

CUT BOX LOCK

4mm solid-wood compartment sides.

Veneer top edge after sawing box in two.

BALL CATCH

LID SUPPORT

INTERNAL BOTTOM PANEL

PARTITION

Mitre joint with tongue for solid-wood sides and ends.

Leather-lined fixed writing slope

DRAWER GUIDE

Cut slot for drawer fronts in end pieces.

TOP PANEL
Veneered 9mm plywood

BOTTOM PANEL
Veneered 9mm plywood. Glue into rebates in sides and ends.

Solid wood or plywood

Pencil box

Machine-dovetail rebates and hollow out centres with a router.

MULTI-STACK SLIDING BOX

Letter racks

DIVISIONS
Acrylic or plywood triangles

90°

45°

SLOTTED WOODEN BASE

BACK

PARTITION

FRONT

BOTTOM

Partitions housed into sides.

ROLL-TOP DESKS

The traditional roll-top desk, with its unique retractable cover or tambour, has always carried with it a measure of status. No doubt this is due partly to the amount of skill (and therefore cost) required to make such a complex item, but there is also the added air of exclusivity implied by the fact that private papers could be hidden from view without even having to tidy them away. The tambour was always made by gluing wooden strips to a canvas backing, but it is possible nowadays to buy tambours constructed from interlocking plastic extrusions.

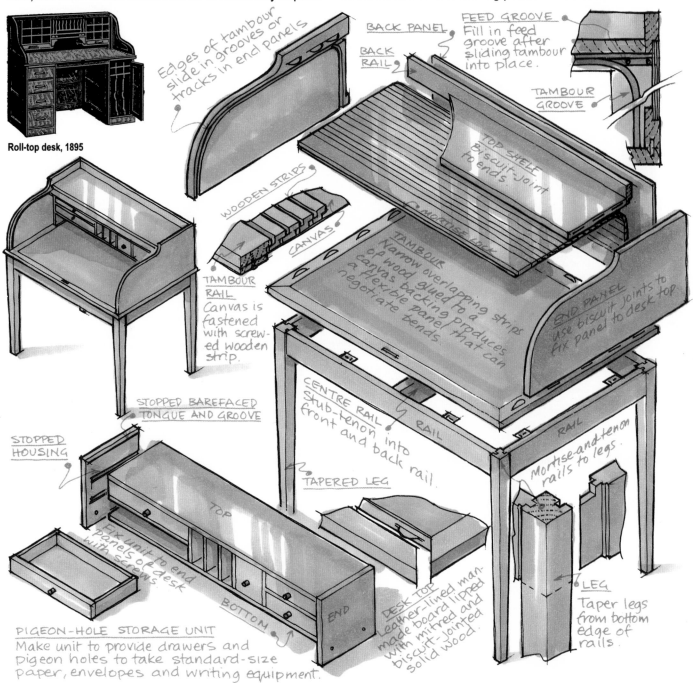

Roll-top desk, 1895

Edges of tambour slide in grooves or tracks in end panels

BACK PANEL

BACK RAIL

FEED GROOVE
Fill in feed groove after sliding tambour into place.

TAMBOUR GROOVE

TOP SHELF
Biscuit-joint to ends.

MORTISE LOCK

WOODEN STRIPS

CANVAS

TAMBOUR RAIL
Canvas is fastened with screwed wooden strip.

TAMBOUR
Narrow overlapping strips of wood glued to a canvas backing produces a flexible panel that can negotiate bends.

END PANEL
Use biscuit joints to fix panel to desk top

RAIL

STOPPED BAREFACED TONGUE AND GROOVE

CENTRE RAIL
Stub-tenon into front and back rail.

RAIL
Mortise-and-tenon rails to legs.

STOPPED HOUSING

TAPERED LEG

TOP

FIX unit to end panels of desk with screws.

BOTTOM

END

DESK TOP
Leather-lined man-made board lipped with mitred and biscuit-jointed solid wood.

LEG
Taper legs from bottom edge of rails.

PIGEON-HOLE STORAGE UNIT
Make unit to provide drawers and pigeon holes to take standard-size paper, envelopes and writing equipment.

FALL-FRONT DESKS

The fall-front desk exists in many forms, known variously as scrutoires, bureau cabinets, secretaires and so on. In essence they all comprise a hinged flap, which when lowered provides a horizontal writing surface, and some form of pigeon-hole storage for stationery. Antique examples frequently include a tall glazed bookcase mounted above the desk compartment. It was also usual to have drawers or cupboards beneath. The concept of a fall-front desk and even a secretaire drawer unit can be easily adapted to a modern style.

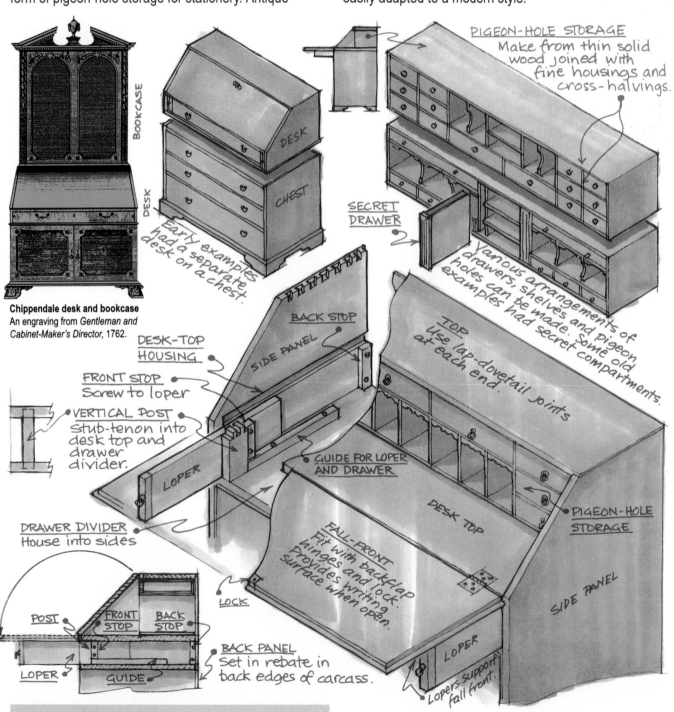

BOOKCASE

DESK

DESK

CHEST

Chippendale desk and bookcase
An engraving from *Gentleman and Cabinet-Maker's Director*, 1762.

Early examples had a separate desk on a chest.

PIGEON-HOLE STORAGE
Make from thin solid wood joined with fine housings and cross-halvings.

SECRET DRAWER

Various arrangements of drawers, shelves and pigeon holes can be made. Some old examples had secret compartments.

BACK STOP

SIDE PANEL

DESK-TOP HOUSING

FRONT STOP
Screw to loper

VERTICAL POST
Stub-tenon into desk top and drawer divider.

LOPER

GUIDE FOR LOPER AND DRAWER

DRAWER DIVIDER
House into sides

TOP
Use lap-dovetail joints at each end.

DESK TOP

PIGEON-HOLE STORAGE

FALL-FRONT
Fit with backflap hinges and lock. Provides writing surface when open.

LOCK

SIDE PANEL

POST

FRONT STOP

BACK STOP

LOPER

GUIDE

BACK PANEL
Set in rebate in back edges of carcass.

LOPER

Lopers support fall front.

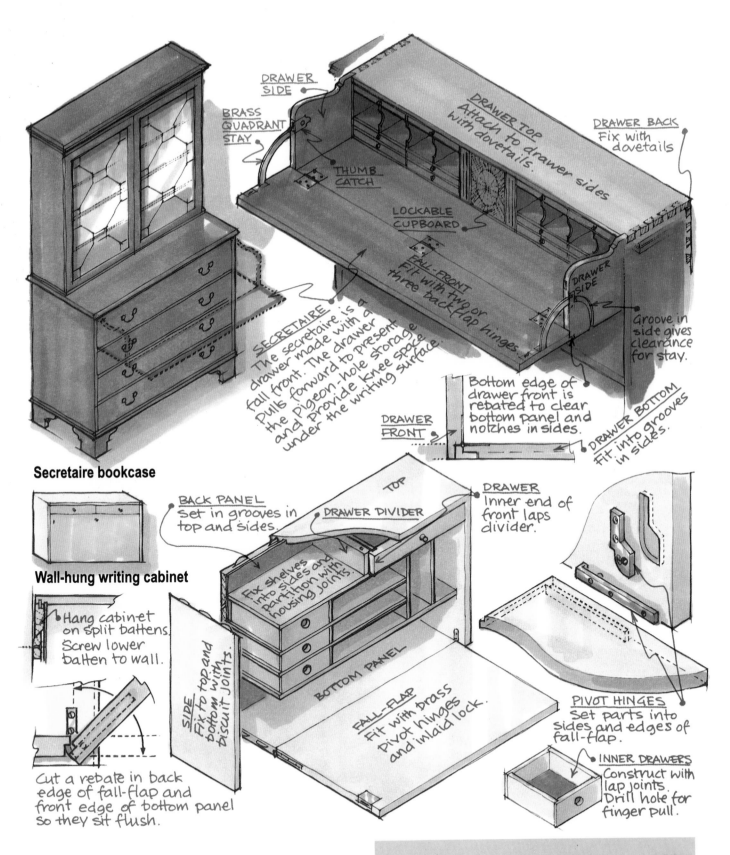

Secretaire bookcase

DRAWER SIDE

BRASS QUADRANT STAY

THUMB CATCH

LOCKABLE CUPBOARD

DRAWER TOP
Attach to drawer sides with dovetails.

DRAWER BACK
Fix with dovetails

DRAWER SIDE

Groove in side gives clearance for stay.

FALL-FRONT
Fit with two or three backflap hinges.

SECRETAIRE
The secretaire is a drawer made with a fall front. The drawer pulls forward to present the pigeon-hole storage and provide knee space under the writing surface.

DRAWER FRONT

Bottom edge of drawer front is rebated to clear bottom panel and notches in sides.

DRAWER BOTTOM
Fit into grooves in sides.

Wall-hung writing cabinet

BACK PANEL
Set in grooves in top and sides.

DRAWER DIVIDER

TOP

DRAWER
Inner end of front laps divider.

Fix shelves into sides and partition with housing joints.

Hang cabinet on split battens. Screw lower batten to wall.

SIDE
Fix to top and bottom with biscuit joints.

BOTTOM PANEL

FALL-FLAP
Fit with brass pivot hinges and inlaid lock.

PIVOT HINGES
Set parts into sides and edges of fall-flap.

INNER DRAWERS
Construct with lap joints. Drill hole for finger pull.

Cut a rebate in back edge of fall-flap and front edge of bottom panel so they sit flush.

HOME OFFICE

New technology and changes in working procedures have encouraged more people to work from home. Conventional paperwork requires well-organized filing systems and materials storage. Computer systems can reduce the amount of paper stored, but the equipment itself occupies a considerable amount of space. If a room is to be used exclusively as an office, then any desk and filing cabinet will suffice – but if the room is also required for other household activities, some means of enclosing the 'office' is an advantage.

KITCHEN FILE DRAWER
Household paperwork is often conducted on the kitchen table. A deep drawer can be converted to take hanging files. Fix metal rods or strips with wooden battens screwed inside the drawer. Hanging frames are also available from stationers.

Rods can be suspended from side to side or front to back.

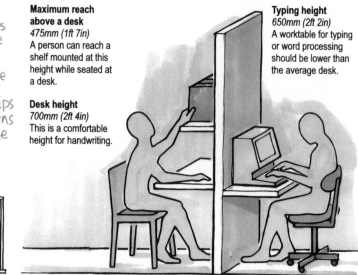

Maximum reach above a desk
475mm (1ft 7in)
A person can reach a shelf mounted at this height while seated at a desk.

Desk height
700mm (2ft 4in)
This is a comfortable height for handwriting.

Typing height
650mm (2ft 2in)
A worktable for typing or word processing should be lower than the average desk.

Desk with mobile storage

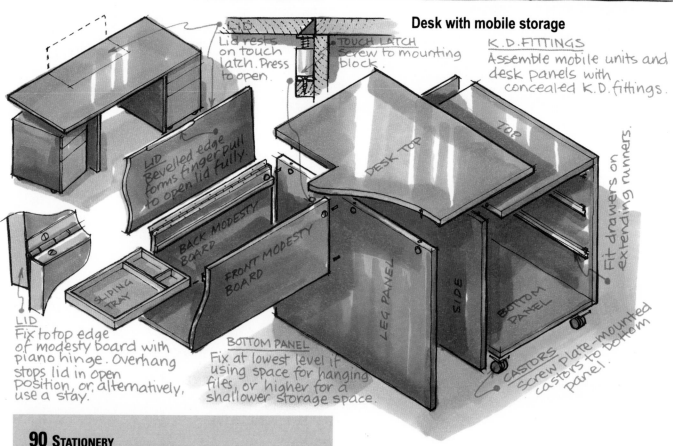

LID
Lid rests on touch latch. Press to open.

TOUCH LATCH
Screw to mounting block.

K.D. FITTINGS
Assemble mobile units and desk panels with concealed K.D. fittings.

LID
Bevelled edge forms finger pull to open lid fully.

BACK MODESTY BOARD

FRONT MODESTY BOARD

SLIDING TRAY

DESK TOP

TOP

LEG PANEL

SIDE

BOTTOM PANEL

Fit drawers on extending runners.

LID
Fix to top edge of modesty board with piano hinge. Overhang stops lid in open position, or, alternatively, use a stay.

BOTTOM PANEL
Fix at lowest level if using space for hanging files, or higher for a shallower storage space.

CASTORS
Screw plate-mounted castors to bottom panel.

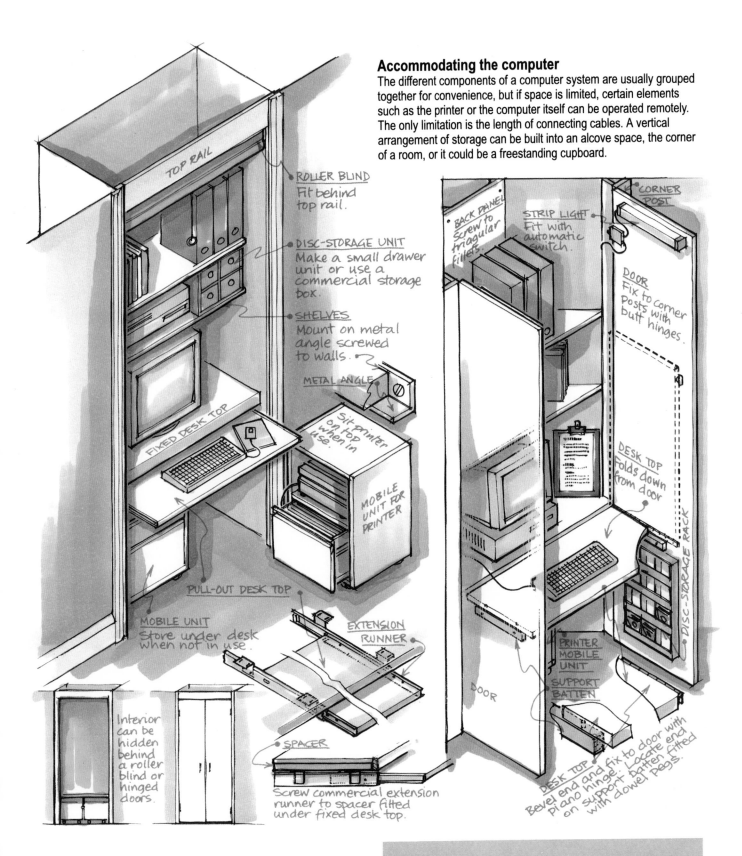

Accommodating the computer

The different components of a computer system are usually grouped together for convenience, but if space is limited, certain elements such as the printer or the computer itself can be operated remotely. The only limitation is the length of connecting cables. A vertical arrangement of storage can be built into an alcove space, the corner of a room, or it could be a freestanding cupboard.

TOP RAIL

ROLLER BLIND
Fit behind
top rail.

DISC-STORAGE UNIT
Make a small drawer
unit or use a
commercial storage
box.

SHELVES
Mount on metal
angle screwed
to walls.

METAL ANGLE

FIXED DESK TOP

Sit printer
on top
when in
use.

MOBILE
UNIT FOR
PRINTER

PULL-OUT DESK TOP

MOBILE UNIT
Store under desk
when not in use.

EXTENSION
RUNNER

Interior
can be
hidden
behind
a roller
blind or
hinged
doors.

SPACER

Screw commercial extension
runner to spacer fitted
under fixed desk top.

BACK PANEL
Screw to
triangular
fillets.

STRIP LIGHT
Fit with
automatic
switch.

CORNER
POST

DOOR
Fix to corner
posts with
butt hinges.

DESK TOP
Folds down
from door

DISC-STORAGE RACK

DOOR

PRINTER
MOBILE
UNIT

SUPPORT
BATTEN

DESK TOP
Bevel end and fix to door with
piano hinge. Locate end
on support batten fitted
with dowel pegs.

11 TV AND HI-FI SYSTEMS

Although they are entirely functional in concept, modern hi-fi systems and television sets, with their electronic displays and panoply of push-buttons and selectors, are visually seductive pieces of engineering.

Most of us are more than happy to display such equipment openly, but some people find its 'high-tech' presence too modern for their tastes, preferring instead to hide it inside period-style storage units.

Records, tape cassettes and compact discs are supplied in packaging that provides sufficient protection for them to be stored on open shelving or wall-hung racks. A large collection of vinyl records will be extremely heavy, and requires strong, securely fixed shelving. See DESIGNING AND PLANNING for how to construct rigid shelves.

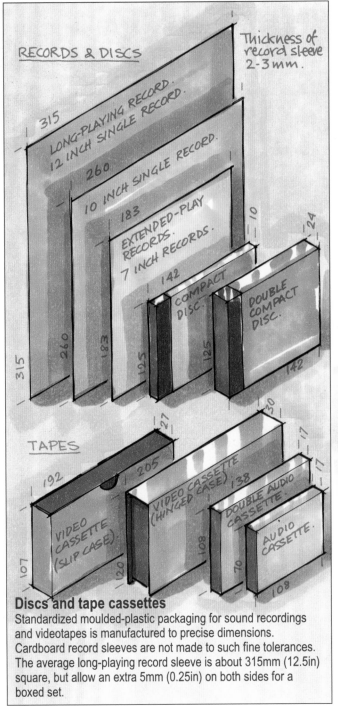

RECORDS & DISCS

Thickness of record sleeve 2-3mm.

315 LONG-PLAYING RECORD. 12 INCH SINGLE RECORD.

260 10 INCH SINGLE RECORD.

183 EXTENDED-PLAY RECORDS. 7 INCH RECORDS.

10

24

142 COMPACT DISC.

DOUBLE COMPACT DISC.

125

315 260 183 125 125 142

TAPES

30 27 17 17

192 205 VIDEO CASSETTE (HINGED CASE) 138 DOUBLE AUDIO CASSETTE.

VIDEO CASSETTE (SLIP CASE). AUDIO CASSETTE.

107 120 108 70 108

Discs and tape cassettes
Standardized moulded-plastic packaging for sound recordings and videotapes is manufactured to precise dimensions. Cardboard record sleeves are not made to such fine tolerances. The average long-playing record sleeve is about 315mm (12.5in) square, but allow an extra 5mm (0.25in) on both sides for a boxed set.

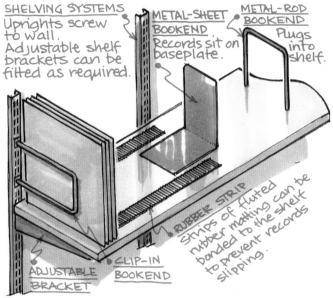

SHELVING SYSTEMS
Uprights screw to wall. Adjustable shelf brackets can be fitted as required.

METAL-SHEET BOOKEND
Records sit on baseplate.

METAL-ROD BOOKEND
Plugs into shelf.

RUBBER STRIP
Strips of fluted rubber matting can be bonded to the shelf to prevent records slipping.

ADJUSTABLE BRACKET

CLIP-IN BOOKEND

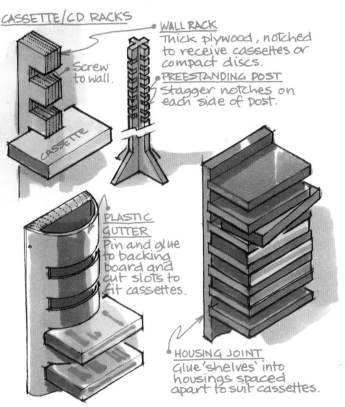

CASSETTE/CD RACKS

WALL RACK
Thick plywood, notched to receive cassettes or compact discs.

PREESTANDING POST
Stagger notches on each side of post.

Screw to wall.

CASSETTE

PLASTIC GUTTER
Pin and glue to backing board and cut slots to fit cassettes.

HOUSING JOINT
Glue 'shelves' into housings spaced apart to suit cassettes.

HI-FI SYSTEMS

The sometimes bewildering choice of hi-fi equipment makes it impossible to design storage that will cater for every eventuality, especially since the more demanding enthusiast is apt to assemble a one-off system to meet his or her particular requirements. If you can foresee a time when you might want to change your hi-fi system, construct storage that can be adapted easily to accommodate different equipment. You may also want to integrate sufficient storage space for your growing collection of discs and tapes. Consider a wall-hung shelf or cabinet for a record-playing deck – a floorstanding unit tends to transmit the slightest vibration to the stylus.

Wall-hung shelves

Floorstanding storage

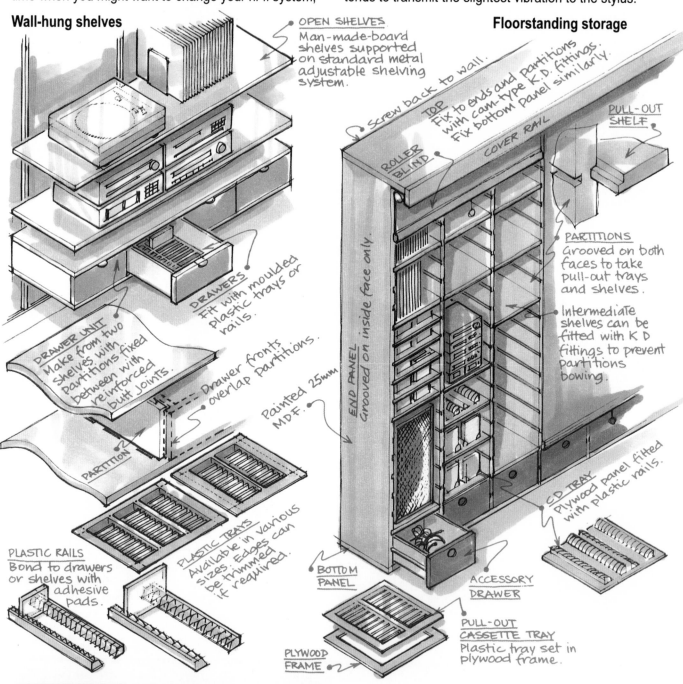

OPEN SHELVES
Man-made-board shelves supported on standard metal adjustable shelving system.

DRAWERS
Fit with moulded plastic trays or rails.

DRAWER UNIT
Make from two shelves with partitions fixed between with reinforced butt joints.

Drawer fronts overlap partitions.

Painted 25mm MDF.

PARTITION

PLASTIC RAILS
Bond to drawers or shelves with adhesive pads.

PLASTIC TRAYS
Available in various sizes. Edges can be trimmed if required.

Screw back to wall.

TOP
Fix to ends and partitions with cam-type K.D. fittings. Fix bottom panel similarly.

COVER RAIL

ROLLER BLIND

END PANEL
Grooved on inside face only.

PULL-OUT SHELF

PARTITIONS
Grooved on both faces to take pull-out trays and shelves.

Intermediate shelves can be fitted with K D fittings to prevent partitions bowing.

CD TRAY
Plywood panel fitted with plastic rails.

BOTTOM PANEL

ACCESSORY DRAWER

PULL-OUT CASSETTE TRAY
Plastic tray set in plywood frame.

PLYWOOD FRAME

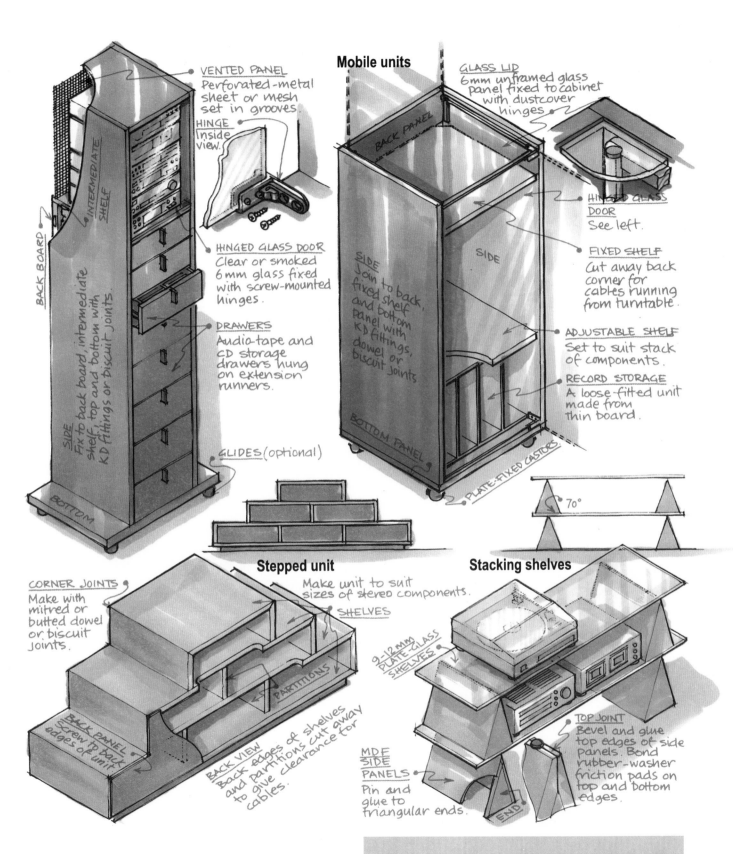

VENTED PANEL
Perforated-metal sheet or mesh set in grooves

HINGE Inside view.

HINGED GLASS DOOR
Clear or smoked 6mm glass fixed with screw-mounted hinges.

DRAWERS
Audio-tape and CD storage drawers hung on extension runners.

GLIDES (optional)

INTERMEDIATE SHELF

BACK BOARD

SIDE
Fix to back board, intermediate shelf, top and bottom with KD fittings or biscuit joints.

BOTTOM

Mobile units

GLASS LID
6mm unframed glass panel fixed to cabinet with dustcover hinges

BACK PANEL

SIDE
Join to back, fixed shelf, and bottom panel with KD fittings, dowel or biscuit joints.

SIDE

BOTTOM PANEL

HINGED GLASS DOOR
See left.

FIXED SHELF
Cut away back corner for cables running from turntable.

ADJUSTABLE SHELF
Set to suit stack of components.

RECORD STORAGE
A loose-fitted unit made from thin board.

PLATE-FIXED CASTORS

70°

Stepped unit

Make unit to suit sizes of stereo components.

SHELVES

CORNER JOINTS
Make with mitred or butted dowel or biscuit joints.

PARTITIONS

BACK PANEL
Screw to back edges of unit

BACK VIEW
Back edges of shelves and partitions cut away to give clearance for cables.

Stacking shelves

9-12 mm PLATE-GLASS SHELVES

MDF SIDE PANELS
Pin and glue to triangular ends.

END

TOP JOINT
Bevel and glue top edges of side panels. Bond rubber-washer friction pads on top and bottom edges.

TV STANDS AND CUPBOARDS

Most TV-set manufacturers supply simple metal stands for their equipment. Some stands also incorporate a shelf for a video recorder. If you don't want your set on display the whole time, you could design a cupboard to house it along with the video machine and tapes. An extending turntable allows you to slide the television out of its storage unit, then rotate the set to the most comfortable angle for viewing.

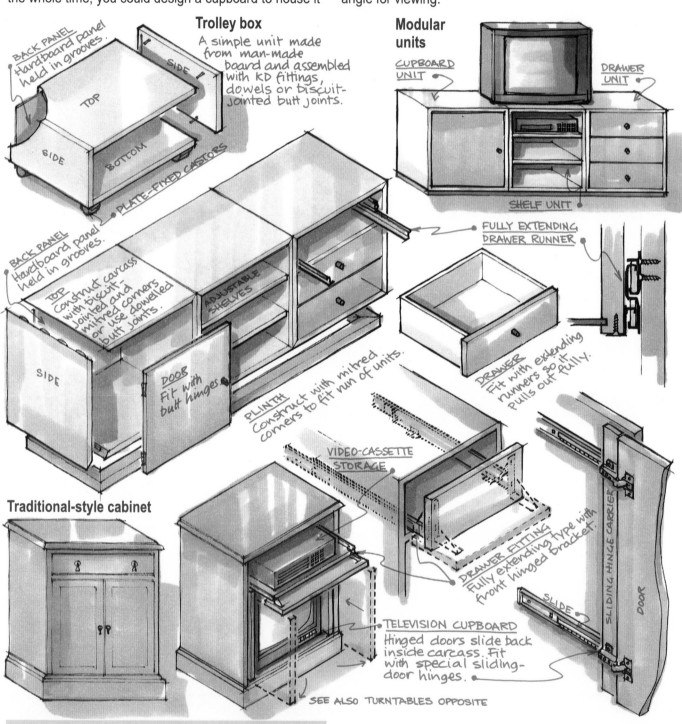

Trolley box

A simple unit made from man-made board and assembled with KD fittings, dowels or biscuit-jointed butt joints.

BACK PANEL Hardboard panel held in grooves.
SIDE
TOP
SIDE
BOTTOM
PLATE-FIXED CASTORS

Modular units

CUPBOARD UNIT
DRAWER UNIT
SHELF UNIT

BACK PANEL Hardboard panel held in grooves.
TOP
Construct carcass with biscuit-jointed and mitred corners or use dowelled butt joints.
ADJUSTABLE SHELVES
SIDE
DOOR Fit with butt hinges.

FULLY EXTENDING DRAWER RUNNER

DRAWER Fit with extending runners so it pulls out fully.

PLINTH Construct with mitred corners to fit run of units.

VIDEO-CASSETTE STORAGE

DRAWER FITTING Fully extending type with front hinged bracket.

SLIDING HINGE CARRIER
SLIDE
DOOR

Traditional-style cabinet

TELEVISION CUPBOARD Hinged doors slide back inside carcass. Fit with special sliding-door hinges.

SEE ALSO TURNTABLES OPPOSITE

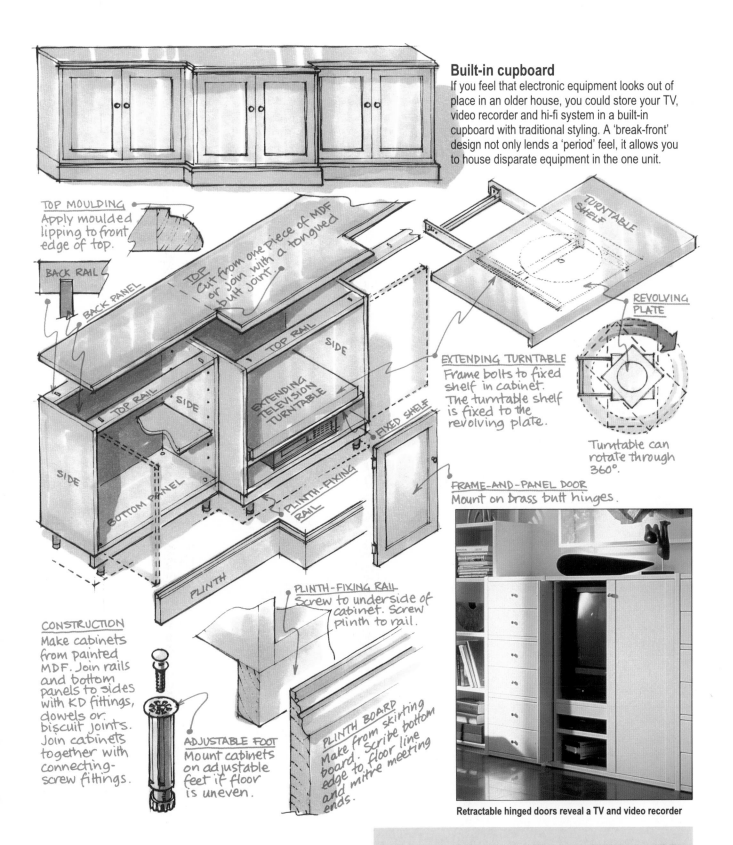

Built-in cupboard

If you feel that electronic equipment looks out of place in an older house, you could store your TV, video recorder and hi-fi system in a built-in cupboard with traditional styling. A 'break-front' design not only lends a 'period' feel, it allows you to house disparate equipment in the one unit.

TOP MOULDING Apply moulded lipping to front edge of top.

BACK RAIL

BACK PANEL

TOP Cut from one piece of MDF or join with a tongued butt joint.

TOP RAIL

SIDE

TOP RAIL

SIDE

EXTENDING TELEVISION TURNTABLE

SIDE

BOTTOM PANEL

PLINTH-FIXING RAIL

PLINTH

TURNTABLE SHELF

REVOLVING PLATE

EXTENDING TURNTABLE Frame bolts to fixed shelf in cabinet. The turntable shelf is fixed to the revolving plate.

Turntable can rotate through 360°.

FIXED SHELF

FRAME-AND-PANEL DOOR Mount on brass butt hinges.

CONSTRUCTION Make cabinets from painted MDF. Join rails and bottom panels to sides with KD fittings, dowels or biscuit joints. Join cabinets together with connecting-screw fittings.

ADJUSTABLE FOOT Mount cabinets on adjustable feet if floor is uneven.

PLINTH-FIXING RAIL Screw to underside of cabinet. Screw plinth to rail.

PLINTH BOARD Make from skirting board. Scribe bottom edge to floor line and mitre meeting ends.

Retractable hinged doors reveal a TV and video recorder

12 COLLECTIONS

Keen collectors, with their specialized knowledge and peculiarly protective instincts, will go to great lengths to preserve and display what to the uninitiated appears to be worthless bric-a-brac. It may be necessary to keep valuable items under lock and key, but the display cases and storage cabinets shown here are designed to allow free access to the collector who wants to use and enjoy a collection without restriction.

Whether they accrue great quantities of material related to their special interest or prefer to acquire a few select items only, most collectors want to display at least some of their acquisitions. Many items can be displayed on open shelves, but more delicate material needs to be protected behind glass.

Divided display box

Glazed boxes

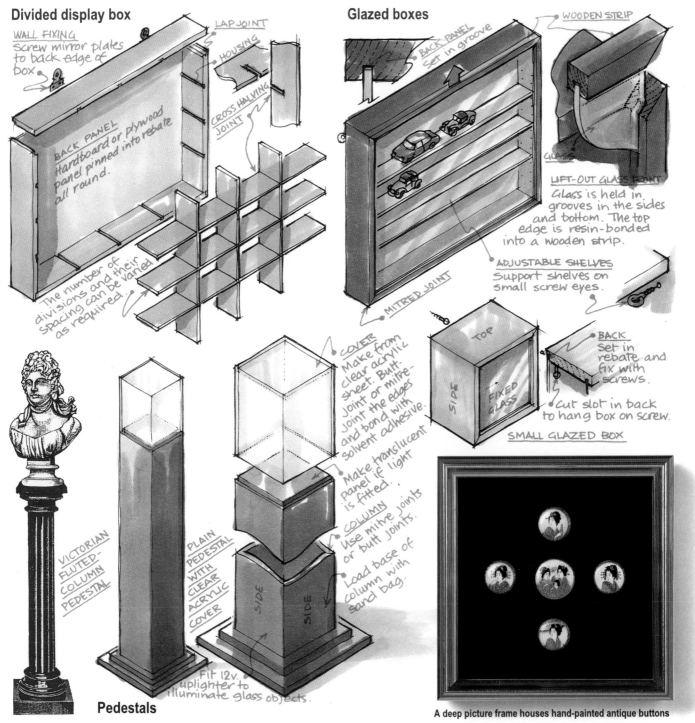

WALL FIXING
Screw mirror plates to back edge of box

LAP JOINT

HOUSING

CROSS HALVING JOINT

BACK PANEL
Hardboard or plywood panel pinned into rebate all round.

The number of divisions and their spacing can be varied as required.

WOODEN STRIP

BACK PANEL set in groove

GLASS

LIFT-OUT GLASS FRONT
Glass is held in grooves in the sides and bottom. The top edge is resin-bonded into a wooden strip.

MITRED JOINT

ADJUSTABLE SHELVES
Support shelves on small screw eyes.

BACK
Set in rebate and fix with screws.

Cut slot in back to hang box on screw.

SMALL GLAZED BOX

TOP

SIDE

FIXED GLASS

COVER
Make from clear acrylic sheet. Butt-joint or mitre-joint the edges and bond with solvent adhesive.

Make translucent panel if light is fitted.

COLUMN
Use mitre joints or butt joints.

Load base of column with sand bag.

VICTORIAN FLUTED-COLUMN PEDESTAL

PLAIN PEDESTAL WITH CLEAR ACRYLIC COVER

SIDE

SIDE

Fit 12v. uplighter to illuminate glass objects.

Pedestals

A deep picture frame houses hand-painted antique buttons

ALCOVE SHELVING

The alcoves on either side of a chimney breast make ideal locations for sturdy display shelving, with hidden bearers for purpose-built shelves screwed securely to the flanking walls. If you need to protect certain items from dust, include some special display shelves fitted with lightweight clear-plastic covers.

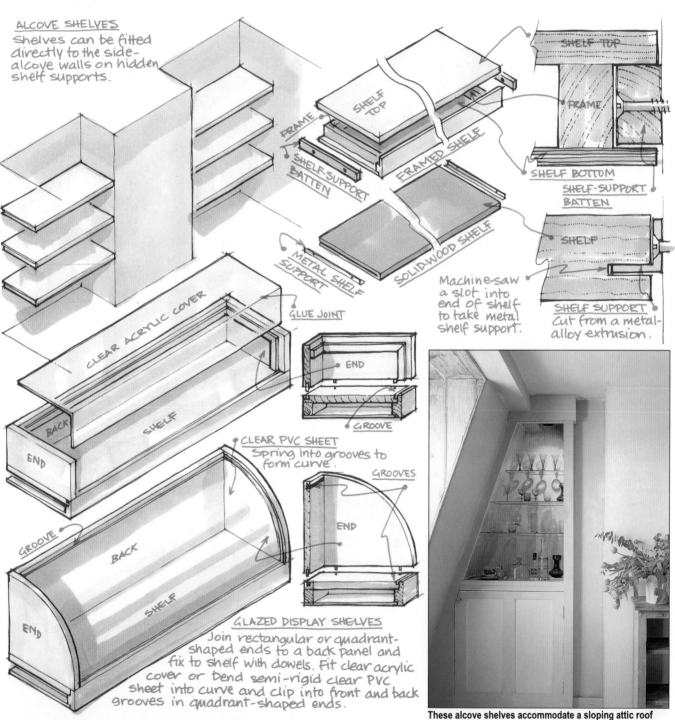

ALCOVE SHELVES
Shelves can be fitted directly to the side-alcove walls on hidden shelf supports.

FRAME

SHELF TOP

SHELF-SUPPORT BATTEN

FRAMED SHELF

METAL SHELF SUPPORT

SOLID-WOOD SHELF

GLUE JOINT

CLEAR ACRYLIC COVER

BACK

SHELF

END

END

GROOVE

CLEAR PVC SHEET
Spring into grooves to form curve.

GROOVES

END

GROOVE

BACK

SHELF

END

SHELF TOP

FRAME

SHELF BOTTOM

SHELF-SUPPORT BATTEN

SHELF

Machine-saw a slot into end of shelf to take metal shelf support.

SHELF SUPPORT
Cut from a metal-alloy extrusion.

GLAZED DISPLAY SHELVES
Join rectangular or quadrant-shaped ends to a back panel and fix to shelf with dowels. Fit clear acrylic cover or bend semi-rigid clear PVC sheet into curve and clip into front and back grooves in quadrant-shaped ends.

These alcove shelves accommodate a sloping attic roof

COLLECTORS' CABINETS

These special-purpose cabinets have been around for as long as there have been collectors to covet them. They are invariably made to the highest standards, usually from costly materials, and are so appealing it is almost worth taking up collecting as an excuse to own one.

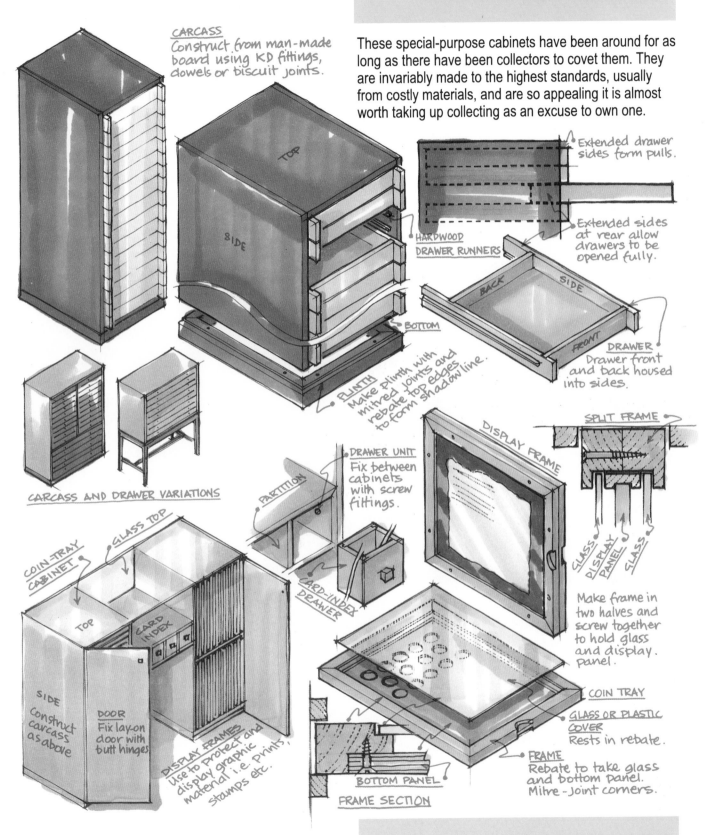

CARCASS
Construct from man-made board using KD fittings, dowels or biscuit joints.

TOP

SIDE

BOTTOM

Extended drawer sides form pulls.

HARDWOOD DRAWER RUNNERS

Extended sides at rear allow drawers to be opened fully.

BACK

SIDE

FRONT

DRAWER
Drawer front and back housed into sides.

PLINTH
Make plinth with mitred joints and rebate top edges to form shadowline.

CARCASS AND DRAWER VARIATIONS

DRAWER UNIT
Fix between cabinets with screw fittings.

PARTITION

CARD-INDEX DRAWER

DISPLAY FRAME

SPLIT FRAME

GLASS DISPLAY PANEL GLASS

Make frame in two halves and screw together to hold glass and display panel.

COIN-TRAY CABINET

GLASS TOP

TOP

CARD INDEX

SIDE
Construct carcass as above

DOOR
Fix lay-on door with butt hinges

DISPLAY FRAMES
Use to protect and display graphic material i.e. prints, stamps etc.

BOTTOM PANEL

FRAME SECTION

COIN TRAY

GLASS OR PLASTIC COVER
Rests in rebate.

FRAME
Rebate to take glass and bottom panel. Mitre-joint corners.

13 TOYS AND GAMES

Whatever you provide to store children's toys and games will be outmoded within a few years, so it's worth considering how you might convert storage to another use as a child grows. Make sure under-bed storage will be large enough for spare blankets, for example; and if possible, make shelving adjustable so that it can be altered to take schoolbooks. Perhaps most important of all, any purpose-built storage unit that is designed to include a bed should be large enough to accommodate a standard single mattress.

Open shelving capable of doubling as toy storage and bookshelves is normally restricted to a child's bedroom. However, as young children need supervision it is clearly advantageous to keep some of their favourite toys in

mobile storage that can be transferred easily to other areas of the house. Even fairly small children can move simple tote boxes from room to room, and the floor can be cleared in minutes at bedtime.

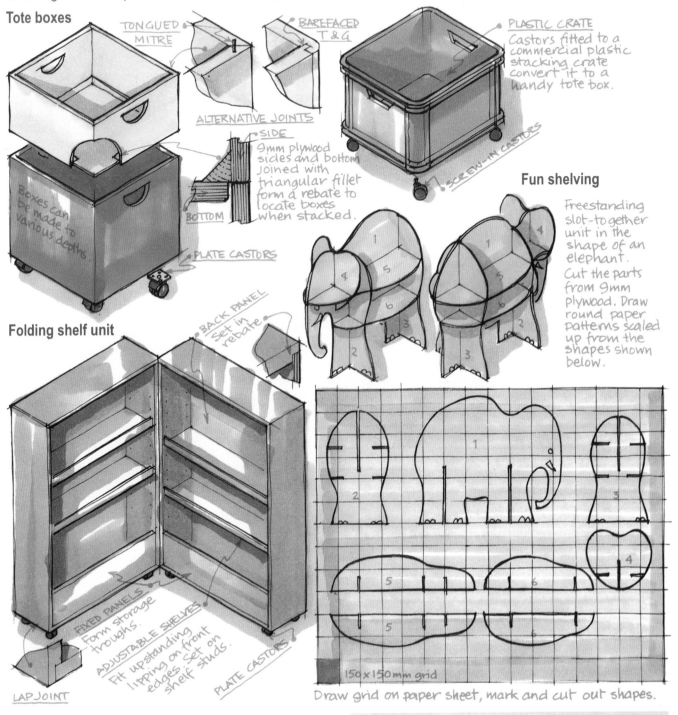

Tote boxes

TONGUED MITRE

BAREFACED T & G

ALTERNATIVE JOINTS

SIDE

9mm plywood sides and bottom joined with triangular fillet form a rebate to locate boxes when stacked.

BOTTOM

Boxes can be made to various depths.

PLATE CASTORS

Folding shelf unit

BACK PANEL set in rebate

FIXED PANELS form storage troughs.

ADJUSTABLE SHELVES. Fit upstanding lipping on front edges. Set on shelf studs.

LAP JOINT

PLATE CASTORS

PLASTIC CRATE

Castors fitted to a commercial plastic stacking crate convert it to a handy tote box.

SCREW-IN CASTORS

Fun shelving

Freestanding slot-together unit in the shape of an elephant. Cut the parts from 9mm plywood. Draw round paper patterns scaled up from the shapes shown below.

150 x 150 mm grid

Draw grid on paper sheet, mark and cut out shapes.

PLAYROOM STORAGE

A child's bedroom has to double as a playroom for much of the time, so keeping an area of the floor clear for spreading out toys and games is a major consideration. Storing toys under a conventional bed is one option, or you could build a raised platform that combines sleeping accommodation with ample storage beneath. Making room for a model-railway layout or car-racing track is always difficult in the average-size bedroom. You might consider suspending one from the ceiling, but only if you can anchor the fixings securely to the joists above.

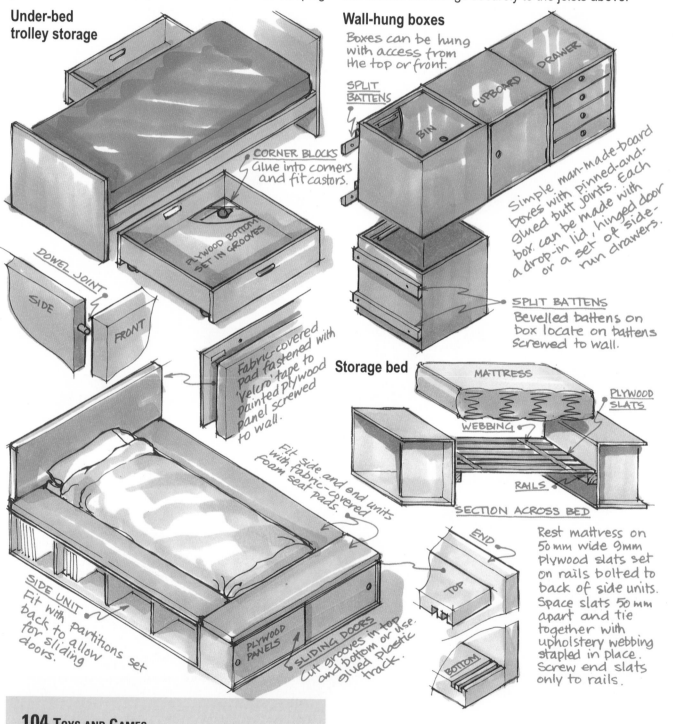

Under-bed trolley storage

CORNER BLOCKS
Glue into corners and fit castors.

PLYWOOD BOTTOM SET IN GROOVES

DOWEL JOINT

SIDE

FRONT

Fabric-covered pad fastened with 'Velcro' tape to painted plywood panel screwed to wall.

Fit side and end units with fabric-covered foam seat pads.

SIDE UNIT
Fit with partitions set back to allow for sliding doors.

PLYWOOD PANELS

SLIDING DOORS
Cut grooves in top and bottom or use glued plastic track.

Wall-hung boxes

Boxes can be hung with access from the top or front.

SPLIT BATTENS

BIN   CUPBOARD   DRAWER

Simple man-made-board boxes with pinned-and-glued butt joints. Each box can be made with a drop-in lid, hinged door or a set of side-run drawers.

SPLIT BATTENS
Bevelled battens on box locate on battens screwed to wall.

Storage bed

MATTRESS

PLYWOOD SLATS

WEBBING

RAILS

SECTION ACROSS BED

END

TOP

BOTTOM

Rest mattress on 50 mm wide 9mm plywood slats set on rails bolted to back of side units. Space slats 50 mm apart and tie together with upholstery webbing stapled in place. Screw end slats only to rails.

Raised-bed unit

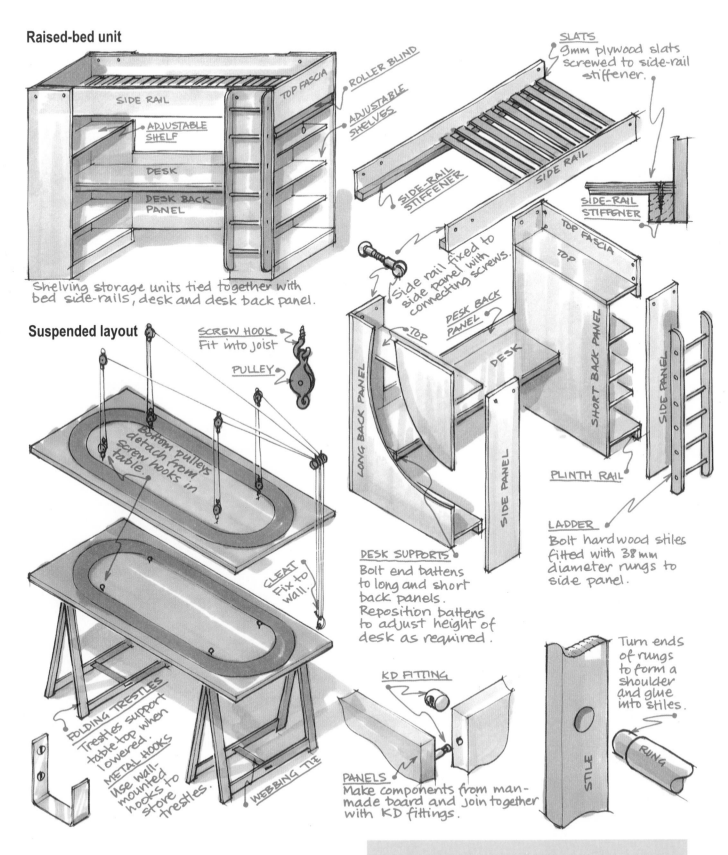

SIDE RAIL

TOP FASCIA

ROLLER BLIND

ADJUSTABLE SHELVES

ADJUSTABLE SHELF

DESK

DESK BACK PANEL

Shelving storage units tied together with bed side-rails, desk and desk back panel.

SLATS
9mm plywood slats screwed to side-rail stiffener.

SIDE-RAIL STIFFENER

SIDE RAIL

SIDE-RAIL STIFFENER

Side rail fixed to side panel with connecting screws.

TOP FASCIA

TOP

DESK BACK PANEL

DESK

SHORT BACK PANEL

SIDE PANEL

LONG BACK PANEL

TOP

SIDE PANEL

PLINTH RAIL

LADDER
Bolt hardwood stiles fitted with 38mm diameter rungs to side panel.

Suspended layout

SCREW HOOK
Fit into joist

PULLEY

Bottom pulleys detach from screw hooks in table.

CLEAT
Fix to wall.

FOLDING TRESTLES
Trestles support table top when lowered. Use wall-mounted hooks to store trestles.

METAL HOOKS

WEBBING TIE

DESK SUPPORTS
Bolt end battens to long and short back panels. Reposition battens to adjust height of desk as required.

KD FITTING

PANELS
Make components from man-made board and join together with KD fittings.

Turn ends of rungs to form a shoulder and glue into stiles.

STILE

RUNG

14 SPORTS EQUIPMENT

Most amateur sporting pursuits are restricted to weekends, and many are seasonal. Consequently, sports equipment needs to be stored, perhaps for long periods, in such a way that it will remain in good working order. If you have the room, you will probably store bulky equipment in the garage or cellar, but if space is limited you may be compelled to adopt more unconventional methods of storage.

Flat dwellers often have no option but to leave a bicycle standing in the hallway – a practice guaranteed to become unpopular with the neighbours. Try to think of somewhere in your home where you could suspend the bicycle upside down from the ceiling, or perhaps hang it from wall-mounted brackets. The methods shown below are so simple that they can be adapted easily to suit other cumbersome items of equipment.

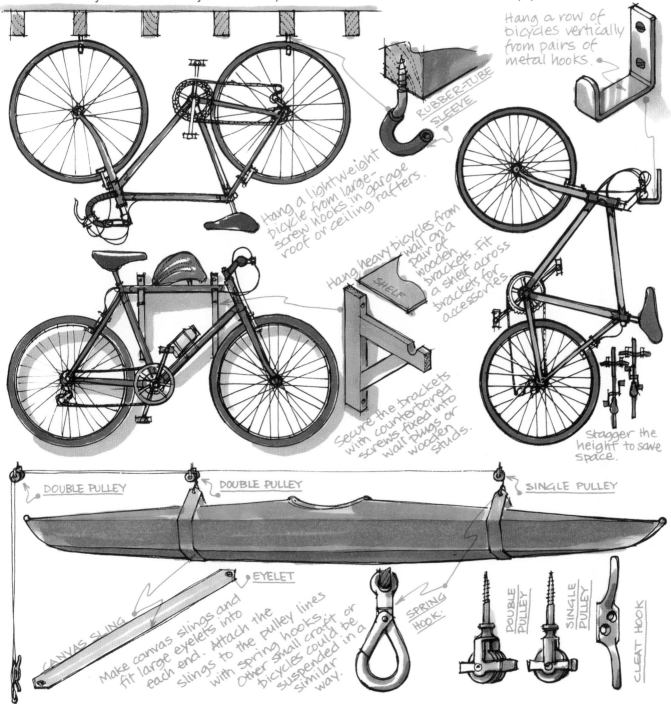

Hang a row of bicycles vertically from pairs of metal hooks.

RUBBER-TUBE SLEEVE

Hang a lightweight bicycle from large-screw hooks in garage roof or ceiling rafters.

Hang heavy bicycles from a wall on a pair of wooden brackets. Fit a shelf across brackets for accessories.

SHELF

Secure the brackets with counterbored screws fixed into wall plugs or wooden studs.

Stagger the height to save space.

DOUBLE PULLEY

DOUBLE PULLEY

SINGLE PULLEY

CANVAS SLING

EYELET

SPRING HOOK

DOUBLE PULLEY

SINGLE PULLEY

CLEAT HOOK

Make canvas slings and fit large eyelets into each end. Attach the slings to the pulley lines with spring hooks. Other small craft or bicycles could be suspended in a similar way.

WALL FITTINGS

Wall-mounted shelving is perfectly adequate for most types of sports equipment, but purpose-made brackets may be more practical for awkwardly shaped items.

Depending on whether or not the equipment needs to be kept under cover, you might fix a bracket in the garage, shed or loft, or even to an outside wall.

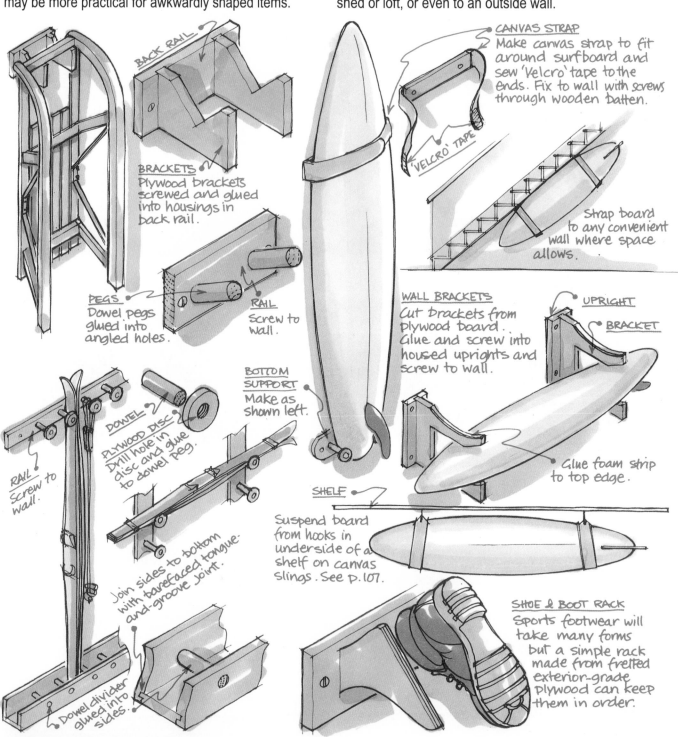

BACK RAIL

BRACKETS
Plywood brackets screwed and glued into housings in back rail.

PEGS
Dowel pegs glued into angled holes.

RAIL
Screw to wall.

RAIL
Screw to wall.

DOWEL
PLYWOOD DISC
Drill hole in disc and glue to dowel peg.

Join sides to bottom with barefaced tongue-and-groove joint.

Dowel divider glued into sides.

CANVAS STRAP
Make canvas strap to fit around surfboard and sew 'Velcro' tape to the ends. Fix to wall with screws through wooden batten.

'VELCRO' TAPE

Strap board to any convenient wall where space allows.

WALL BRACKETS
Cut brackets from plywood board.. Glue and screw into housed uprights and screw to wall.

BOTTOM SUPPORT
Make as shown left.

SHELF
Suspend board from hooks in underside of a shelf on canvas slings. See p.107.

UPRIGHT

BRACKET

Glue foam strip to top edge.

SHOE & BOOT RACK
Sports footwear will take many forms but a simple rack made from fretted exterior-grade plywood can keep them in order.

GENERAL-PURPOSE STORAGE

Many sporting activities require a number of small and disparate items, as well as specialized clothing and footwear. In most homes they simply clutter the wardrobe or are thrown under the stairs, whereas a specially adapted cupboard or purpose-made chest would be tidier and much more convenient.

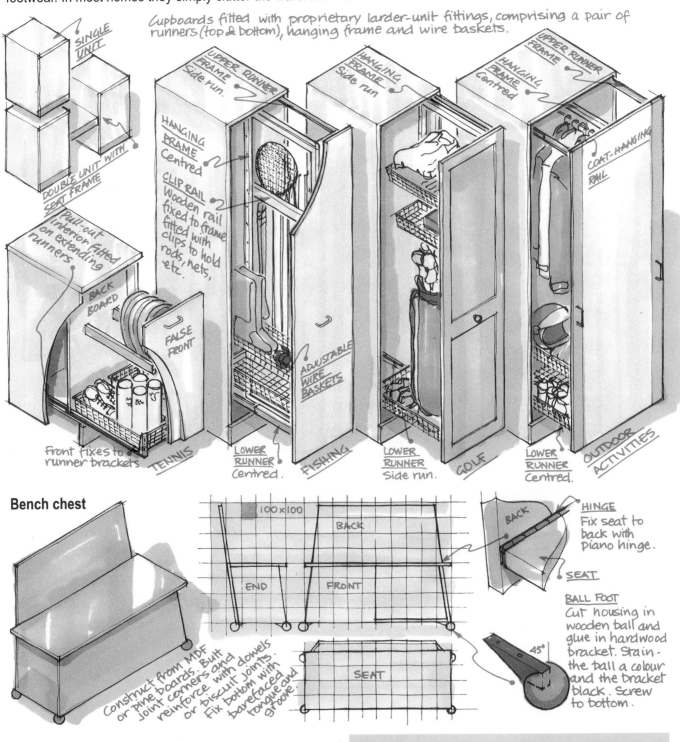

SINGLE UNIT

DOUBLE UNIT WITH SEAT FRAME

Cupboards fitted with proprietary larder-unit fittings, comprising a pair of runners (top & bottom), hanging frame and wire baskets.

UPPER RUNNER FRAME Side run.

HANGING FRAME Centred

CLIP RAIL Wooden rail fixed to frame fitted with clips to hold rods, nets, etc.

HANGING FRAME Side run

UPPER RUNNER FRAME

HANGING FRAME Centred

COAT-HANGING RAIL

Pull-out interior fitted on extending runners

BACK BOARD

FALSE FRONT

ADJUSTABLE WIRE BASKETS

Front fixes to runner brackets

TENNIS

LOWER RUNNER Centred.

FISHING

LOWER RUNNER Side run.

GOLF

LOWER RUNNER Centred.

OUTDOOR ACTIVITIES

Bench chest

Construct from MDF or pine boards. Butt joint corners and reinforce with dowels or biscuit joints. Fix bottom with barefaced tongue and groove.

100 x 100

BACK

END

FRONT

SEAT

BACK

HINGE
Fix seat to back with piano hinge.

SEAT

BALL FOOT
Cut housing in wooden ball and glue in hardwood bracket. Stain the ball a colour and the bracket black. Screw to bottom.

45°

Nowadays comparatively few people are content to maintain a house and garden with basic handtools. The booming DIY market, spurred on by tool manufacturers, has seen to it that more and more households are equipped with sophisticated toolkits and workshops. However, tools and materials are not cheap, and one needs to protect what is a considerable investment with adequate storage.

A rudimentary repair kit, comprising a pair of scissors and basic needles and threads, can be stored in any small box or even in a rolled fabric pouch tied with laces. Embroiderers and dressmakers, however, accumulate numerous coloured cottons, which need to be selected and matched carefully, plus copious amounts of fabric remnants and paper patterns, and an extensive variety of tools and equipment. Pin cushions and simple racks make accessible storage for small frequently used needlecraft accessories.

Pin cushions

Cotton-reel racks

Worktop tidy

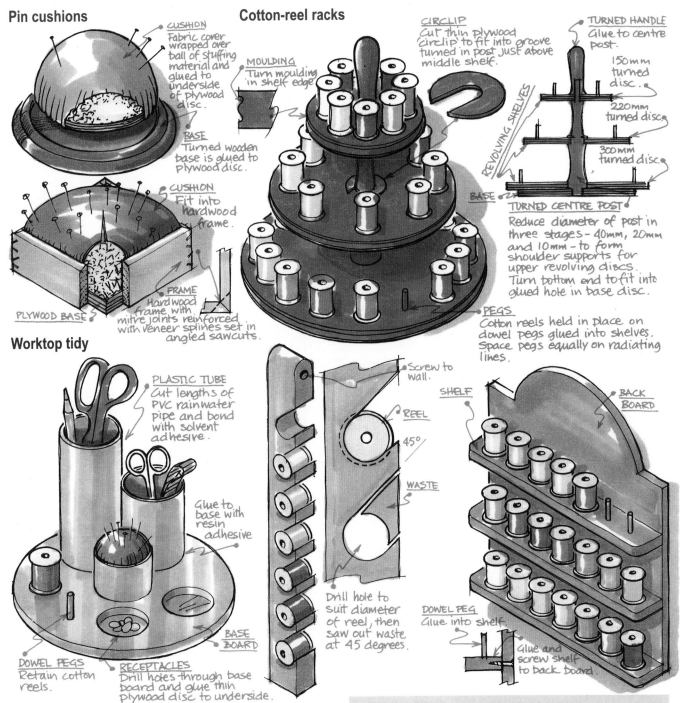

CUSHION
Fabric cover wrapped over ball of stuffing material and glued to underside of plywood disc.

MOULDING
Turn moulding in shelf edge.

BASE
Turned wooden base is glued to plywood disc.

CUSHION
Fit into hardwood frame.

FRAME
Hardwood frame with mitre joints reinforced with veneer splines set in angled sawcuts.

PLYWOOD BASE

CIRCLIP
Cut thin plywood 'circlip' to fit into groove turned in post just above middle shelf.

TURNED HANDLE
Glue to centre post.

150mm turned disc.

220mm turned disc.

300mm turned disc.

REVOLVING SHELVES

BASE

TURNED CENTRE POST
Reduce diameter of post in three stages – 40mm, 20mm and 10mm – to form shoulder supports for upper revolving discs. Turn bottom end to fit into glued hole in base disc.

PEGS
Cotton reels held in place on dowel pegs glued into shelves. Space pegs equally on radiating lines.

PLASTIC TUBE
Cut lengths of PVC rainwater pipe and bond with solvent adhesive.

Glue to base with resin adhesive

Screw to wall.

REEL

45°

WASTE

SHELF

BACK BOARD

DOWEL PEG
Glue into shelf.

Glue and screw shelf to back board.

Drill hole to suit diameter of reel, then saw out waste at 45 degrees.

DOWEL PEGS
Retain cotton reels.

RECEPTACLES
Drill holes through base board and glue thin plywood disc to underside.

BASE BOARD

SEWING BOXES

If you have the space, devoting a chest of drawers to storing sewing materials and fabrics is an excellent solution. Keep folded fabric, wool and patterns in the larger drawers, and divide the smaller ones with lift-out trays for cottons, tools and equipment. Otherwise, why not make a set of traditional Shaker-style boxes or a portable storage unit that can be stowed beneath your workbench or beside an armchair?

Traditional Shaker-style box

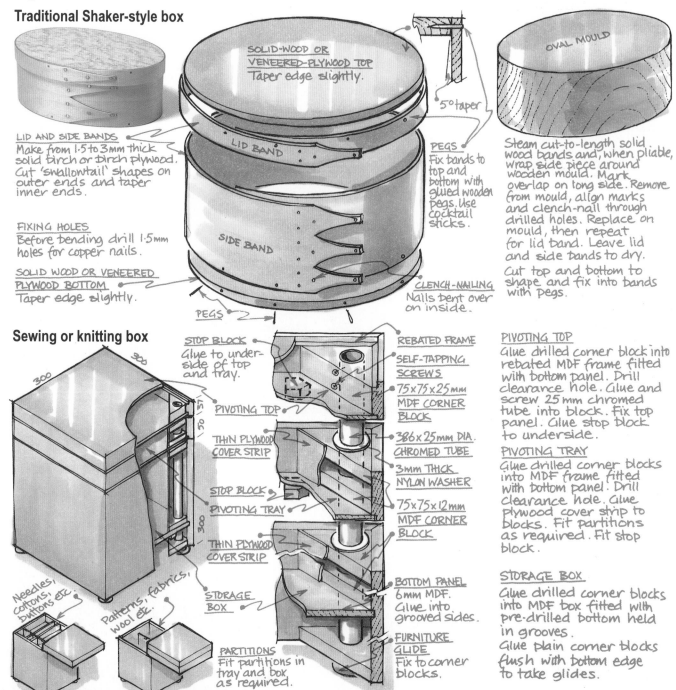

SOLID-WOOD OR VENEERED-PLYWOOD TOP
Taper edge slightly.

OVAL MOULD

5° taper

LID BAND

SIDE BAND

LID AND SIDE BANDS
Make from 1·5 to 3mm thick solid birch or birch plywood. Cut 'swallowtail' shapes on outer ends and taper inner ends.

FIXING HOLES
Before bending drill 1·5mm holes for copper nails.

SOLID WOOD OR VENEERED PLYWOOD BOTTOM
Taper edge slightly.

PEGS

PEGS
Fix bands to top and bottom with glued wooden pegs. Use cocktail sticks.

CLENCH-NAILING
Nails bent over on inside.

Steam cut-to-length solid wood bands and, when pliable, wrap side piece around wooden mould. Mark overlap on long side. Remove from mould, align marks and clench-nail through drilled holes. Replace on mould, then repeat for lid band. Leave lid and side bands to dry.
Cut top and bottom to shape and fix into bands with pegs.

Sewing or knitting box

STOP BLOCK
Glue to underside of top and tray.

PIVOTING TOP

THIN PLYWOOD COVER STRIP

STOP BLOCK

PIVOTING TRAY

THIN PLYWOOD COVER STRIP

STORAGE BOX

Needles, cottons, buttons etc.

Patterns, fabrics, wool etc.

PARTITIONS
Fit partitions in tray and box as required.

REBATED FRAME

SELF-TAPPING SCREWS

75×75×25mm MDF CORNER BLOCK

386×25mm DIA. CHROMED TUBE

3mm THICK NYLON WASHER

75×75×12mm MDF CORNER BLOCK

BOTTOM PANEL
6mm MDF. Glue into grooved sides.

FURNITURE GLIDE
Fix to corner blocks.

PIVOTING TOP
Glue drilled corner block into rebated MDF frame fitted with bottom panel. Drill clearance hole. Glue and screw 25mm chromed tube into block. Fix top panel. Glue stop block to underside.

PIVOTING TRAY
Glue drilled corner blocks into MDF frame fitted with bottom panel. Drill clearance hole. Glue plywood cover strip to blocks. Fit partitions as required. Fit stop block.

STORAGE BOX
Glue drilled corner blocks into MDF box fitted with pre-drilled bottom held in grooves. Glue plain corner blocks flush with bottom edge to take glides.

A properly organized workshop makes for a safer and more efficient working environment. Keep your tools and materials in an orderly fashion so that they can be found and retrieved easily. There is very little point in keeping every scrap of board or useful offcuts if you can't find them when they are needed. If possible, store flammable materials elsewhere, perhaps in a separate shed or lean-to. For safety's sake, install good artificial lighting and place your workbench adjacent to any windows. Provide a first-aid kit and keep it prominently displayed.

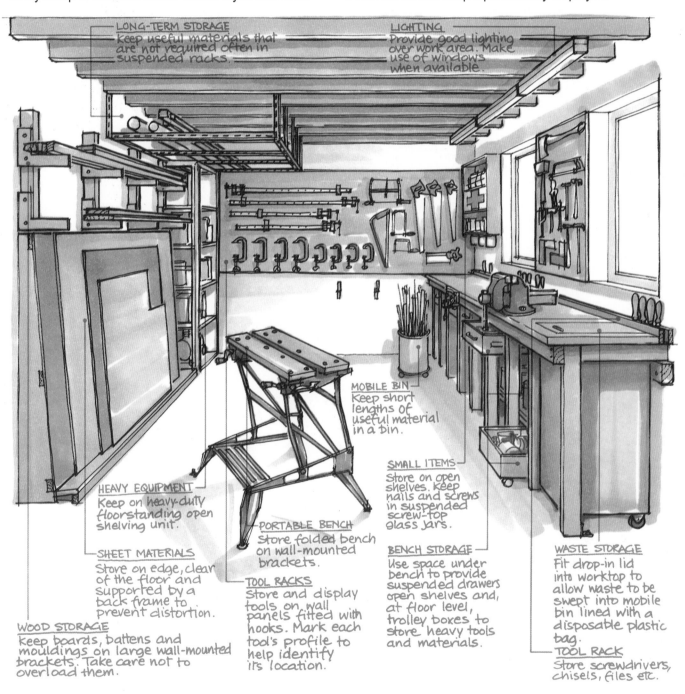

LONG-TERM STORAGE
Keep useful materials that are not required often in suspended racks.

LIGHTING
Provide good lighting over work area. Make use of windows when available.

MOBILE BIN
Keep short lengths of useful material in a bin.

HEAVY EQUIPMENT
Keep on heavy-duty floorstanding open shelving unit.

PORTABLE BENCH
Store folded bench on wall-mounted brackets.

SMALL ITEMS
Store on open shelves. Keep nails and screws in suspended screw-top glass jars.

SHEET MATERIALS
Store on edge, clear of the floor and supported by a back frame to prevent distortion.

TOOL RACKS
Store and display tools on wall panels fitted with hooks. Mark each tool's profile to help identify its location.

BENCH STORAGE
Use space under bench to provide suspended drawers open shelves and, at floor level, trolley boxes to store heavy tools and materials.

WASTE STORAGE
Fit drop-in lid into worktop to allow waste to be swept into mobile bin lined with a disposable plastic bag.

WOOD STORAGE
Keep boards, battens and mouldings on large wall-mounted brackets. Take care not to overload them.

TOOL RACK
Store screwdrivers, chisels, files etc.

TOOL RACKS AND SHELVING

Tools that are left lying around on the bench or dumped ignominiously in a canvas bag or cupboard quickly loose their cutting edges and make for hopelessly inaccurate work. Wall-mounted racks are cheap to make and keep tools conveniently close to hand. Store heavier tools and equipment on strong shelves or home-made brackets.

Shelving

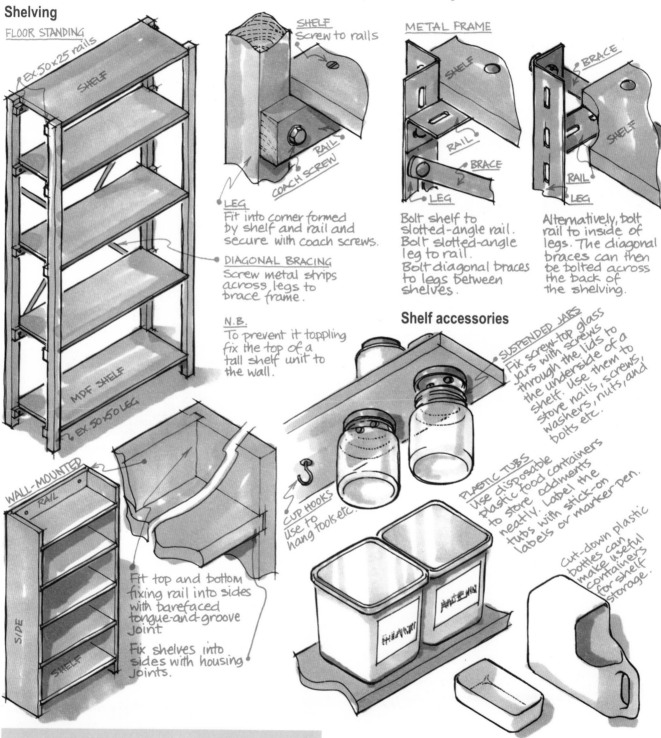

FLOOR STANDING
Ex.50x25 rails
SHELF
MDF SHELF
Ex.50x50 LEG

SHELF
Screw to rails

LEG
Fit into corner formed by shelf and rail and secure with coach screws.

COACH SCREW
RAIL

DIAGONAL BRACING
Screw metal strips across legs to brace frame.

N.B.
To prevent it toppling fix the top of a tall shelf unit to the wall.

METAL FRAME
SHELF
RAIL
BRACE
LEG

Bolt shelf to slotted-angle rail. Bolt slotted-angle leg to rail. Bolt diagonal braces to legs between shelves.

BRACE
SHELF
RAIL
LEG

Alternatively, bolt rail to inside of legs. The diagonal braces can then be bolted across the back of the shelving.

Shelf accessories

SUSPENDED JARS
Fix screw-top glass jars with screws through the lids to the underside of a shelf. Use them to store nails, screws, washers, nuts, and bolts etc.

PLASTIC TUBS
Use disposable plastic food containers to store oddments neatly. Label the tubs with stick-on labels or marker pen.

Cut-down plastic bottles can make useful containers for shelf storage.

CUP HOOKS
Use to hang tools etc.

WALL-MOUNTED
RAIL
SIDE
SHELF

Fit top and bottom fixing rail into sides with bareface tongue-and-groove joint.

Fix shelves into sides with housing joints.

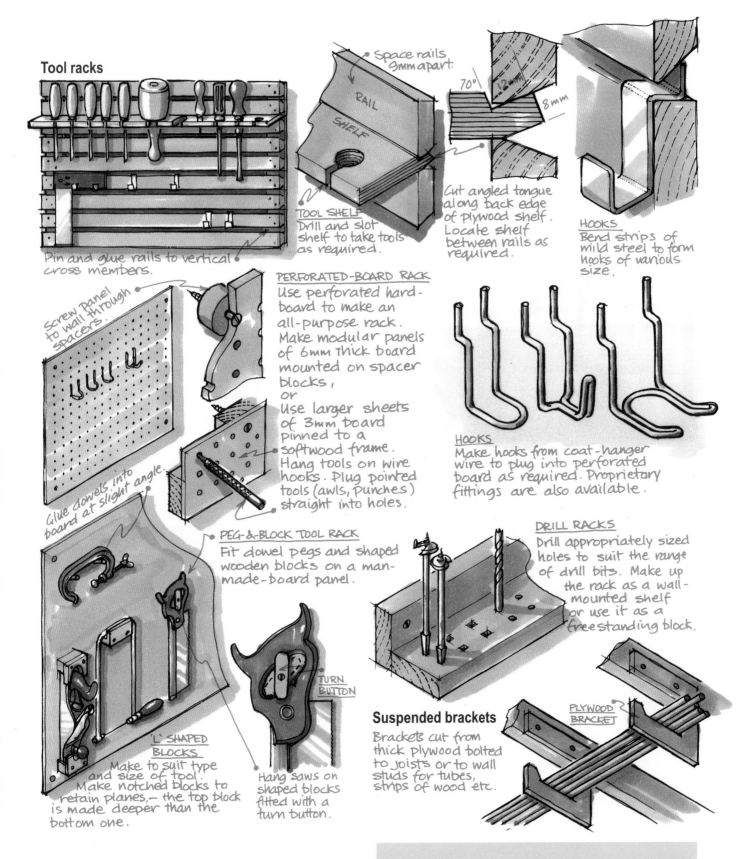

Tool racks

Pin and glue rails to vertical cross members.

Space rails 9mm apart.

RAIL

SHELF

TOOL SHELF
Drill and slot shelf to take tools as required.

70°   12mm   8mm

Cut angled tongue along back edge of plywood shelf. Locate shelf between rails as required.

HOOKS
Bend strips of mild steel to form hooks of various size.

Screw panel to wall through spacers.

PERFORATED-BOARD RACK
Use perforated hardboard to make an all-purpose rack. Make modular panels of 6mm thick board mounted on spacer blocks, or
Use larger sheets of 3mm board pinned to a softwood frame. Hang tools on wire hooks. Plug pointed tools (awls, punches) straight into holes.

HOOKS
Make hooks from coat-hanger wire to plug into perforated board as required. Proprietary fittings are also available.

Glue dowels into board at slight angle.

PEG-&-BLOCK TOOL RACK
Fit dowel pegs and shaped wooden blocks on a man-made-board panel.

DRILL RACKS
Drill appropriately sized holes to suit the range of drill bits. Make up the rack as a wall-mounted shelf or use it as a freestanding block.

'L'-SHAPED BLOCKS
Make to suit type and size of tool. Make notched blocks to retain planes,— the top block is made deeper than the bottom one.

TURN BUTTON

Hang saws on shaped blocks fitted with a turn button.

Suspended brackets

PLYWOOD BRACKET

Brackets cut from thick plywood bolted to joists or to wall studs for tubes, strips of wood etc.

GARDEN EQUIPMENT

Most people acquire far more handtools than they used to for gardening and outdoor building projects and just about everyone has a powered lawnmower and possibly other machine tools as well. Some people own ladders in order to prune trees or collect fruit, and a large family

probably has a sizeable set of folding garden chairs and a table. Very few garden sheds, the traditional repository for the wheelbarrow and a few tools, are large enough for all this equipment. One is therefore forced to organize extra storage space in the garage, cellar or workshop.

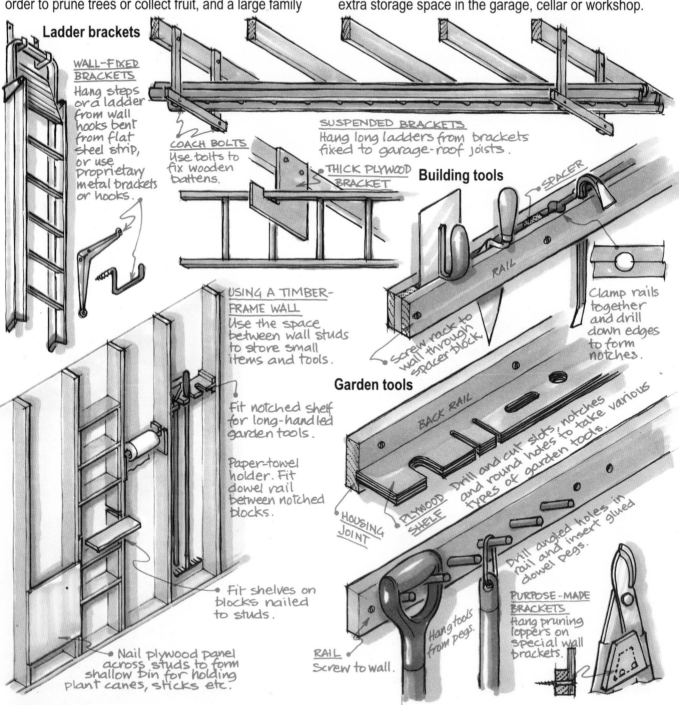

Ladder brackets

WALL-FIXED BRACKETS
Hang steps or a ladder from wall hooks bent from flat steel strip, or use proprietary metal brackets or hooks.

COACH BOLTS
Use bolts to fix wooden battens.

SUSPENDED BRACKETS
Hang long ladders from brackets fixed to garage-roof joists.

THICK PLYWOOD BRACKET

Building tools

SPACER

RAIL

Clamp rails together and drill down edges to form notches.

screw rack to wall through spacer block

USING A TIMBER-FRAME WALL
Use the space between wall studs to store small items and tools.

Fit notched shelf for long-handled garden tools.

Paper-towel holder. Fit dowel rail between notched blocks.

Garden tools

BACK RAIL

Drill and cut slots, notches and round holes to take various types of garden tools.

PLYWOOD SHELF

HOUSING JOINT

Drill angled holes in rail and insert glued dowel pegs.

Fit shelves on blocks nailed to studs.

Nail plywood panel across studs to form shallow bin for holding plant canes, sticks etc.

RAIL
Screw to wall.

Hang tools from pegs.

PURPOSE-MADE BRACKETS
Hang pruning loppers on special wall brackets.

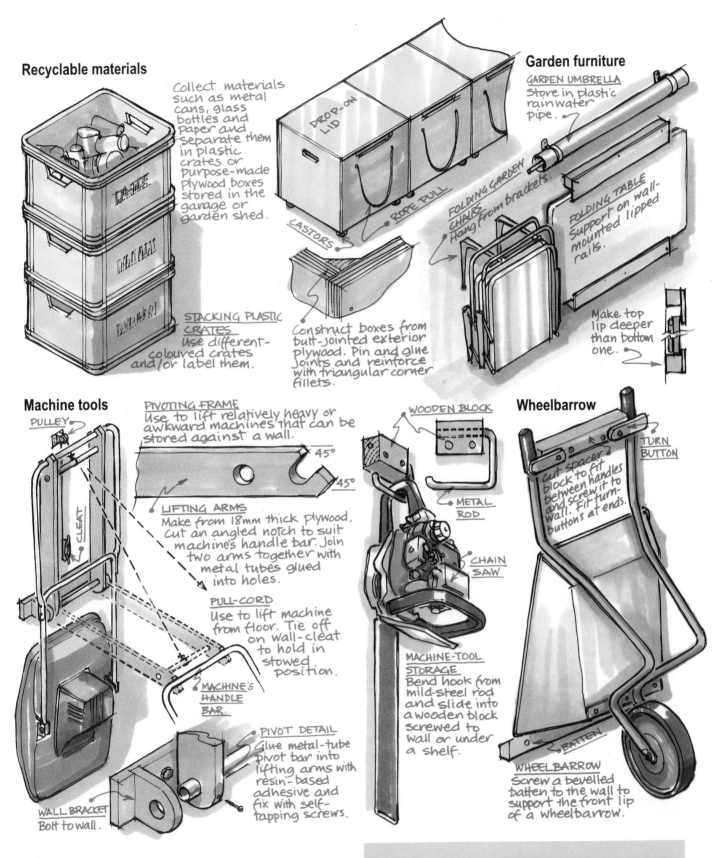

Recyclable materials

Collect materials such as metal cans, glass bottles and paper and separate them in plastic crates or purpose-made plywood boxes stored in the garage or garden shed.

DROP-ON LID

ROPE PULL

CASTORS

STACKING PLASTIC CRATES
Use different-coloured crates and/or label them.

Construct boxes from butt-jointed exterior plywood. Pin and glue joints and reinforce with triangular corner fillets.

Garden furniture

GARDEN UMBRELLA
Store in plastic rainwater pipe.

FOLDING GARDEN CHAIRS
Hang from brackets.

FOLDING TABLE
Support on wall-mounted lipped rails.

Make top lip deeper than bottom one.

Machine tools

PULLEY

PIVOTING FRAME
Use to lift relatively heavy or awkward machines that can be stored against a wall.

45°
45°

LIFTING ARMS
Make from 18mm thick plywood. Cut an angled notch to suit machine's handle bar. Join two arms together with metal tubes glued into holes.

CLEAT

PULL-CORD
Use to lift machine from floor. Tie off on wall-cleat to hold in stowed position.

MACHINE'S HANDLE BAR

PIVOT DETAIL
Glue metal-tube pivot bar into lifting arms with resin-based adhesive and fix with self-tapping screws.

WALL BRACKET
Bolt to wall.

WOODEN BLOCK

METAL ROD

CHAIN SAW

MACHINE-TOOL STORAGE
Bend hook from mild-steel rod and slide into a wooden block screwed to wall or under a shelf.

Wheelbarrow

TURN BUTTON

Cut spacer block to fit between handles and screw it to wall. Fit turn-buttons at ends.

BATTEN

WHEELBARROW
Screw a bevelled batten to the wall to support the front lip of a wheelbarrow.

16 LONG-TERM STORAGE

Chapter

Much valuable storage space is often occupied by possessions we use perhaps once or twice a year, or which we cannot bear to part with even though they have outlived their usefulness. And yet in the most well-organized house there are bound to be empty spaces that could be utilized for long-term storage.

Most attics are probably already employed for long-term storage, but you may be able to organize the space more efficiently. There's often additional storage capacity behind the partition walls of a bedroom conversion and even the loft enclosed by a modern low-pitched roof can be of some use. Check before loading an attic that the joists are strong enough, and lay a chipboard floor to prevent someone putting a foot through the ceiling.

Window seat and cupboards

Eaves storage

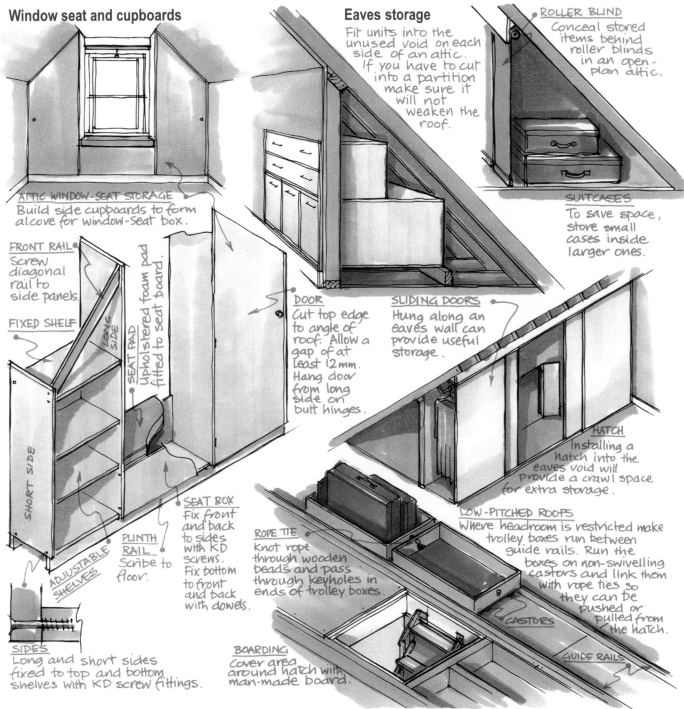

ROLLER BLIND
Conceal stored items behind roller blinds in an open-plan attic.

Fit units into the unused void on each side of an attic. If you have to cut into a partition make sure it will not weaken the roof.

ATTIC WINDOW-SEAT STORAGE
Build side cupboards to form alcove for window-seat box.

FRONT RAIL
Screw diagonal rail to side panels.

FIXED SHELF

LONG SIDE

SEAT PAD
Upholstered foam pad fitted to seat board.

DOOR
Cut top edge to angle of roof. Allow a gap of at least 12mm. Hang door from long side on butt hinges.

SLIDING DOORS
Hung along an eaves wall can provide useful storage.

SUITCASES
To save space, store small cases inside larger ones.

SHORT SIDE

ADJUSTABLE SHELVES

PLINTH RAIL
Scribe to floor.

SEAT BOX
Fix front and back to sides with KD screws. Fix bottom to front and back with dowels.

ROPE TIE
Knot rope through wooden beads and pass through keyholes in ends of trolley boxes.

HATCH
Installing a hatch into the eaves void will provide a crawl space for extra storage.

LOW-PITCHED ROOFS
Where headroom is restricted make trolley boxes run between guide rails. Run the boxes on non-swivelling castors and link them with rope ties so they can be pushed or pulled from the hatch.

CASTORS

GUIDE RAILS

SIDES
Long and short sides fixed to top and bottom shelves with KD screw fittings.

BOARDING
Cover area around hatch with man-made board.

UNEXPLOITED SPACES

Accessibility is not critical for long-term storage, so you can capitalize on locations that are unsuitable for everyday use and take advantage of vacant spaces that can only be reached with a step ladder. Stretch your imagination and you can come up with even more possibilities. Most people have never considered making use of the void under the floor, for example, let alone building exterior weatherproof cupboards.

Under cellar stairs

Store bulky seasonal items clear of the floor on wide shelves suspended from the underside of cellar stairs.

END STOP Prevents stored items encroaching on the stair treads.

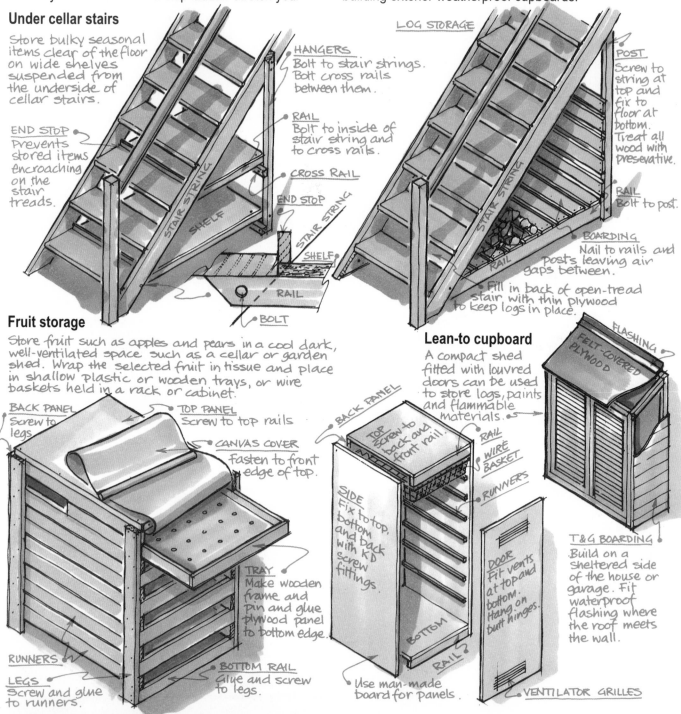

HANGERS Bolt to stair strings. Bolt cross rails between them.

RAIL Bolt to inside of stair string and to cross rails.

CROSS RAIL

END STOP

STAIR STRING

SHELF

RAIL

BOLT

LOG STORAGE

POST Screw to string at top and fix to floor at bottom. Treat all wood with preservative.

STAIR STRING

RAIL Bolt to post.

BOARDING Nail to rails and posts leaving air gaps between.

RAIL

Fill in back of open-tread stair with thin plywood to keep logs in place.

Fruit storage

Store fruit such as apples and pears in a cool dark, well-ventilated space such as a cellar or garden shed. Wrap the selected fruit in tissue and place in shallow plastic or wooden trays, or wire baskets held in a rack or cabinet.

BACK PANEL Screw to legs

TOP PANEL Screw to top rails

CANVAS COVER Fasten to front edge of top.

TRAY Make wooden frame and pin and glue plywood panel to bottom edge.

RUNNERS

LEGS Screw and glue to runners.

BOTTOM RAIL Glue and screw to legs.

Lean-to cupboard

A compact shed fitted with louvred doors can be used to store logs, paints and flammable materials.

BACK PANEL

TOP Screw to back and front rail.

SIDE Fix to top, bottom and back with KD screw fittings

RAIL

WIRE BASKET

RUNNERS

DOOR Fit vents at top and bottom. Hang on butt hinges.

BOTTOM

RAIL

Use man-made board for panels.

FLASHING

FELT-COVERED PLYWOOD

T&G BOARDING Build on a sheltered side of the house or garage. Fit waterproof flashing where the roof meets the wall.

VENTILATOR GRILLES

Stairwell storage

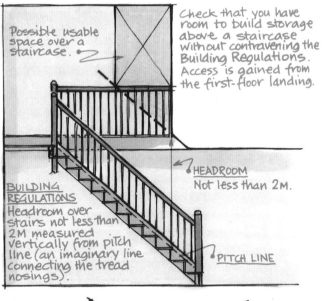

Possible usable space over a staircase.

Check that you have room to build storage above a staircase without contravening the Building Regulations. Access is gained from the first-floor landing.

HEADROOM
Not less than 2M.

BUILDING REGULATIONS
Headroom over stairs not less than 2M measured vertically from pitch line (an imaginary line connecting the tread nosings).

PITCH LINE

Making full use of floor-to-ceiling storage capacity in a bedroom

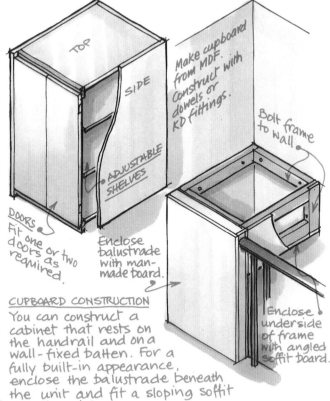

TOP

SIDE

ADJUSTABLE SHELVES

Make cupboard from MDF. Construct with dowels or KD fittings.

Bolt frame to wall.

DOORS
Fit one or two doors as required.

Enclose balustrade with man-made board.

Enclose underside of frame with angled soffit board.

CUPBOARD CONSTRUCTION
You can construct a cabinet that rests on the handrail and on a wall-fixed batten. For a fully built-in appearance, enclose the balustrade beneath the unit and fit a sloping soffit over the stairs.

Underfloor storage

Use the space under a floor to build in a suspended box.

Make a lid from cut floorboards joined with crosspieces.

Cut floor boards flush with a joist.

CUT JOIST

TRIMMER
Cut one joist back and nail in trimmers to support cut ends.

BOX
Make from exterior-grade plywood and nail to joists.

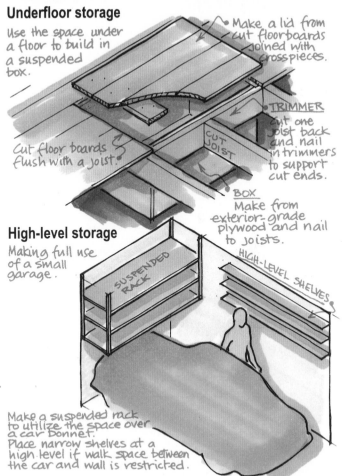

High-level storage

Making full use of a small garage.

SUSPENDED RACK

HIGH-LEVEL SHELVES

Make a suspended rack to utilize the space over a car bonnet.
Place narrow shelves at a high level if walk space between the car and wall is restricted.

Chapter 17

REFERENCE

The nature of storage is such that making cabinets and boxes usually requires basic woodworking skills, including the ability to make strong and accurate joints. However, unless you want to make some of the more ambitious pieces of storage furniture, you don't have to be a skilled craftsman. If you can cut pieces of wood square and true, you already have the requisite skills to make simple, practical items, but being able to choose from at least the more common framework and cabinet joints extends your options considerably.

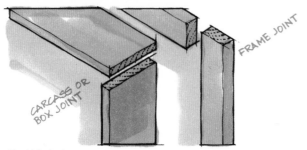

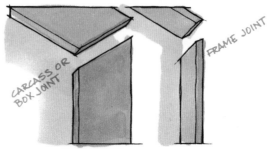

Butt joints

Square-cut butt joints are used to make cupboards and boxes, and to construct simple frames. Because end grain does not glue well, butt joints are usually reinforced with nails or internal corner blocks. Metal brackets or plywood corner plates are also used to brace butt joints, especially for a rough framework. Knock-down fittings are often employed to hold wide butt joints together for carcasses built from man-made boards.

Cutting and assembling the joint
To make a simple glued joint, first mark the shoulders of the joint with a knife and, using a bench hook to hold each workpiece, cut the ends square with a backsaw (**1**). Trim the end grain with a sharp block plane.

Apply adhesive to the mating surfaces and assemble the joint, then pin it dovetail-fashion using lost-head nails (**2**). Punch the nail heads below the surface. Alternatively, clamp the joint and rub glued wooden blocks on the inside (**3**). Leave the glue to set before removing the cramps.

1 Cut the ends square with a saw

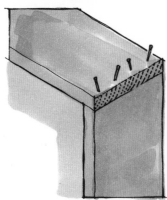

2 Drive in nails at an angle

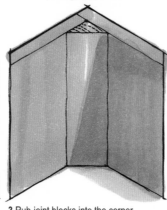

3 Rub-joint blocks into the corner

Mitre joints

Mitres make neat corner joints, and are essential when constructing frames from moulded sections. Glue alone is sufficient to hold a lightweight mitred frame together; but if sturdier construction is required, mitre joints can be reinforced like square butt joints. Wide mitre joints for a deep box or carcass, for example, are often reinforced internally with a plywood tongue. This sort of joint is more easily cut by machine.

Cutting and assembling the joint
Make a right-angle mitre joint by sawing the ends of two components to an angle of 45 degrees. This can be done by eye, but it is much easier if you use a mitre box to guide the saw blade (**1**). Shave each mitre with a plane. Assemble a single glued joint in a special mitre cramp, or use a web cramp to apply pressure to the four corners of a frame while the adhesive sets.

Reinforcing the joint
Unless the joint contains a loose plywood tongue that is included as the joint is assembled (see edge-to-edge joints), reinforcement is usually added to strengthen the joint after the glue has set. Mitre joints are often pinned and the nail heads driven below the surface of the wood. Another method is to glue strips of veneer into slots sawn across the corner (**2**). Plane the veneer flush with the wood after the glue has set.

1 Place the work in a mitre box

2 Reinforce a mitre with strips of veneer

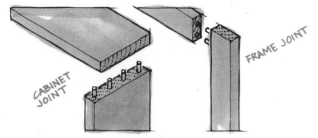

CABINET JOINT

FRAME JOINT

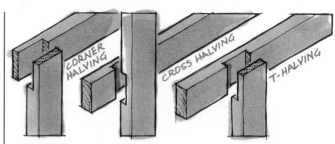

CORNER HALVING

CROSS HALVING

T-HALVING

Dowel joints

A dowel joint, used for both frame and carcass construction, is basically a butt joint reinforced with short wooden pegs glued into holes drilled in each component. Ready-made fluted dowels are available in different sizes, or you can cut your own from lengths of hardwood dowelling. The diameter of each dowel should be about half the thickness of the wood to be joined, and its length should be approximately five times its own diameter. Even the smallest joint needs a minimum of two dowels to prevent a rail twisting, and allow 100 to 150mm (4 to 6in) between dowels along a wide carcass joint. The outermost dowels should never be less than 6mm (0.25in) from the edges of the joint.

Marking the joint with centre points

You can buy or hire sophisticated dowelling jigs that alleviate the necessity to mark out the joint, but using small metal points to mark one half of the joint from the other is much cheaper and just as accurate.

Use a marking gauge to score the centre line on the end grain of one component (1) and make a cross to mark the position of each dowel (2). Drill holes for the dowels on the crosses. Insert a proprietary centre point into each hole (3) and, using a home-made right-angle jig as a guide (4), press the centre points into the side of the other component. Drill dowel holes on the small indentations left by the points.

Assembling the joint

Put glue in each hole, and tap the dowels into one component, then assemble and clamp the joint. Wipe off excess glue squeezed from the joint, and leave the workpiece in cramps until the glue sets.

1 Score the centre line on the end grain

2 Mark the dowel centres with a pencil

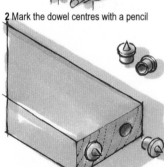

3 Insert a centre point in each hole

4 Press the points into the side grain

Halving joints

Halving joints can be adapted to join lengths of wood at a corner or T-joint, or where two components cross one another. Normally, each half of the joint is identical; but the joint can also be used to join different-size components, provided the rebates or housings are cut to the same depth.

Cross halving joints

Pencil the width of one component on the other (1). Lay the two components side by side on a bench and use a try square and knife to mark the shoulder lines clearly on both pieces of wood (2), then continue the lines half way down both edges of the components (3). With a marking gauge set to half the thickness of the wood, score a line between the marks on all the edges (4).

Place both components side by side again and, using a backsaw, cut just on the waste side of the shoulder lines. Make one or two extra saw cuts across the waste to make it easier to remove with a chisel (5). Chisel out the waste, working towards the middle and keeping the blade angled slightly upwards (6). Turn the wood around and cut from the other side in the same way. With most of the waste removed, pare down to the scored line (7). Check the fit, then glue both halves together.

3 Continue the lines over the edges

4 Score the half-way mark on each edge

5 Make saw cuts across the waste

6 Chop out the waste with a chisel

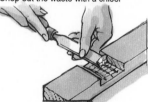

7 Pare down to the scored line

1 Mark the width of the joint

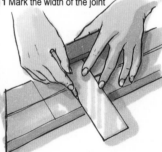

2 Mark the shoulders with a try square

T-halving joint

The housing in the crosspiece is cut as described opposite. Mark out a matching tongue on the end of the other component (1), allowing a little extra on the length of the tongue. To make the tongue, hold the workpiece at an angle in a vice and saw down to the shoulder on one edge (2), keeping to the waste side of the line. Turn the work around and saw down to the shoulder on the opposite edge. Finally, saw down square to the shoulder line (3). Remove the waste by sawing across the shoulder line (4). Glue and assemble the joint; after the adhesive has set, plane the end of the tongue flush with the crosspiece.

1 Mark out the tongue

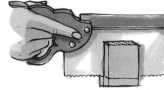

3 Then saw square across the joint

2 Saw to the shoulder on both sides

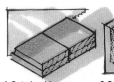

4 Cut off the waste with a saw

Corner halving joint

To construct a corner joint, make two identical tongues as described above, but cut their shoulders simultaneously (1). Having glued the joint, reinforce it with screws (2) or with glued dowels that pass right through both pieces of wood.

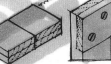

1 Cut shoulders   **2** Screw-fix joint

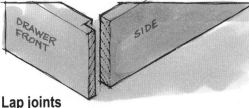

Lap joints

Although they are not as strong as dovetails, lap joints are frequently used for joining a drawer front to the drawer sides. Lap joints are pinned and glued like butt joints.

Cutting the joint

Cut the square-ended board and use it to mark out the width of the rebate on the other component (1). Set a marking gauge to about one-third of the timber's thickness and mark out the tongue (2). Saw out the waste.

1 Mark the width of the rebate

2 Mark the inner face of the tongue

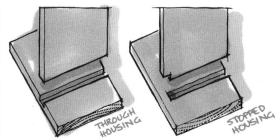

THROUGH HOUSING   STOPPED HOUSING

Housing joints

Housing joints are ideal for fixing shelves inside a cupboard or bookcase. A stopped housing is designed to be invisible from the front. An electric router is the best tool for cutting housings, especially across a wide board, but they can be cut by hand as described below.

Cutting a through housing

Square the end of the shelf and use it to mark the width of the housing on the other component (1). With a marking gauge set to about one third of the board's thickness, mark the depth of the housing on both edges (2). Saw along both sides of the housing, keeping just on the inside of the marked lines (3). Chisel out the waste, cutting from both sides towards the middle (4), then use a paring chisel to level the bottom of the housing. Glue the joint at each end of the shelf and place a sash cramp across the work until the adhesive sets.

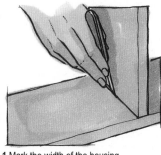

1 Mark the width of the housing

2 Score the bottom of the housing

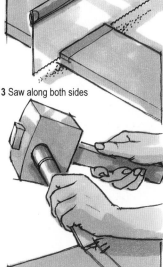

3 Saw along both sides

4 Chop out the waste with a chisel

Cutting a stopped housing

Mark out the housing as described above, but stop about 18mm (0.75in) short of the front edge. To provide a saw clearance, cut out about 50mm (2in) of the housing at the stopped end, first with a drill and then with a chisel to square the shoulders (1). Saw down both sides of the housing and chop out the remainder of the waste with a chisel. Saw a notch in the front corner of the shelf to fit over the stopped end of the housing (2), so that the front edges of both components will lie flush when they are assembled.

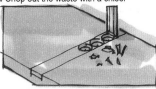

1 Square the stopped end with a chisel

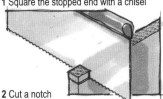

2 Cut a notch

HOUSING OR GROOVE

TONGUE

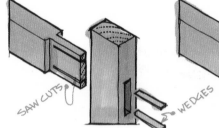
SAW CUTS

WEDGES

HAUNCH

Barefaced tongue-and-groove joints

A barefaced tongue-and-groove joint, also known as a barefaced housing, is stronger than a standard housing and can be used as a corner joint.

Marking and cutting the tongue
With a marking gauge set to about one third the thickness of the vertical component, score the shoulder line for the tongue on the side of the horizontal member (1). Continue this line halfway down both edges. Mark the width of the tongue across the end grain (2) and down both edges to meet the other gauged lines. Saw out the waste and, if necessary, pare down to the shoulder line with a shoulder plane.

Marking and cutting the groove
Use the tongue to mark the width of the groove across the vertical member, and remove the waste as described for cutting a housing joint.

1 Mark the shoulder line for the tongue

2 Mark the width of the tongue

Mortise-and-tenon joints

Mortise-and-tenon joints are essential for traditional frame-and-panel construction, and they are also used extensively for making underframes from relatively slim sections of timber. Various forms of the joint exist to fulfil slightly different functions.

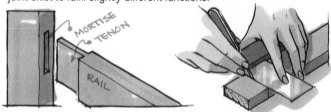
MORTISE
TENON
RAIL

Standard mortise and tenon
As a rough guide, the thickness of a tenon is usually about one third the width of the horizontal rail, and it penetrates about three quarters of the way through the vertical component.

Mark the width of the mortise, using the horizontal rail as a guide, then mark the shoulder of the tenon all round the rail (1). Use a mortise gauge (a marking gauge with two points) to mark both the mortise and tenon (2).

Cut the waste from both sides of the tenon as described for cutting a T-halving joint. Remove most of the waste from the mortise with a drill, and chop out what's left with a chisel (3). Glue and assemble the joint using sash cramps.

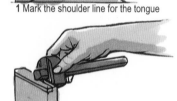
1 Mark the tenon shoulder on the rail

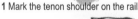
2 Gauge the mortise and tenon

3 Square up the mortise with a chisel

Through mortise and tenon
A tenon that passes right through the upright component can be spread with wedges, increasing the strength of the joint considerably.

Make the tenon slightly longer than the width of the upright, then make two saw cuts along the tenon, stopping just short of the shoulders (1). Having cut the mortise, use a chisel to pare a shallow taper at each end of it (2). Glue and assemble the joint, then drive two glued hardwood wedges into the saw cuts to spread the tenon in the mortise (3). When the glue has set hard, plane the end of the tenon and the wedges flush with the upright.

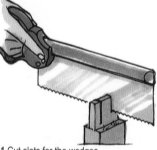
1 Cut slots for the wedges

2 Taper the mortise with a chisel

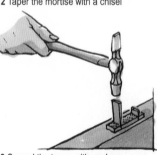
3 Spread the tenon with wedges

Haunched mortise and tenon
A haunched mortise and tenon is used to make frames with strong right-angle corners. The joint is designed to reduce the size of the mortise, thus preventing it breaking out at the end of the upright component, while the short stub or haunch supports the top edge of the rail. The length of the haunch is usually equal to the thickness of the tenon; the width of the haunch should be about one third the width of the tenon (1).

Cut the mortise in the usual way, then make the cutout for the haunch by sawing down both sides (2). Chop out the waste between the saw cuts with a narrow chisel (3). Make a full-width tenon as described previously, then saw away the top corner to leave a haunch of the required size (4).

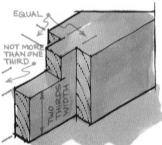
EQUAL
NOT MORE THAN ONE THIRD
TWO THIRDS WIDTH
1 Proportions of a haunched tenon

2 Saw down both sides of the cutout

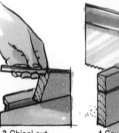
3 Chisel out the waste

4 Saw off the top corner

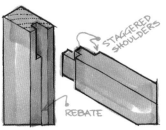

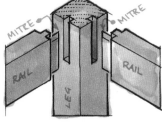

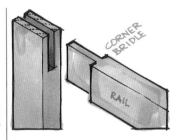

Rebated-frame mortise and tenon
A special version of the haunched mortise and tenon is required for frame-and-panel construction. The tenon is made with staggered shoulders to accommodate the panel rebate.

Corner mortise and tenon
Two joints per leg are required when constructing an underframe with haunched mortise and tenons. Cut mitres on the end of the tenons so they meet snugly at right angles inside the leg.

Bridle joints
A bridle joint, though similar to a mortise and tenon, is not quite as strong when used to construct the corner of a frame. It is, however, a much easier joint to make.

Corner bridle joint
Set a mortise gauge to mark equal-size tongues, one centred on the horizontal rail and two on the vertical component (1). Each tongue should be slightly longer than the width of the workpieces.

Use a tenon saw to remove the waste from each side of the tongue on the rail (see T-halving joint). Clamp the vertical member in a vice and make two saw cuts down to the shoulder line (2). Chop out the waste with a narrow chisel. Glue and assemble the joint, and plane the ends of the tongues flush once the glue has set. Reinforcement is not normally required, but you can introduce screws or glued dowels if you want an extra-strong joint.

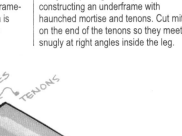

Twin mortise and tenon
A chest of drawers features a number of rails that are turned on their sides. These rails are made with twin tenons side by side. Mark out the tenons with a mortise gauge (1), and use the same tool to score two mortises on the upright component. Chop out the twin mortises (see standard mortise and tenon).

Use a tenon saw to cut down beside each tenon on the waste side of the marked lines (2), then saw along the shoulders to remove the corner waste from both sides (3). Cut the waste from between the tenons with a coping saw (4). Finally, square up the shoulder between the tenons with a chisel.

1 Mark the tongues on both components

2 Saw down to the shoulder

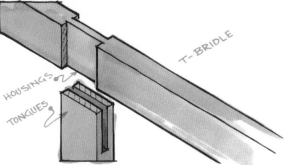

T-bridle joint
Make a T-joint with two tongues on the vertical member as described above.

To cut a housing on each side of the horizontal rail, first saw along the shoulder lines (1), taking care not to cut too deeply and weaken the crosspiece. Place the work against the stop of a bench hook (2), and chisel out the waste as if you were making housings for a cross halving joint.

1 Mark out the twin tenons

3 Saw across each shoulder

2 Saw down beside each tenon

4 Remove the waste with a coping saw

1 Saw along the shoulder lines

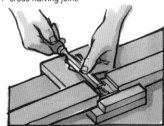

2 Support the work on a bench hook

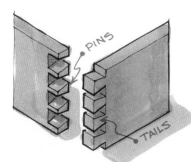

Dovetail joints

A dovetail joint, with its fan-shape 'tails' and matching 'pins', is perhaps the strongest joint of all for constructing boxes and cabinets from solid-wood boards. A through dovetail is visible on both sides of a corner, whereas a lapped dovetail joint can be seen from one side only. Both types of dovetail are used for making drawers in the traditional manner.

Softwood joints require fewer and coarser tails than similar joints in hardwood. Mark out tails with a 1-in-6 slope for softwood and a 1-in-8 slope for hardwood (**1**). The size and number of tails vary according to the width of the boards, but as a general guide the tails should be equally spaced and wider than the pins.

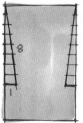 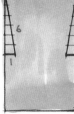

Hardwood dovetail   Softwood dovetail

Through dovetail joint

With both components cut square, set a cutting gauge (a marking gauge with a small blade instead of a metal point) to the thickness of the wood. Mark the shoulder line all round the tail component (**1**) and across the two wide faces of the other component.

To mark out the tails, draw a pencil line across the end grain 6mm (0.25in) from each edge, then divide the distance between these lines into an even number of equal parts. The marks represent the middle of 6mm (0.25in) gaps between the tails. Using a try square, draw the gaps on the end grain (**2**). Draw the slope of the tails on both faces of the workpiece, using an adjustable bevel (**3**) or a small dovetail template. Mark the waste clearly with a pencil in order to avoid confusion later.

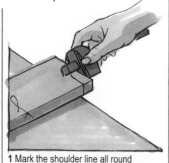

1 Mark the shoulder line all round

2 Mark the gaps between the tails

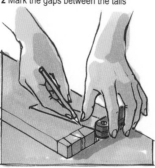

3 Mark the sloping sides of the tails

Cutting the tails

Clamp the wood in a vice with one side of the tails vertical. Using a dovetail saw, cut down one side of each tail on the waste side of the line (**4**). Reposition the wood and saw down the other side of each tail. Set the wood horizontally and cut away the corner waste, following the shoulder line on each edge (**5**). Remove most of the waste from between the tails with a coping saw (**6**) before trimming the shoulders with a narrow chisel (**7**).

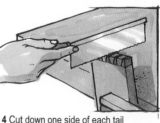

4 Cut down one side of each tail

5 Cut away the corner waste

6 Cut the waste from between the tails

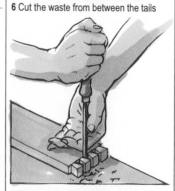

7 Trim the shoulders with a chisel

Marking and cutting the pins

To mark the pins, rub chalk onto the end grain and set the wood upright in a vice. Lay the tails precisely on the chalked end and mark their shape with a knife or a pointed scriber (**8**). Use a try square to extend the lines down to the shoulders on each face of the wood (**9**). Hatch the waste with a pencil.

Saw down each side of the pins (**10**), then remove the waste between them with a coping saw and chisel.

Check the fit, then glue and assemble the joint (**11**). Wipe away the excess adhesive with a damp rag and, when the glue has set, clean up the joint with a sharp smoothing plane.

8 Mark the pins with a scriber

9 Extend the lines down to the shoulder

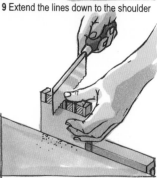

10 Saw down each side of the pins

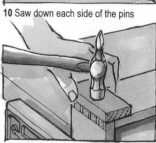

11 Tap the glued joint together

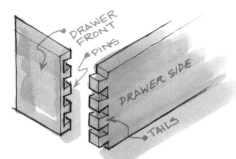

Lapped dovetail joint

With a lapped dovetail, the length of the tails should be about three quarters the thickness of the pin component. Mark out and cut the tails as described opposite.

With a cutting gauge set to the length of the tails, mark the lap line across the end grain of the pin component (1). Reset the gauge to the thickness of the tail component and mark a shoulder line on the inside face of the pin component (2). Chalk the end grain and mark the pins from the tails (3). Square the lines down to the inside shoulder line and mark the waste.

Holding the saw at an angle, cut down each side of the pins on the waste side of the lines (4). Chop out the waste with a chisel, first by cutting across the grain (5) then by paring down to the lap line (6). Glue and assemble the joint.

1 Mark the lap line across the end grain

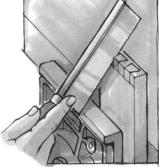

4 Saw at an angle to cut the pins

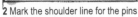

2 Mark the shoulder line for the pins

5 Chop out the waste with a stout chisel

3 Mark the pins from the tails

6 Pare down to the lap line

Machine-made dovetails

If you need to make several lapped dovetails, it is worth hiring a powered router and a special dovetail-cutting jig. Two components are clamped together in the jig, slightly offset and inside out. Run the dovetail router cutter in and out of the jig fingers, then remove the components and turn them the right way round for assembly.

Jig for routing lapped dovetails

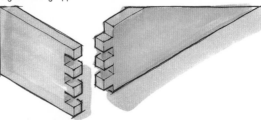

Comb joints

A comb joint (also known as a finger joint) is similar to a dovetail though not as strong. It is normally cut by machine, but it is relatively easy to make by hand.

Making the joint

Set a cutting gauge to just over the thickness of the wood, and mark shoulder lines all round on each component. Clamp both pieces of wood together in a vice and divide their width into an odd number of equal parts. Square the lines down the sides to the shoulder lines. Hatch the waste in such a way that the gaps in one half of the joint will be opposite fingers on the other (1).

Separate the components and cut down the sides of each finger with a dovetail saw (2). Remove most of the waste between the fingers with a coping saw and clean up the shoulders with a chisel. Saw out the corner waste on the shoulder lines of one component (3). Glue and assemble the joint between cramps, and when the adhesive has set plane the ends of the fingers flush.

1 Mark the waste

2 Cut down beside each finger

3 Remove the corner waste

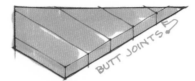

Edge-to-edge joints

Edge-to-edge joints are used to make wide solid-wood panels from several narrower boards. Arrange the boards so that the end-grain growth-ring patterns alternate (1). This will even out any tendency for the panel to bow as the wood shrinks. Also, try to keep the direction of the grain constant from board to board in order to make it easier to clean up the surface with a plane later. Number the boards sequentially so that you can keep them in order.

Butt joints

In most cases, glued butt joints are quite sufficient. Clamp adjacent boards back to back in a vice, and plane all the edges straight and square. Even if you cannot manage to produce perfectly square joints, the boards will still lie flat provided you always keep the same faces aligned. Prepare each joint in the same way.

Lay the boards over some battens on a bench top. Apply a thin film of glue to each edge and rub them together until the boards lie flush with one another. Place a sash cramp at each end of the panel, with strips of softwood protecting the edges of the boards and scraps of hardboard beneath the cramp bars to prevent them bruising the surface of the wood (2). If necessary, tap the joints with a hammer and block to set them flush (3). Wipe off excess glue with a damp rag and turn the panel over. Place a third cramp across the middle of the panel (4). Wipe excess glue from this side of the panel and leave it in cramps until the adhesive sets hard. When you remove the cramps, check that all the joints are perfectly flush and, if necessary, shave the surface with a finely set plane.

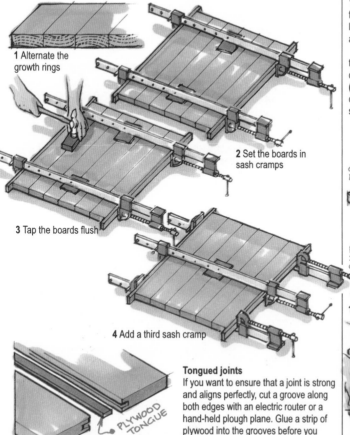

1 Alternate the growth rings

2 Set the boards in sash cramps

3 Tap the boards flush

4 Add a third sash cramp

Tongued joints

If you want to ensure that a joint is strong and aligns perfectly, cut a groove along both edges with an electric router or a hand-held plough plane. Glue a strip of plywood into the grooves before you clamp the work.

PLYWOOD TONGUE

Biscuit joints

Although a special power tool is required in order to cut a biscuit joint, it is included here because it has proved to be an ideal joint for cabinetwork. Butt joints, mitres and edge-to-edge joints are reinforced with small compressed-beech 'biscuits' that fit into slots machined in the edge of solid-wood or man-made boards. Glue causes the biscuits to swell in the slots, creating a tight fit and an extremely strong joint.

Biscuit jointer

The biscuit jointer is a miniature circular saw with an adjustable fence that allows you to position the saw blade accurately on the workpiece. Pressing down on the spring-loaded tool plunges the blade into the wood to a predetermined depth, cutting a short slot for a single biscuit. You can also slide the jointer along the work to cut continuous grooves.

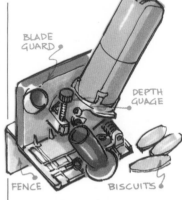

BLADE GUARD

DEPTH GUAGE

FENCE

BISCUITS

Making a butt joint

Having drawn the centre line of the joint on the work, mark the centre of each slot, spacing the centre marks about 100mm (4in) apart. Adjust the jointer fence to place the blade over the centre line. Align the tool with each slot mark and plunge the blade into the work (1).

To cut matching slots in the edge of the other component, clamp the work flat on a bench and rest the tool on its side (2). Make an edge-to-edge joint by cutting slots in both components in the same way.

CENTRE LINE

BISCUIT-SLOT CENTRES

1 Align the tool with each slot centre

2 Cut slots in the edge of the workpiece

Making a mitre joint

Some jointers are supplied with an angled fence for cutting slots for a mitre joint with the work laid flat on a bench (3). If the tool is fitted with a standard fence only, it is still possible to cut slots in a bevelled edge by clamping the work so that it overhangs the bench (4).

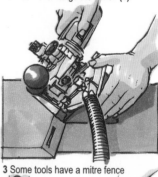

3 Some tools have a mitre fence

4 Or use a standard fence for mitres

An appreciation of what hardware is available can lead to many an idea for storage furniture. The way a cupboard is constructed could depend entirely on a cunning knock-down fitting, for example, or perhaps it is a discreet hinge that inspires you to design a startlingly simple storage range. The following pages illustrate fixings and fittings that are often used for constructing storage units. Your local supplier will probably stock many of them, but you may have to obtain some of the more unusual items from a specialist ironmonger or mail-order company.

Knock-down fittings

Mechanical fixings are used a great deal by manufacturers that supply self-assembly storage units. Many of the same knock-down fittings are now available through the DIY trade and are ideal for constructing cupboards and boxes from man-made boards. All you need is the ability to cut square butt joints and the means to drill holes precisely.

Chipboard inserts
It is impossible to make a satisfactory fixing in the edge of chipboard using ordinary woodscrews alone. However, to make surprisingly strong butt joints, push nylon inserts into pre-drilled holes. The inserts expand and grip the core of the chipboard as woodscrews are inserted.

Tee nuts and bolts
A machine screw with a special toothed nut is used to erect a framework or to bolt wooden components to a board. A hole is drilled through both components at once. The nut is tapped into the hole at the back of one component, and the bolt passed through the hole in the other.

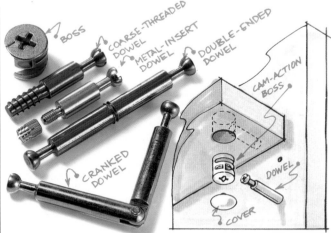

Cam fittings
With this type of fitting, the rounded head of a dowel projecting from one component locates in a slot in a cam-action boss dropped into a hole drilled in the other component. Turning the boss with a screwdriver pulls the two components together. There are several varieties of dowel. The standard straight dowel has a coarse-threaded tip that screws straight into the wood, or is made to fit a number of plastic or metal inserts. Also, there is a straight double-ended dowel for edge-to-edge joints, or a cranked one for clamping mitre joints.

Screw connectors
Coarse-threaded screws are designed to make fixings in chipboard without inserts. Using a standard cross-head screw-driver, a countersunk screw connector is driven into a narrow pilot hole drilled in the edge of the board.

Another version of the cam fitting comprises a cranked nylon peg that plugs into the edge of one component and fits into a circular boss recessed in the other. Turning a cross-head screw in the boss actuates the cam action and tightens the joint.

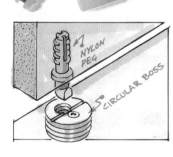

Screw sockets
Threaded metal sockets are used as a means of bolting together solid-wood components and man-made boards. Each socket is driven into a bored hole with a screwdriver until it lies just below the surface. A machine screw fits the threaded hole in the centre of the socket.

Block joints
One of the simplest, though somewhat obtrusive, knock-down fittings consists of two interconnecting plastic blocks that join panels at right angles. With one block screwed to each component, a clamping bolt or a tapered metal plate pulls the two together.

Cabinet connectors
Bolt two cupboards or wardrobes side by side with moulded-plastic or all-metal cabinet connectors. The ribbed 'nut', which is plugged into a hole drilled in one side panel, remains stationary while the threaded bolt is inserted from inside the other cupboard. The fitting can be dismantled easily when required.

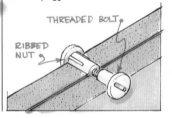

Hinges

It pays to familiarize yourself with the various door and flap hinges, especially those that permit you to open lay-on doors mounted side by side. However, unless the hinge prevents a door opening further than 90 degrees, don't design it to swing towards a bank of drawers built alongside. Sooner or later someone will forget to push a drawer home and, if the door is opened wide, the resulting leverage against the corner of the drawer will tear the door off its hinges.

Butt hinges
The traditional butt hinge is made with wide flaps for large cupboards and wardrobes, and narrow ones for fine cabinets and boxes. For good-quality work, avoid flimsy hinges with shallow screw recesses and slack knuckle joints. Inset and lay-on doors can be hung from butt hinges.

Lift-off hinges
Lift-off hinges are decorative butt hinges used to hang items such as a dressing-table side mirror that you might want to detach when moving house. Lift-off hinges are made for left-hand and right-hand opening.

Flush hinges
A flush hinge is easy to fit because you don't have to cut recesses in the wood for the flaps. However, the hinge should only be used to hang lightweight doors.

Piano hinges
A piano hinge is a lightweight butt hinge 2m (6ft 6in) long, used where a particularly strong fixing is required. Piano hinges are cut to fit a workpiece.

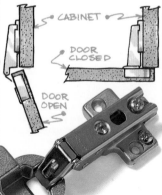

Concealed cabinet hinges
Concealed hinges are made specifically for lay-on doors butted edge to edge, and are capable of adjustment so that a row of doors can be aligned precisely. The hinge is designed to throw the door clear of its neighbour as it swings open to an angle of between 90 and 170 degrees, depending on the particular design. Spring-loaded versions keep the door closed. Concealed hinges are normally made with a circular boss that fits securely in a hole drilled in the back of the door and a baseplate that screws to the side of the cupboard.

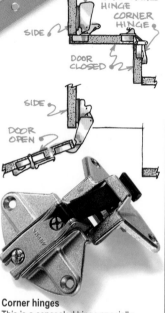

Corner hinges
This is a concealed hinge specially designed for kitchen corner cupboards equipped with three-quarter revolving shelves. Corner hinges link the two halves of a cranked door which is attached to the cupboard itself with wide-angle concealed cabinet hinges.

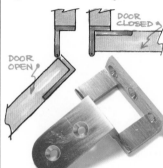

Cranked hinges
A solid-brass cranked hinge is normally used for fine cabinetwork incorporating lay-on doors. A door can be swung through an arc of 180 degrees.

Glass-door hinges
This hinge is ideal for modern display cabinets or hi-fi units. A glass door up to 800mm (2ft 8in) high and 350mm (1ft 2in) wide can be hung from just two of these hinges, and without having to drill the glass. They are slid onto the top and bottom corners of the door and held firmly in place with plastic screws on the inside. If necessary, the door can be detached to provide easier access when fitting hi-fi equipment.

A slightly different version is screwed into semi-circular recesses cut into the top and bottom panels of a cupboard. The same hinge can be used for left-hand and right-hand opening.

Cylinder hinges
Although they can be used to hang normal inset or lay-on doors, these hinges are especially suitable for folding doors that need to be opened a full 180 degrees. The hinges fit into holes drilled in the wood and are invisible when the door is closed.

Soss invisible hinges
Used in the same situations as cylinder hinges but for heavier-weight doors.

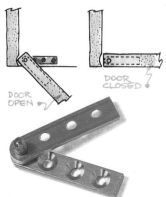

Centre hinges
Recessed into the top and bottom edges of a door, this type of hinge is practically invisible when closed. It can also be used to fit lids and fall flaps.

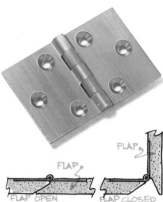

Backflap hinges
With its wide flaps recessed into the wood, the traditional solid-brass backflap hinge is used for attaching a fall flap to a bureau or drinks cabinet.

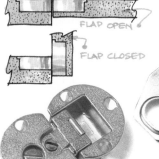

Flush-fitting flap hinges
This type of adjustable hinge permits a lay-on fall flap to lie flush when open.

Pivot hinges
A pivot hinge leaves the surface of a fall flap completely clear. One half of the hinge is recessed into the edge of the flap, and the other half into the side panel. The hinge is made with an integral stop that supports the open flap in the required position.

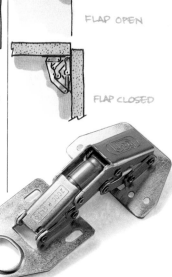

Lift-up-flap hinges
These hinges are designed for attaching lay-on flaps to high-level cupboards. A spring-loaded version holds the flap in the raised position.

Catches
Small, usually inconspicuous catches are used to keep cupboard doors or fall flaps closed. However, you will probably need a fairly powerful surface-mounted magnetic catch to secure a heavy door.

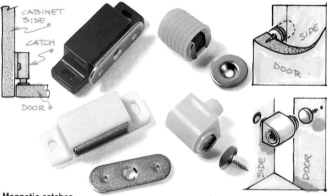

Magnetic catches
This type of catch often consists of a small encased magnet that is screwed inside a cabinet or plugged into a hole drilled in the side panel. Alternatively, a cylindrical version is located in a hole drilled in the edge of the panel. The magnet attracts a small metal striker plate screwed to the back of the door.

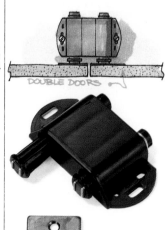

Magnetic touch latches
A cupboard fitted with a touch latch does not need a handle. Pressing on the door operates a spring inside the fitting that pushes the door open.

Ball catches
The neatest ball catch is nothing more than a spring-loaded steel ball trapped in a cylindrical brass case that is inserted in the edge of a cupboard door. As the door is closed, the ball springs into a recess cut or pressed in a small metal striker plate screwed to the carcass.

Surface-mounted double ball catches are also available for heavier doors, but they are more obtrusive.

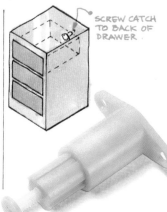

Drawer latches
Pressure applied to the drawer front causes this special touch latch to push out a drawer from behind. The fitting can be adapted to open a lift-up desk flap.

Locks and bolts

Although they provide a measure of privacy, any small finely made lock or bolt fitted to storage furniture and boxes can be forced by a determined thief.

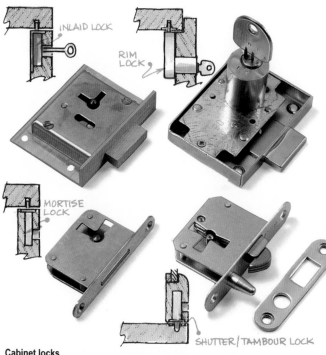

INLAID LOCK

RIM LOCK

MORTISE LOCK

SHUTTER / TAMBOUR LOCK

Cabinet locks

The traditional cabinet lock is used to secure drawers or cupboards. A surface-mounted rim lock is screwed directly to the inside of a lay-on door or overlapping drawer. Inset doors and drawers can be fitted with a neater inlaid lock that lies flush with the surface of the wood, or a slim mortise lock that is buried in a narrow slot cut in the edge of the door or drawer. A similar mortise lock for tambours or boxes with lift-up lids has a hooked bolt that engages the striker plate when the key is turned. Cabinet locks are often made with two keyholes at right angles to each other so they can be mounted either horizontally or vertically. Left-hand and right-hand versions are available.

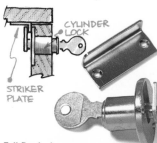

CYLINDER LOCK

STRIKER PLATE

Fall-flap locks

A fall-flap cylinder lock is designed to lie flush with the inside surface of a fold-down writing surface or counter top. The key, which can only be removed when the flap is closed, is pushed in and turned to operate a cranked bolt that locates behind a hooked striker plate.

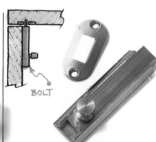

BOLT

Door bolts

On a twin-door cupboard, one door is often fitted with a pair of small surface-mounted or flush bolts on the inside. Bolts shoot into the top and bottom panels, or possibly an intermediate shelf. The other door is usually locked or fitted with a catch.

INNER DOOR

OUTER DOOR

DRILLED HOLE

KEY TIP

Sliding-door locks

A special cylinder lock is designed to secure overlapping sliding doors. The lock, which is fitted in the outer door, is operated by a push button that sends a bolt into a socket recessed in the other door. Turning a key withdraws the bolt.

A similar lock is made for glass sliding doors. With this design, the tip of the key is left behind when the key is withdrawn from the lock. The tip projects from the back of the lock, immobilizing both doors until the key is re-engaged.

Shelf supports

Some shelves are integral structural components, but most cupboard shelving is either supported on small permanently fixed shelf studs or rests on adjustable supports that make optimum use of storage space.

Nailable studs

Simple plastic studs are nailed to the carcass sides. It is essential to level the studs accurately or the shelf will rock.

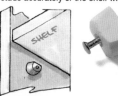

SHELF

1 NAILABLE STUD

Plug-in studs

Vertical adjustment is achieved with shelf studs that plug into regularly spaced holes drilled inside the cabinet. Friction is enough to keep wooden shelves in place, but glass-shelf studs are either grooved for extra security or are made with sprung safety catches that prevent the shelf tilting accidentally.

SHELF

WIRE SUPPORT

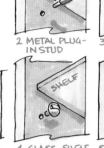

2 METAL PLUG-IN STUD

3 PLASTIC PLUG-IN STUD

4 GLASS-SHELF STUD

5 SPRUNG GLASS SHELF STUD

Wire shelf supports

A shelf with a stopped groove cut in each end slides onto a bent-wire support plugged into two holes drilled in the carcass. Wire shelf supports are extremely strong and are invisible once the shelf is in place.

Door and flap stays

A stay is a mechanism designed primarily to support a fall flap in a horizontal position, taking the strain off the hinges. However, stays are also used to stop a hinged door opening more than 90 degrees, and to support heavy chest lids or high-level lift-up doors.

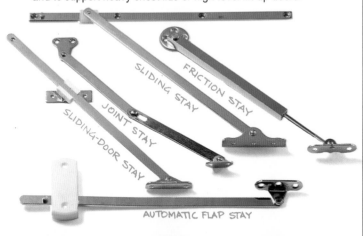

SLIDING STAY
FRICTION STAY
JOINT STAY
SLIDING-DOOR STAY
AUTOMATIC FLAP STAY

JOINT STAY SLIDING STAY FRICTION STAY

Fall-flap stays

The simplest stay is screw-fixed at both ends and has a riveted joint approximately halfway along the arm that breaks to allow the stay to fold back inside the cabinet. A better-quality version slides silently on a bar fixed horizontally or vertically on the inside of the carcass. A friction stay controls the movement of the flap so that it falls slowly and smoothly under its own weight. It is usually possible to regulate the amount of friction.

 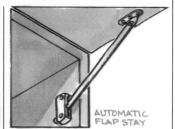

SLIDING-DOOR STAY AUTOMATIC FLAP STAY

Door stays

A door stay restricts the swing to a maximum of 90 degrees. It is designed to prevent a heavy door being ripped off its hinges by being levered accidentally against an adjacent door, or a bank of drawers or some similar obstruction.

Lift-up-flap stays

Some stays are designed to lock automatically when a lift-up flap is raised. The stays are released for closure by lifting the flap slightly before allowing it to fall. A friction stay will prevent a flap slamming shut. Stays are also used to support heavy lids.

Drawer runners

Traditionally drawers are made to slide on wooden runners built into the carcass, but a pair of precision-made roller-guided runners makes for exceptionally smooth movement even when a drawer is loaded to capacity.

Extending drawer runners

Folded-metal runners, screwed to each side of a drawer, slide silently on nylon-covered steel rollers and provide adequate support even when fully extended. The drawer cannot be pulled out of the cabinet accidentally, but can be removed when required. Drawer width is reduced by approximately 25mm (1in) to accommodate a pair of runners. All extending runners are designed for reasonably heavy drawers, but check the recommended load-carrying capacity of a pair of runners before you fit them.

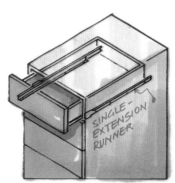

SINGLE-EXTENSION RUNNER

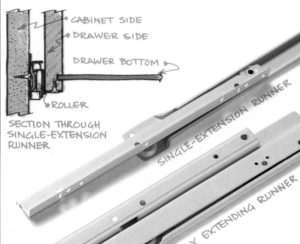

CABINET SIDE
DRAWER SIDE
DRAWER BOTTOM
ROLLER

SECTION THROUGH SINGLE-EXTENSION RUNNER

SINGLE-EXTENSION RUNNER

FULLY EXTENDING RUNNER

FULLY EXTENDING RUNNER

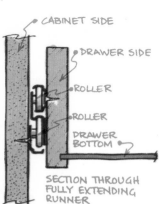

CABINET SIDE
DRAWER SIDE
ROLLER
ROLLER
DRAWER BOTTOM

SECTION THROUGH FULLY EXTENDING RUNNER

Extension options

Drawers fitted with single-extension runners cannot be opened further than normal bottom-run or side-run drawers.

Fully extending runners continue to support a drawer while permitting it to be pulled clear of the carcass.

Handles

A handle or finger grip is often formed as an integral part of a door or drawer. However, there are numerous ready-made fittings to choose from. Although they are essentially functional pieces of hardware, handles can enhance or spoil the appearance of storage furniture, so select them carefully to suit the style and scale of the workpiece.

Cabinet handles
The classic cabinet drawer handle is suspended from a pivot at each end. It is available in a variety of forms, including the distinctive swan-neck handle and the stronger plate handle.

Ring pulls
This is similar in construction to a drop handle, but the ring always hangs from the top of the backing plate.

Drop handles
A single teardrop-shaped grip or decorative ring is suspended from the centre of a drop-handle backplate. This type of handle is used for lightweight doors and small drawers.

Flush handles
A pivoted ring or D-shaped handle lies flush with a thick solid-brass backing plate that is recessed into the drawer front and fixed with countersunk woodscrews.

Drawer pulls
One-piece pressed-metal drawer pulls were originally used on military chests, and similar handles are to be found on numerous Victorian drawer fronts. They provide a firm grip on heavy drawers.

Door and drawer knobs
Traditional rounded door and drawer knobs are made from wood, metal, ceramic and glass, in a variety of sizes to suit storage ranging from wardrobes to collectors' cabinets. Modern-style knobs are often made from plastic. The method of attachment may be a screw that projects from the back of the knob or, alternatively, an ordinary woodscrew or machine screw passed through a hole in the wood into the knob.

Sliding-door handles
Circular or rectangular recessed finger grips are made from wood, metal or plastic for gluing into sliding doors.

Glass-door handles
Small handles can be clamped to the edge of a hinged glass door. Holes are drilled in sliding doors to accommodate circular recessed handles.

D-handles
These slim metal, plastic or wooden handles suit simple modern furniture. They are usually made with threaded inserts in each end to accommodate small machine screws.

Adhesives are a more permanent alternative to the mechanical fixings that are designed to hold components together. For certain tasks you need a particular glue that is formulated for joining a specific material, but it also pays to stock your workshop with a small range of general-purpose adhesives.

Woodworking adhesives

Glue made from animal skins and bones was once used extensively for every aspect of cabinet construction, from joint making to veneering. Many traditionalists still prefer to use animal glue, even though it has to be melted down in a special glue pot before it assumes a usable liquid consistency. However, it is far more convenient to use modern woodworking glues, some of which are ready to use without any preparation.

PVA glue
Polyvinyl-acetate adhesive, also known as white glue, is perhaps the most widely available and cheapest woodworking glue on the market. It is a ready-to-use emulsion of PVA suspended in water, and has an almost indefinite shelf life, provided it is kept sealed in its plastic dispenser in a reasonably warm environment. PVA adhesive forms a tough, invisible, though slightly flexible glue line. The standard glue is not water-resistant, so make sure you buy the exterior-grade version if your project needs to be fully waterproof.

Urea-formaldehyde glue
Unlike a water-based glue that sets by evaporation, a urea-formaldehyde glue cures as a result of a chemical reaction. It is often sold as a powder which, once mixed with water, forms an excellent gap-filling water-resistant glue.

Normally the glue is applied to both halves of a joint, but there are other versions that need a separate catalyst or 'hardener' that is applied to one half of a joint while the powdered component mixed with water is spread on the other. With these two-part adhesives, the curing process does not begin until the joint is assembled – a considerable advantage if you are constructing a large complicated piece such as a frame-and-panel wardrobe.

When handling urea-formaldehyde glues, you should ventilate your workshop and wear protective gloves and spectacles.

Applying woodworking glue
Be sure to spread adhesive on the inside of a joint such as a mortise and tenon, for example, as most of the glue can be scraped from the tenon as it is inserted.

Contact adhesives

A contact adhesive is spread onto both mating surfaces, then allowed to dry. When the glued surfaces are brought together, bonding is instant. Convenient as this is for some operations, it leaves no room for error. Consequently, some contact adhesives allow for slight adjustment until pressure is applied with a roller. The usual solvent-based glues are extremely flammable and exude fumes that some people find unpleasant. However, there are safer water-based glues, but they take longer to set.

Contact glues for veneers
Standard contact adhesives are used for gluing melamine laminates to kitchen worktops. Wood veneers can also be applied with a contact adhesive, but you should use a softer, gel-like version, which spreads easily.

General-purpose adhesives

There are some adhesives that can be used to glue a range of disparate materials. The hot-melt glues are included under this heading because, although specific adhesives may be recommended for particular materials, the same tool is used to liquefy and apply a whole range of glues.

Epoxy-resin glue
This is a two-part glue comprising a resin and a hardener that are mixed in equal proportions. The most common form of epoxy-resin glue, available in tubes from practically any hardware store, has a comparatively thick consistency. In cold weather, it pays to warm the tubes on a radiator before preparing the glue. When mixed, the glue is yellowish in colour, but it is almost invisible once it has set.

Standard epoxy-resin glue is not really suitable for woodworking, but it forms an extremely strong bond between metals, plastics and other diverse materials.

Hot-melt glues
Hot-melt glues are usually made in the form of cylindrical sticks for use with an electrically heated applicator or 'gun'. Different types of glue are available for wood and other materials. This comparatively crude way of applying glue is unsuitable for close-fitting joints such as dovetails, but it is an extremely fast and efficient technique for building rough utilitarian structures.

Another form of hot-melt adhesive is ideal for veneering. A thin paper-like sheet of glue is sandwiched between a wood veneer and the structural groundwork. Running a heated domestic iron over the veneer melts the glue and bonds the veneer in place.

Cyanoacrylate glue
Cyanoacrylate adhesives, the so-called 'super glues', come close to being truly universal adhesives. They bond practically anything in seconds, although the absorbent nature of wood tends to draw the adhesive away from the glue line before bonding is complete. Cyanoacrylate adhesives, normally sold in small dispensers, are too expensive for gluing large surface areas. These glues are, therefore, usually reserved for small-scale workpieces. Make sure you have some of the special solvent to hand before using cyanoacrylate adhesive in case you accidentally get glue on your skin.

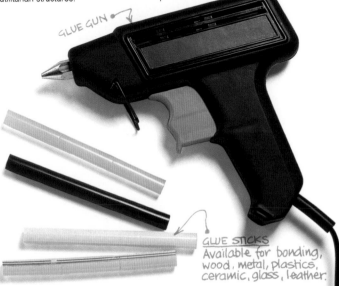

GLUE GUN

GLUE STICKS
Available for bonding, wood, metal, plastics, ceramic, glass, leather.

MAN-MADE BOARDS

The development of man-made boards has profoundly influenced the design and construction of storage furniture. Previously, only solid timber was available, and considerable skill was required to make and assemble wide flat boards of even thickness that would not suffer from warping and splitting with changes in humidity.

Stable man-made boards changed all that. In just a few hours, you can now make a cabinet that would have taken days of painstaking work to produce before the advent of factory-made preveneered boards. Below are some of the more common boards that you will find at any good timber merchant.

Plywood

Plywood is a laminated material made by gluing thin sheets of wood together in layers to form boards of various thicknesses. The grain of alternate sheets (known as plies) are set at right angles to one another to reduce the tendency for wood to move as it shrinks or swells. Normally, plywood is made with an odd number of plies for balanced construction. Decorative veneers are often used for the surface or 'face' plies. To reduce manufacturing costs, a slightly inferior surface veneer may be used on the back.

Blockboard and laminboard

Blockboard is more stable than plywood and is an excellent structural material. It is constructed with a core of fairly substantial solid-wood strips with two veneers glued on each side. The face veneers usually run parallel to the core, the others at right angles to it. Laminboard is similar in construction, but with a core of narrower softwood strips glued side by side. It is often selected for a workpiece that is to be veneered, because the narrow strips are less likely to show through on the surface.

Plywood
Relatively cheap board, comprising three birch plies only, is often used for drawer bottoms. Being flexible, it can also be nailed or glued over a curved frame, forming a tough rigid skin.

Preveneered plywood
Thin plywood with a decorative face veneer is an ideal material for cabinet backs. It is also used nowadays as a substitute for sheets of solid wood in frame-and-panel construction.

Multi-ply board
Strong structural plywood boards are composed of a number of cross-banded veneers. Use exterior-grade water-resistant plywood for built-in storage around showers or in bathrooms.

Blockboard
Although it's a strong rigid material, perfect for most furniture applications and shelving, blockboard invariably requires edging with solid-wood lippings.

Laminboard
Laminboard is superior to blockboard in stability, largely due to its core of fine softwood strips. Its face ply often runs across the board, so that any additional veneer runs parallel to the core.

Chipboard
Chipboard with a core of coarse particles sandwiched between outer layers of fine high-density particles has a smooth surface suitable for paint or varnish.

Chipboard edging
Rolls of preglued edging are sold for covering the raw edges of melamine-faced and wood-veneered chipboard. Using a warm iron, press matching strips along the edge of a board and, when it cools, plane or sand the overhang flush.

Chipboard

Small particles of softwood are bonded together under pressure to create flat sheets of chipboard. Having no particular grain direction, chipboard has no tendency to twist or bow. However, excessive moisture will cause ordinary chipboard to swell and eventually disintegrate. Some grades of chipboard can be painted successfully; others are made with a surface texture that is too coarse for paint but perfect for veneering. Preveneered and plastic-covered board is also available in a wide range of standard-size panels.

Medium-density fibreboard

A relative newcomer to the DIY trade, medium-density fibreboard (MDF) is fast becoming one of the more popular materials. Being made from reconstituted wood fibres bonded with synthetic-resin adhesive, it has a uniform texture throughout. Consequently, planing and edge-moulding MDF results in exceptionally smooth surfaces. MDF takes paint finishes well, and preveneered or plastic-covered boards are ideal for carcass construction and shelving.

Hardboard

Hardboard is made by compressing wet fibres at a high temperature so that the wood's natural resins cause the fibres to bond into an homogeneous stable sheet. Impregnating the fibres with oil and resin produces a stronger tempered hardboard that is also water resistant. Most sheets of hardboard have one smooth face only, but it is also possible to obtain duo-faced hardboards and other more decorative varieties. Most timber yards sell thin hardboard only, but better suppliers stock boards up to 12mm (0.5in) thick.

Plastic-covered board
The thin melamine foil applied to this type of chipboard is not designed for heavy wear, but is nevertheless an excellent water-resistant finish for cabinets and shelves.

Veneered chipboard
Wood-veneered board only needs light sanding before varnishing, oiling or polishing. A limited range of hardwood veneers is available.

MDF
This is an exceptionally stable board that makes an excellent substrate for veneers. Its uniform density makes for secure fixings using woodscrews and knock-down fittings.

Hardboard
This is a cheap high-density fibreboard used for drawer bottoms and to make rigid back panels for cupboards.

Decorative hardboard
This variety of hardboard is surfaced with plastic foil in plain colours or printed with wood-grain effects. Single-faced and duo-faced boards are used for inexpensive panelling.

Perforated hardboard
Perforated hardboard is sometimes employed for its decorative qualities, but it is perhaps more frequently used to make storage racks for tools suspended from home-made wire hooks.

FINISHES

A surface finish is primarily intended to protect wood from staining and prevent it becoming dirty. To most people, however, the way a finish enhances the appearance of a workpiece is perhaps the prime consideration.

Paint, varnish and lacquer

Paint, varnish and lacquer are similar in many ways, not the least being that they are sprayed or, more commonly, brushed onto the surfaces of a workpiece. Certain varnishes and paints are almost identical in composition, the main difference being that paint contains pigments that make it opaque and colourful.

Solvent-based paint
Virtually all solvent-based household paints are suitable for storage furniture. They are made by suspending solid pigment in a synthetic resin such as vinyl, acrylic or polyurethane. Most paint finishes are built up in layers; a primer coat, two undercoats, and a glossy, matt or semi-matt top coat. However, some heavily pigmented paints are designed to cover a workpiece with only one coat.

Polyurethane varnish
Modern polyurethane varnish is heat-resistant, waterproof and extremely hardwearing. Though most varnishes are

colourless, they nevertheless greatly enrich the colour of the underlying wood. There are, however, tinted varieties that lend the wood a definite hue without obliterating the grain pattern. Varnishes are made to dry with a high-gloss, matt or semi-matt finish.

Cold-cure lacquer
A cold-cure lacquer does not begin to set until it is mixed with a catalyst. This type of lacquer is normally transparent, but black and white lacquers are also available. Cold-cure lacquer is exceptionally tough and dries with a gloss or matt finish.

Wax polishes

Wax polish is an attractive mellow finish that actually improves with age. Proprietary polishes are either translucent, for finishing pale woods, or are made in a range of brown shades to create a darker or antique patina.

Cream polishes
Cream wax polish, which is liquid enough to be brushed onto the wood, tends to sink into the pores. At least two or three applications are required to build up a protective coating.

Paste polish
This is a wax polish with a thicker consistency that is applied with a ball of very fine wire wool or a lint-free rag. Once the polish dries, it is buffed to a shine with a soft duster.

Wood-finishing oil

Oil is a traditional finish for naturally oily hardwoods, such as teak, but it leaves a satisfying sheen on practically any timber, including softwoods. Don't use oil on the inside of a cupboard or drawers that contain anything that would be stained by contact with oiled timber.

Danish and teak oils
Some traditionalists like to use tung oil or linseed oil, but these finishes take a minimum of 24 hours to dry between applications. Commercially prepared wood-finishing oils contain additives that

shorten the drying time considerably. Heat and water tend to leave white stains temporarily on an oiled surface, but if they don't disappear of their own accord you can efface them with fresh oil.

French polish

French polish is not used widely these days because it is a comparatively fragile finish. Alcohol and water leave white stains on the surface, and the soft polish scratches easily. However, it is a handsome finish for any traditionally styled piece of storage furniture.

Brushing French polish
Professional French polishers usually apply the finish with a soft wad called a rubber, but it is a technique that takes time and practice to perfect. However, brushing French polish is manufactured

with an additive that slows down the normally rapid drying process so that it can be painted onto the wood. It also produces a more durable finish than is possible with traditional French polish.

UNFINISHED WOOD
PRIMER
UNDERCOAT
TOP COAT

PAINT

VARNISH

CLEAR LACQUER

BLACK LACQUER

WAX

OIL

FRENCH POLISH

None of the wood finishes described opposite are difficult to apply, but it helps if you work in a relatively dust-free environment and use clean brushes or applicators.

It is essential that you work in good light – preferably daylight. Some finishes exude quite unpleasant fumes, so ventilate your workplace and wear a respirator.

Preparing wood for finishing
No surface finishes, especially clear varnishes, lacquers and polishes, will disguise a poorly prepared surface. Holes, dents and cracks should be filled, and the wood sanded smooth.

Cellulose filler
Before applying an opaque finish, use ordinary decorator's cellulose filler to prepare the surface. Mix the powdered filler with water to a smooth creamy paste, and apply it to the surface with a flexible filling knife. Let the filler dry, then sand with medium-grade garnet paper.

Stopper
For transparent varnish or lacquer, use a filler paste known as stopper. It is made in a variety of woodlike colours. Press stopper into cracks and dents with a flexible knife, and allow the filler to set hard before you sand it flush.

Wax sticks
Hard carnauba-wax sticks are ideal for filling minor blemishes before you apply wax polish, but seal the wood first with French polish. Use a warm blade to melt the tip of a stick, then press the soft wax into cracks and holes. Once it hardens, scrape the wax flush, then burnish it with the smooth back of abrasive paper.

Sanding the surface
Even if it has not been necessary to fill blemishes, you should still sand wood smooth before you apply any finish. Raise the wood fibres by wetting the surface with a damp rag. Leave it to dry, then wrap a strip of medium-grade garnet paper round a cork block and sand in the direction of the grain. Continue to sand the wood with progressively finer grades of paper until the surface feels smooth to the touch. Pick up the wood dust with a 'tack rag' (a cloth impregnated with sticky resins).

Melt a wax stick with a warm blade

Oiling timber
Some people prefer to apply oil with a soft cloth, rubbing it into the grain, but with large flat surfaces it is slightly faster to paint it on.

Coating a surface with oil
Decant some oil into a shallow dish or paint kettle, and paint it liberally onto the wood. Avoid splashing oil onto adjacent surfaces when you are finishing built-in storage, and don't allow oil to collect in pools. Leave the finish to soak into the wood for a few minutes, then wipe over the surface with a clean rag to absorb excess oil and spread it evenly. Paint on a second coat six hours later, and leave it to dry overnight. Apply one more coat, then buff with a soft cloth.

Using wax polish
Before applying wax polish, seal the surface with one coat of varnish or French polish. This not only prevents the wax being absorbed too deeply into the wood, it also protects the wood from dirt that could sink through the soft wax finish. Lightly sand the sealer coat with fine silicon-carbide paper.

Polishing the wood
Paint on a generous coat of liquid wax, then about one hour later buff the surface with a soft rag. Apply a second, thinner coat, this time with a cloth pad, rubbing in the direction of the grain. Buff the surface as before and add a third coat. Leave the final coat to harden for several hours, then burnish the wax vigorously with a soft duster.

Alternatively, apply a paste polish with a small ball of 0000-grade wire wool, then buff the surface with a duster.

Applying varnish
Before you apply a clear or tinted varnish, seal the wood with varnish that has been diluted by 10 to 20 per cent. Rub it on with a rag, in the direction of the grain, and leave it to dry.

Painting on full-strength varnish
Paint a coat of full-strength varnish onto the wood, brushing in all directions and finishing with light brush strokes in the direction of the grain. Blend the wet edges of varnish as you gradually cover the surface, but avoid dragging the brush through varnish that has begun to set or you may leave bristle marks in the finish. If this should happen, leave the varnish to harden overnight, then rub it down lightly with silicon-carbide paper (wet-and-dry paper), and apply a fresh coat.

Painting wood or boards
Paint is applied like varnish, but you must build up a protective coat using primer, undercoat and top coat.

Building a protective coat
Seal bare wood with a coat of white or pink primer. This is a cheap paint that flows easily and prevents absorption of subsequent coats. Once the primer sets, paint the wood with at least two coats of heavily pigmented undercoat. White or grey undercoat dries to a matt finish that is ideal for the final top coat.

Using cold-cure lacquer
Because this type of lacquer cures as a result of a chemical reaction, it is essential that you follow precisely the manufacturer's instructions for mixing the components. It is also important to make sure the wood is clean, as any trace of grease or wax can delay the setting of the lacquer.

Applying lacquer
Brush on a liberal coat of lacquer in the direction of the grain only – don't spread it like varnish or paint. Work fairly quickly to blend the wet edges before the lacquer begins to set. After a couple of hours, rub the surface lightly with fine silicon-carbide paper to remove brush marks, then wipe off the dust. Apply a second coat of lacquer two hours later, followed by a third.

Painting with French polish
Before it begins to harden, Brushing French polish has a liquid consistency that makes it easy to apply with a clean, soft paintbrush.

Applying the polish
Brush on an even coat with straight parallel strokes, blending the wet edges. After 15 to 20 minutes, sand the polish lightly with dry silicon-carbide paper, then apply two more coats in the same way. To give the surface an attractive sheen, rub it lightly with a ball of very fine wire wool dipped in wax polish, then burnish with a duster.

Waxing a French-polished surface
Apply wax polish with wire wool, rubbing in the direction of the grain.

INDEX